BHARAT FIRST

Dr. Ambedkar's Contribution to Nation Building

BHARAT FIRST

Dr. Ambedkar's Contribution to Nation Building

A first-ever presentation of the roadmap, vision and mission for India's development

Kishor Makwana

PRABHAT PRAKASHAN

Published by
PRABHAT PRAKASHAN PVT. LTD.
4/19 Asaf Ali Road,
New Delhi-110 002 (INDIA)
e-mail: prabhatbooks@gmail.com

ISBN 978-93-5562-042-2
BHARAT FIRST
by Shri Kishor Makwana

Edition
2026

Price
₹ 600.00 (Rupees Six Hundred only)

Printed at
R-Tech Offset Printers, Delhi

Dedicated to...

The honourable Prime Minister
Shri Narendra Modiji
who envisaged and worked towards
realisation of the dreams
of
Dr. Babsaheb Ambedkar...

My Thoughts...

Evaluation of a life and life's work of any epoch maker is not only a difficult but is almost impossible for a common man. The main reason behind it is that such trailblazers touch many different issues concerning society and the nation during their limited lifespan. Most people tend to study, concentrate and highlight only one trait of a great personality and then people start believing in only that quality of the person. It might have been possible that dwarfs measure him with a smaller yardstick and giants with a somewhat bigger one, while some self-proclaimed leaders had completely different viewpoints; but the fact is that all of them had different yardsticks for judging according to their own limited knowledge and ability to discern. Such analysis and characterisation of that great personality have many drawbacks and create a very different image of the personality in the society. Another fact is that such great people have never been popular during their lifetime because their vision and work was beyond their own times. They were invariably ahead of time and that made them even more difficult to be judge or evaluated.

One such person was Dr. Bhimrao Ambedkar, who not only drew up India's Constitution or was a fighter against untouchability, or an economist or reformist demanding women's empowerment, or a leader fighting for the rights of the oppressed and backward castes, he was an inveterate leader who thought only about his nation and devoted his life to building it. His actual personality was so great that it was beyond the imagination of the common leaders. For him, the only *mantra* was 'nation first' and he talked of a new philosophy which emphasised that 'every citizen should feel that he/she is treated for and with liberty, equality and fraternity.'

Dr. Babasaheb delivered speeches and wrote many articles and books reflecting his clear and direct views on 'nation first'. If we study his life properly and minutely, then we can realise that he was not just a leader but a true *statesman* of his time. His contribution to nation building is unbeatable. He should be compared with great personalities like Abraham Lincoln, Martin Luther King, Frederick the Great of Russia or Kremlin of England.

Nation building is not an easy task; it's rather easier to establish a political party, to acquire power and adopt tactics to retain that power or agitate, confuse and misguide the masses.

It is essential for nation builders to have in-depth knowledge about everything, like history of the nation, religious traditions, political history, social traditions, culture and people's mind. A great and glorious political leader represents his own generation; later the future generation remembers him for his contribution in the past. This is because his work and vision affect the lives of the generations to come. It is said that 'statesmen overshadow the future'.

The following even characteristics are essential for any nation builder:

1. Clear vision of the nation.
2. Dedication to the cause of nation building.
3. In-depth study and knowledge of nation building as well as social structure.
4. Good character.
5. Organisational power.
6. Provide road-map for nation building.
7. Extraordinary leadership qualities.

Dr. Babasaheb Ambedkar was one such great personality, whose life was endowed with all the above-mentioned qualities.

His point of view towards India and national problems can clearly be understood on the basis of the following three statements and his life's goal.

'To work for the upliftment of society of Untouchables is a great service to the nation. To strive for their upliftment is to serve the Indian nation and the world' (*Janata* magazine, June 1932).

'If you want the development of our nation and if we want to be respected among the leading nations of the world, then efforts should be made for that and there should be internal unity in any nation, any society' (*Mooknayak* magazine, vol. 13, 21 July, 1920).

'I do not believe in any kind of discrimination. I am Indian first, then Hindu or Muslim. This is not acceptable to me. In fact, I am Indian first and Indian forever. Such an attitude is conducive to India's independence' (4 April, 1938; at Mumbai Assembly on the occasion of bifurcation of Karnataka).

Concerned about the development of the nation, he wrote in *Mooknayak* magazine (vol. 15, 28 August, 1920) : 'Look at our large nation – what is its condition and what was the condition of small Japan which today is the Japan that has progressed and established its place among the major nations of the world. The artificial caste distinction that exists in Hindustan today also existed there, but the people of Samurai caste known as upper class in their society, abandoned their racial seniority and made their ignorant and miserable brethren wise and happy. This earned their love towards the nation and created a new national spirit of oneness, leading to the elevated state of the motherland there.'

In this book, I have made a humble effort to convey Dr. Ambedkar's national contribution to the masses. As such, my lectures given to the youth at Hemchandracharya University, Patan and at the Orange Literature Festival in Nagpur, are elaborated upon to highlight Babasaheb's unique contribution to nation building. The young generation should know, understand and ponder on the invaluable contribution of this builder of the nation, because not much is written on this particular aspect of Dr. Ambedkar. I have made this humble effort and I am confident that the new insight gained through this book will arouse the curiosity of the readers to conduct more study and research. Thanks: Dr. Ami Upadhyay, Dr. Hardipsinha Gohel, Vatsal Thakkar...

—Kishor Makwana

Just a few words more:

I had very little or no opportunity to read about Babasaheb Ambedkar and his life-work prior to this book by Shri Kishorbhai Makwana. In fact, my information about Ambedkar was next to none and so, it was a challenge taken by me to translate (paraphrase) this book from Gujarati into English because, normally I prefer to translate books, subject of which may not be familiar to me, but likely to be of my interest. It was for the first time that I got involved in a subject which had been different to my sphere of learning. As luck would have it, not only was the subject really interesting, it also proved beneficial to me.

As stated by Kishorbhai in the preface of this book, it is indeed difficult to characterize a man with such a high character, like Dr. Bhimrao Ambedkar aka Babasaheb Ambedkar, who was a multi-faceted personality who reached the highest position in every facet of life.

I believe that most people are unable to gauge the real character of Dr. Babasaheb Ambedkar; however, as Kishorbhai said, there are many external reasons as well. Like, particular political parties and many such organisations and institutions, that are influenced by communism,, tried to portray only a few and select aspects of a man's personality in such a way that he would not be labelled as being extraordinary because that would serve their vested interests and particular agenda; the pity is that they have been successful in their mission. It is no wonder that Dr. Babasaheb Ambedkar has been depicted in a blue coloured bust-size statue erected outside numerous Dalit colonies across the country or as a full-size statue in front of a government building or a busy square of a city or town with a copy of the Indian Constitution held in one hand and the index finger of the other hand pointing up in the air! This became the image of Dr. Babasaheb Ambedkar for the common Indian belonging to any community, race or religion.

This book aims to break this illusive image of Babasaheb, who has been made to appear a dwarf by small-minded Dalit and other political leaders to fulfil their political interests. This book shows all the possible faces and facets of Dr. Babasaheb through historical proofs. I strongly recommend that the youth of India, especially the Dalit youth, should read this book at least once, so as to become familiar and proud of Dr. Babasaheb for innumerable reasons and, if possible, try to make his dream come true i.e. uplift of Hindu religion and curb on any further division of society on the basis of caste or religion.

—Vatsal Thakkar

Phases of Dr. Ambedkar's Life Journey

A great life story of Dr. Babasaheb Ambedkar can be divided into nine different phases.

Phase One

April, 1891 to December, 1917

- Dr. Bhimrao Ramji Ambedkar was born on 14 April, 1891 at the military headquarters in Mhow, Indore district, (Madhya Pradesh). He was the 14th offspring of father Ramji Sakpal and mother Bhimabai.
- Bhimrao entered the Satara Government English High School, where a loving teacher, Krushnaji Keshavji Ambedkar gave him his own surname 'Ambedkar' to replace his original surname, 'Ambavadekar' as an identity, out of love and affection towards his pupil.
- Subedar (Babasaheb's father) shifted to Mumbai from Satara with his family.
- Bhimrao studied at the famous Elphinstone High School at Mumbai. He cleared his matriculation examination in 1907, thus becoming the first person from the Harijan (untouchable) community in Maharashtra to clear this exam.
- Krushnaji Keluskar, a teacher from Arya Samaj and one who also gifted his own book *Buddha Charitra* (*Buddha's Character* to Bhimrao) and Mr. Damodar Savlaram Chande, owner of Nirnaya Sagar Press fixed a meeting between Bhimrao and Maharaja Sayajirao Gaekwad of Vadodara State when the latter visited Mumbai.

- The Maharaja granted a monthly scholarship of Rs. 25 to Bhimrao to pursue his college education.
- Babasaheb acquired his graduation degree from Mumbai University and took up the job of an accountant at the office of Accountant General of Vadodara state (15 January, 1913). He stayed at home of Atmaram Shastri, who was also known an Arya Samaji, but, Babasaheb was shortly forced to return to Mumbai on 1 February, 1913 on account of his father's serious illness.
- The Maharaja of Vadodara granted a scholarship of yearly 230 (British) pounds to Bhimrao to go to USA for higher studies in USA in 1913.
- He joined the Columbia University.
- He completed his studies and joined the London School of Economics and Political Science to attain an M.Sc. degree followed by D.Sc. in the same subject in 1916. But it so happened that he could not complete his doctorate as he had to return to India because the tenure of his scholarship had got over.
- He joined as Finance Secretary Vadodara state on 21 August, 1917 but left midway on account of encountering a humiliating experience in racism because of which he returned to Mumbai in 1917.
- He accepted the job of a professor at Sydenham College, Mumbai in December, 1917.

Phase Two

July, 1917 to September, 1920

He resumed his studies after a gap of three years in December, 1920 and began participating in public life when some important events took place during this phase.

- Presentation to the Southborough Committee in 1917.
- Meeting with Kolhapur Maharaja Shahuji Maharaj in 1920.
- Inauguration of his first Marathi fortnightly *Mooknayak* 1920.
- Participation in a convention on the deprived community of Mumbai Province.

Phase Three

April, 1923 to November, 1930

This phase marked the initial period of Dr. Babasaheb's public life. He founded his social movement during this phase when some of the major events –took place.

- Establishment of Dr. Ambedkar's first social group called the Bahishkrit Hitkarini Sabha (Society for Welfare of the Outcastes) in 1924.
- Presentation to the Hilton Young Commission in 1925, who founded the Reserve Bank of India in 1935.
- Appointment as member at the Mumbai Province Legislative Council in 1927.
- Launch of a public movement called the Mahad Agitation in 1927.
- Cremation of the epic *Manusmriti* in the presence of a large crowd of people in 1927.
- Publication of Marathi fortnightly *Bahishkrit Bharat* (Deprived India) in 1927.
- Publication of Marathi fortnightly *Janata* (People) in 1930.

Participation in the All India Convention of Deprived Class at Nagpur in 1930. In this phase, Dr. Ambedkar left an indelible mark on the social movement in the country at the provincial level. His contribution was so impressive that the British government invited him to the Round Table Conference in London. He was one of the two delegates selected to represent the untouchables from across British India. This was the stepping stone to his rise to national-level politics.

Phase Four

November, 1930 to August, 1936

This phase started with his participation in the first Round Table Conference and announced his formal entry into politics with the launch of his political party, called the Independent Labour Party. The principal events in this phase were:

- First meeting with Mahatma Gandhi in August, 1931.
- Participation in the First Round Table Conference from November, 1930 to January, 1931. Attended Second Round Table Conference from September to December, 1931.

- Gandhi-Ambedkar dispute with Gandhi going on a fast to oppose the special voting rights to untouchables at the Round Table Conference; signing of the Gandhi-Ambedkar pact or the Pune Pact in September, 1932.
- Third Round Table Conference between November and December, 1932.
- Appointment as president of Employee's Union at Mumbai Municipal Corporation in 1934.
- Announcement to be separated from the Hindu religion, which created turmoil in the country in October, 1935.
- Formation of political party called the Independent Labour Party which marked his formal entry into politics.

Phase Five

1937 to July, 1942

Dr. Ambedkar rose as a prominent labour leader in Mumbai Province. The major events of this phase were as follows:

- Notable success for Independent Labour Party in Mumbai Provincial Assembly elections in 1937.
- People's Movement against *Khoti* system in 1937.
- People's Movement against *Mahar Watan* in 1937.
- Protest against the Track Disputes Bill in 1938 and widespread recognition as a labour leader.
- He told the untouchable workers to beware of communists and portrayed himself a staunch enemy of the communists.

In this phase, due to Dr. Ambedkar's important contribution, he was appointed as a labour member of the Executive Council of the Viceroy, i.e. as Labour Minister.

Phase Six

July, 1942 to May, 1946

This was the most remarkable phase of Dr. Ambedkar's life, when he worked as a minister in the British Government, handling important portfolios, like labour and employment, power, minerals and water management as a member of the Executive Council of Viceroy. He also completed two other important tasks along with his commendable performance as a minister.

- Established a new political party with wide support and called it the Scheduled Caste Federation (S.F.C.) in July, 1942.

- Founded an educational organisation known as the People's Education Society (P.E.S.) in July, 1945.

Phase Seven

May, 1946 to July, 1946

This short phase was very uncertain and a restless period for Dr. Ambedkar, who was not included in the new ministry of the newly formed Executive Government on 19 June, 1946 after dissolution of the Executive Council of the Viceroy. Babu Jagjivan Ram was selected to head the ministry in his place. This restlessness ended in July, 1946 when he was selected on the committee for constitution of Bengal province. Major events in this phase were:

- Formation of Executive Government at the Centre.
- Launch of agitation against the scheme announced by three cabinet ministers of the British Government. The movement spread to places like Mumbai province, Kanpur, Lucknow, etc.

Phase Eight

July, 1946 to September, 1951

This was an impressive phase as it was in this period that Dr. Ambedkar was appointed in the Constituent Assembly and it ended with his resignation from the Union Cabinet as Law Minister in September, 1951. In this phase, he engaged himself in the reconstruction of an independent India. Most important historical events of this phase remained as follows:

- Appointment in the Constituent Assembly of Bengal province in July, 1946.
- Re-appointment in the Constituent Assembly of Mumbai in July, 1947.
- Appointment as the first Law Minister of independent India in August, 1947.
- Appointed as president of the Draft Committee for Indian Constitution in August, 1947.
- Approval of the Indian Constitution drafted by him in November, 1950.

Dr. Ambedkar, in this phase, is remembered for his unique and historical work in the formulation of the Indian Constitution. Above that, Dr. Ambedkar became the first Law Minister of the country and he laid the foundation for the law infrastructure of modern India. He soon resigned as Law Minister because of his differences with then Prime Minister Jawaharlal Nehru over the Hindu Code Bill.

Phase Nine

September, 1951 to 6 December, 1956

In this final phase, Dr. Ambedkar started distancing himself from active politics. He showed his passionate individualism by abandoning Hinduism and embracing Buddhism, which was a part of Indian culture. Important events of this phase were;

- First General Elections were held in 1952.
- He contested this election and lost in 1952.
- Became a member of Rajya Sabha (Upper House of Parliament) in 1952.
- He started a publication entitled *Prabuddha Bharat* (Enlightened India) in February, 1956.
- Adopted Buddhism with five Lakh followers in October, 1956.
- He died on 6 December, 1956.

Contents

1

On the Path of Historical Revolution

Dr. Babasaheb Ambedkar has been propagated essentially as a leader of the oppressed and a builder of the Indian Constitution because of which his image has been limited to these two identities. In reality, he was a great and global personality, much above than of many of his contemporary leaders. He was an economist, historian, expert in foreign policy, guardian of the nation, law expert, specialist in labour problems, scholar on religious matters and of course, a saviour of labourers. He was a writer and a journalist, one of the best educationists and a professor. He was a staunch supporter of women empowerment. It would be unfair if someone would evaluate him, based on only one aspect because such an introduction would always remain incomplete.

The detailed study of his life helps one to observe clearly five major turning points in his life–extensive studying in the beginning of life, then striving to weed out untouchability and demanding equality against social imparity, becoming a guardian of democracy, and chalking out the Constitution before renouncing Hinduism and embracing Buddhism. One can see different shades of his unique personality on all these five turning points of his life–his compassion, sensitivity and struggle for community brotherhood as the untouchables had been oppressed for centuries, his loyalty towards the nation and concern for the nation's future.

It is difficult to understand the life of an epoch-maker and it is even more difficult to evaluate it objectively because such a person of excellence has touched many aspects of the society and life of the nation in his limited lifetime. Often, people emphasise only a particular aspect of this great man's life and spread the word that it was his life's contribution, measuring him with their own yardstick. In fact, it is an incomplete analysis of the great man, who could think far ahead of his time without concern for his reputation as a visionary par excellence. The common man is prone to reject any changes or even modification in his traditional life as their argument is that since it has continued for the last so many years without causing any harm, then why change things now? It's also known as herd mentality, reminding one of the Sanskrit idiom which says that 'if this well has salty water, so what? This is our ancestral well from which we used to drink water and if they didn't stop drinking it, then why should we change it?' This tendency among people is common in our society and social traditions as well. People tend to abide by age-old traditions which are illogical and redundant and have no meaning in life. It was only some reformists who challenged these weird traditions and they were none other than Narsinh Mehta, Jyotiba Phule, Swami Dayanand Saraswati, Swami Vivekananda, Mahatma Gandhi, Vir Savarkar, Dr. Babasaheb Ambedkar, and others.

It is important for us to learn and accept some of the misunderstandings that occurred during the life time of Bharat Ratna Dr. Babasaheb Ambedakar and why they occurred. One major misunderstanding arose among the followers of the Congress much before the country's Independence. They doubted whether Dr. Ambedkar could be considered a nationalist leader and were more interested in categorising him as a leader of the Untouchables. Dr. Ambedkar came to social life in 1920 and started presenting his views lucidly and boldly. He established an organisation named Bahishkrit Hitakarini Sabha (Society for Welfare of Exiled) in 1924 in order to remove the difficulties of the untouchables and place their grievances before the government. The founding principles of the Sabha were 'educate, organise and agitate'. One can easily get a glimpse of his greatness and positivity during the inaugural lecture to this organisation. He selected

Chimanlal Setalwad as the president of the organisation and all members of its executive committee were drawn from the *Suvarna* or upper caste. This showed that he was devoid of a narrow or limited vision; his goal in life was to establish a Hindu society free from the disgusting tradition of untouchability and casteism.

He also delivered a brief speech to the workers at that time. He said, "I have gained this knowledge for the all-round development of society, so that I can work honestly for that goal. I will not use this power of knowledge only for my family and community; I have drawn plans for the progress of the society. And both communities–the touchables and the untouchables–stand to benefit if my plans work out." He did not harbour any negative feelings against any community; on the contrary, he wished for the ultimate welfare of both the communities. He expressed his life's goal in the following words in that meeting, "There are plenty of complex challenges against untouchables. I know that I won't be able to solve all their problems, but I am sure I will be able to place these challenges in front of the entire world and compel them to take note of it. These challenges are mountainous like the Himalayas but I am going to smash my head against that mountain. Just remember one thing, no matter whether I win over that mountain or not, but on seeing my wounded forehead, these seventy million untouchables would be willing to sacrifice themselves to win over the Himalayas. But, no one will be able to save you if you incite adverse feelings in your own people."

His life's aim was to liberate the untouchables from the horrors of untouchability and for which, he carried out many *satyagrahas* (agitations). He launched an agitation to be allowed to draw water from Chavdar Lake in Mahad in 1927 and in 1929, he launched the 'temple entry' *satyagraha*. This *satyagraha* was organised at three main places in Maharashtra–at the Kalaram temple in Nashik, the Parvati temple in Pune and the Ambamata temple in Amravati. He was clear in his views and all his agitations were carried out to restore the basic rights of the untouchables. He made a clear declaration that if an untouchable was a Hindu, he should also get all rights that the upper-caste Hindus enjoyed. He was convinced that it was the practice of untouchability and casteism that had caused a lot of damage to the nation. He even echoed these sentiments during the *satyagraha* at Mahad's Chavdar Lake on 25 November, 1927. He also wrote that discrimination on the basis of *higher* and *lower* castes had caused more harm to the nation and "some people think that our movement is meant only to remove the stain of untouchability and make us *Suvarna* (upper caste). It is not only the untouchables who have been harmed by the atrocities; it has also harmed the upper castes, making the nation suffer the most." He said at the Berar Province Untouchables Conference organized at Amravati on 13 November, 1927, "This work of social reforms is not only in our interest; it is in the interest of the country. Hindu society cannot survive until the bias based on the *chaturvarna* system is eliminated. Social values are important for an intact and a conflict-free society. The inhumane structure of society must be changed so that our country becomes stronger.'

He also said the same during the Mahad *satyagraha* on 25-27 December, 1927, "We are here today to remove inequality from the Hindu society and unite it...We have to change the inhumane structure of the society to make our country stronger."

He founded the Samaj Samata Sangh in 1928 and in which he was accompanied by Shridhar Pant, son of Lokmanya Tilak. The main objective of the organisation was to bring about equality among people. In order to bridge the gap between the untouchables and the upper castes, programmes like communion, sacred thread (*janeu*) ritual and mass festivals were organised. Up to 1935, Babasaheb played the role of a Hindu reformer, but when he realised that neither untouchability could not be eradicated nor social inequality eliminated, he changed the course of his thoughts. Eventually he sought refuge in Buddhism.

Dr. Babasaheb considered the philosophy of Hinduism as the best, but he also regretted that the philosophy was not reflected in practice. In an editorial in *Bahishkrit Bharat* (Exiled India) on 22 April, 1927, he wrote thus under the title 'Principles of Hinduism': "The doctrine of Hinduism is many times more egalitarian than the doctrine of Christianity and Islam. Hinduism fearlessly says that 'humans are God's children; they are a form of God.' No one is higher and no one is lower here; all of us are forms of God and this is the great principle of this religion." He believed that there is no better base to establish an egalitarian society than this principle.

Despite this, the Hindu society did not grant equality seen in the Christian or Muslim society. "Above all, if someone tries to establish such an egalitarian society, then resistance comes from within the Hindu society itself. This makes one doubt if the Hindus really know much about Hinduism themselves? It is not expected that action and ideas are always in confluence with religion; there may be differences sometimes, but then they need to be corrected. It becomes necessary to match them with religious ideology."

Ambedkar's ideas as the best visionary reformer of Hinduism were reflected in most of the editorials he wrote in *Bahishkrit Bharat*. He said in one of his editorials: "The power of Hindu society has been eroded by casteism."

He wanted equality in Hindu religion; in fact, he wanted a change in the fundamentals of Hinduism for which he organised a *satyagraha* at the Mahad Chavdar Lake, demanding entry for untouchables into temples. It was not at all easy for him as he had set out to break age-old traditions. Such traditions included prohibition of entry for untouchables into temples and objection to utilise water from public ponds and wells; so much so that they were even deprived of education. Babasaheb had to break all such traditions. In a sense it was a rebellion against a tradition that had been continuing for years in the name of religion. One has to understand his role in this revolt to introduce social equality. Babasaheb said: "Until now, like Mahatma Gandhi, we used to consider untouchability as a curse in Hinduism, but now our attitude has changed and we consider untouchability as a curse on ourselves."

Babasaheb's ideas were difficult to be absorbed by those who had been following the traditions for ages. It is a human tendency to not think seriously unless the situation demands and that does not necessarily apply only to the Hindu society; it is common across the human race. People do not change traditions, unless an extremely difficult situation arises not only for the common people but also for religious and political leaders. As per Babasaheb's explanation of this phenomenon, "The one who is set on a certain path will keep going on it with his eyes closed as long as the path is straight. He doesn't feel the need to ask anyone anything until he comes across the crossroads, when he would stop and start thinking as to which path will take him where. This clearly means that no one thinks of good or bad about their traditions unless difficulties or obstacles arise along the way. Similarly, the main reason for the practice of untouchability, which has been going on since ages, is that the untouchables have never opposed this practice. Had they protested, the practice of untouchability would have ended by now."

Because of his agitation for the rights of untouchables in the Hindu society, Babasaheb was identified as the leader of untouchables only. Unfortunately, it was not realised by the people at that time that Dr. Babasaheb was the leader of the entire Indian society, working for the upliftment of all communities. Very few contemporaries of his understood the importance of his mission. Shri Savarkarji (Veer Savarkar) was one prominent leader among them to support the *satyagraha* at Chavdar Lake in Mahad. He said that treating the members of one's own society in a way worse than animals was tantamount to insulting, not only mankind, but also one's own soul. Hindus should put an end to such unjust and suicidal practices for the betterment of humanity; practices like water becoming impure on by the touch of an untouchable and the same turning pure by sprinkling the urine of an animal; "this is despicable."

Just as Dr. Babasaheb Ambedkar's struggle was against social inequality, it was also against the Hindu scriptures that supported social inequality. The Hindu scriptures supported the *chaturvarna* caste system which was not acceptable to Babasaheb, who burned a copy of *Manusmriti*, a religious text, as a symbol of rejection of the religious basis of untouchability.Why does a Hindu follow racism and untouchability? Answering this question, he said, "The arrogant followers of Hinduism raise the issue that there are two parts of Hinduism-one is philosophy and the other is practice. Philosophically, untouchables are the same as touchables, but in practice, untouchables are quite unequal and unholy than touchables. It is unrighteous to make any social dealings with them. If the basis of this logic is to ignore philosophy and give importance only to conduct, then why this same logic cannot be adopted in political matters? People would create a stir, when a staunch imperialist man like Mr. Curzon says that 'it is not possible to follow the elements of the Queen's manifesto'. Isn't it a shame that these same people prefer to follow practices and say that philosophy is not useful in religion?"

Because of Babasaheb's harsh criticism of Hindu traditions, customs and Hindu theology, the tradition-bound Hindus called Babasaheb anti-Hindu, a heretic. Babasaheb knew the truth that a common Hindu person was traditionally very religious, very faithful to deities and religious traditions and could not leave his beliefs so easily, but he was determined to bring about a change in the society. He knew that people would not accept his work and ridicule him but he did not care about people's unpleasant reactions for he was like a beacon showing the path to traditionalists. Babasaheb's contemporaries failed to realise that he was thinking of the interests of the entire Hindu community as a friend, guide and a patriot.

It cannot be said that the society made any effort to understand his mission in life even after he is no more. Forget the common man, even a learned man like Arun Shourie is not willing to give importance to Babasaheb and his work. Arun Shourie's book titled *Worshipping False God* was published in 1997 wherein he made four allegations against Babasaheb: (1) Babasaheb opposed the freedom movement; (2) he joined hands with the British to acquire materialistic comforts; (3) he is not the architect of the Indian Constitution but merely gave final touches to the draft constitution prepared by B.N. Rao; (4) He accepted Buddhism as an opportunistic step. Whether it is Arun Shourie or the Dalit intellectuals, they have done a grave injustice to this great man by confining him to a certain frame.

There were two types of slavery during British rule in India– first it was political slavery which was encouraged by the British and second was social slavery imposed by the upper-caste Hindus and their theology. The Congress and other parties were engaged in fighting against the British as they desired political freedom. Similarly, Babasaheb too did not want British rule, but his question was: "Will political freedom abolish the social suppression of untouchables? If that doesn't happen, we will remain slaves; only the rulers will change." That is why his question was whether the untouchables would get political and social freedom while demanding political freedom from the British?

He had his own views on how the Hindu society had imposed social slavery on the untouchables. His speech on elimination of caste system is the best in this context. In a nutshell, he said that we cannot make long-lasting progress in any field without achieving social equality. He raised some questions in the following speech: "Untouchables are your brothers...but you forbid such a large chunk of society from the right of education. So how do you qualify to rule the country? You forbid the untouchables to use public reservoirs, and even forbid them to use common roads. You even forbid them from wearing clothes and jewellery of their choice; they are not even allowed to eat the food of their choice. Then, are you eligible for political rights?"

Babasaheb said that a political revolution invariably takes place only after a social and religious revolution; and that constitutes the course of history. Citing the example of India, he said that there was a socio-cultural revolution before Chandragupta's political revolution. Similarly, many saints of Maharashtra contributed to Shivaji's political revolution. He also cited the example of Guru Nanak, who brought about socio-cultural awakening. He gave importance to cultural unity along with social unity. The essence of his saying was as follows:

1. The order of formation of Hindu society is based on heterogeneity.
2. Caste is determined by birth and no one can change it.
3. Instead of work, the 'workers' are divided on the basis of caste.
4. The caste system is based on a person's economic status. The lower castes are forced to carry out extremely inferior and deplorable duties.
5. Freedom in choice of occupation is not given.
6. All these things have a religious basis.
7. The caste system is considered to be God-made and so it is immutable.

Babasaheb's direct question was, "The Congress may be right as far as political freedom is concerned, but what about our freedom? Are you going to free us from social slavery or not? Will we get all those rights which ordinary Hindus have, such as entry into temples, entry into public places, right to own property, right to choose occupation? In short, what are you going to do for our social freedom?"

It is particularly noteworthy in this context that Swami Vivekananda also raised similar questions. He said, "The upper castes want (political) freedom, as they want to maintain the lower castes as their slaves." His words meant that some of the youth were conducting public meetings to acquire greater power. "The British are laughing at us for such a move. One who does not want to give freedom to others does not deserve freedom for self. Imagine what would happen if the British handed over power to you? Those who will be in power will try to suppress others. They will never let power go out of their hands. Slaves need power to enslave others..."

Babasaheb knew that the Congress did not consider him a nationalist or a patriot. Speaking at the Round Table Conference on 19 January, 1930, he said, "By saying that the nationalists of India would call me a racist for which I am not afraid of. India is a strange country where even patriotic people are strange because these patriotic people not only view their own brothers in a condition worse than animals, but never raise a voice against it. These patriots know that men and women are deprived of human rights for no reason, but the sensibility to help them has not yet awakened within them. They also know that a large section of the people is not allowed to enter common public businesses, but they forget their duty to provide opportunities of justice and protection to this deprived class of society. They are aware of evil practices that are harmful to human beings and society, but they do not feel disgust at such cankering practices. These patriots have only one demand–they want rights for their own class. I am glad that I do not belong to such a class of patriots. I belong to a class where democracy is of utmost importance. We wish to bring this goal into practice in every sphere of life."

Till 1935, Babasaheb considered the untouchables as a class of Hindu society. The politics of that time was totally different. All political parties considered untouchables as a part of Hindu society just for their own political gain. On the other side, the British were applying the 'divide and rule' policy as it was more favourable for them. They ensured that Hindus and Muslims would never live together; at the same time they wanted the various castes of Hindu society to keep fighting among themselves. But, Babasaheb never fell prey to this policy of the British; he always considered the nation first. The nation was paramount for him. He blamed the upper castes in Hindu society for the deplorable condition of untouchables. He challenged, "Please tell us what is the relationship between Hindu society and untouchables?" He pointed out that rituals, such as mass meals and mass marriages, were essential for social unity. Even Veer Savarkar considered the following seven acts as shackles of Hindu society, *sparshbandi* (untouchability), *rotibandi* (ban on meals), *betibandi* (ban on marriage), *sindhubandi* (prohibition of sea travel), *vedbandi* (prohibiting of learning the *Vedas*), *shuddhibandi* (prohibiting untouchables from entering the mainstream society). Similarly, Dr. Ambedkar also considered the three prohibitions as shackles of greater Hindu society–*lagnabandi* (ban on inter-caste marriage), *bhojanbandi* (ban on meals) and *halava-malavabandi* (ban on meeting each other). He believed that all the people in the country "should live as one united society, where such bans would not exist. Two such rituals (namely, marriage and mass meal) can unite the upper class with the untouchables, but both are not in existence in the society. Even a discussion on such issues creates havoc within the people. Forget about inter-marriages and participation in mass meals, even a common symbiosis is not possible in these two classes of Hindu society. Then what is the link which can bring the untouchable Hindus into the mainstream society? It is true that both these classes–upper class and untouchables–of the society flourished under the umbrella of the same religion and same culture. But, that is not the complete picture; if they all are components of one society because of hailing from the same culture, then the word 'society' proves redundant. And there is a big difference in the society as well. Since the culture and society are two different entities, it may be possible that the culture of one society is the same, but people of the same culture may not be a part of one society. Such a rule applies everywhere. All Europeans, for example, grew up as Christians in the same culture. They all follow the same religion and worship the same god–Jesus Christ.

All their rites and rituals are same from birth to death, but that doesn't meant hey are all from the same society. Despite belonging to the same religion, they are parts of different communities, like French, German, Italian, Bulgarian, Spanish, Portuguese, etc. The same applies to Hindus as well: touchables (upper class) and untouchables are two different societies. As it is untrue and rather foolish to consider all the people living in Europe to belong to the same society, similarly it is no less foolish to say that there is one single society of touchables and untouchables simply because they have grown up in the same Hindu culture. In fact, there is no such element which connects the touchables and the untouchables. Untouchables can be a part of Hinduism but they are not a part within the Hindu society at all."

"Whatever it may be, the most surprising phenomenon is that the touchables who have not so far been treating the untouchables in a proper manner are now suddenly showing love towards them; they want them to stay within the Hindu society. I just want to ask, 'Who is urging them not to separate from the Hindus? How is this possible when there is no social relationship between the two? Both of us are different societies. Then what is wrong in being politically different when we are already socially different from each other? When you say we belong to the same society, then why were so many atrocities meted out to us? When some untouchable asks this simple question, the so-called scholarly Hindus try to shut him up with some irrelevant arguments."

"The upper-caste Hindus do not consider the untouchables as their own people or a part of the *chaturvarna* (four-caste) society. They are considered even lower than the Shudras (the lowest caste according to the *chaturvarna* system). In other words, the Hindus have pushed them out of their society. Hindus of all four *varnas* (classes) do not deal with the untouchables in any manner–neither by way of sharing meals with them nor through marriage relationships. Even touching them is considered unholy. Strict rules have been laid out not to deal with untouchables in any way. Those who fight against slavery are known as freedom fighters but, those who are fighting for social freedom are labelled as traitors! One has to suffer imprisonment to be free from political slavery, has to suffer oppression from foreign monarchies and even death;

but the fight for social freedom has to be fought with one's own brothers. One has to experience insults, humiliation and at times even thrashing from them."

The British and other foreigners could be identified immediately;, even the common man can immediately recognise an Arab, Turk, Pathan, Iranian, Iraqi as the Muslims are not our people. That's why those who fight against them are called patriots, but the person who struggles against the natives will never be called a patriot in his lifetime. This is because his work is far ahead of his time. His contemporaries can never understand him. Even the next two generations may be confused about his work. Babasaheb's contribution to nation building, to society-building will begin to be understood only after three or four generations after his death. It is necessary to glance at the history of the world to know the worth of Babasaheb's social struggle. There were about four million slaves in America in 1860. In order to liberate them, a civil war broke out. It was South v/s North and it was the worst war ever fought on American soil. About six lakh twenty thousand soldiers were killed and almost as many were wounded. Adding civilians to it, the death toll reached over 13 lakh. This meant that American society had to pay a very high price for giving social freedom to slaves. If the loss of property, ruined towns and families are taken into account, then the horrors of this civil war can be understood. Wounds of war cripple human beings. The State revolution that took place in France was aimed at liberating the common people from slavery of the monarchy. That revolution was as fierce and violent as the American Civil War. France may be smaller than any state in our country, but 40,000 people were killed in this revolution between 1793 and 1794. They had to pay a heavy price for achieving liberty, equality and fraternity.

There was also a communist revolution in Russia. This revolution took place to give freedom, justice and economic equality to the poor. About six million people were killed during Lenin's rule and about 30 million died during Stalin's leadership. In order to establish a state of equality in Russia and to liberate the agricultural labourers as well as slaves, those who had wealth were branded as capitalists and put to death. Such statistics break the heart. Figures of death may be in thousands, lakhs or crores, but the seriousness of the death toll is realised when one loses one's brother or daughter in the war. The destruction of the family and its world in this revolution does not come to anyone's notice.

Babasaheb made a comparison between the slavery of untouchables in India and the slavery in Rome, proving that the slavery of untouchables in India was the worst. Slaves would become rebels when you make them feel that they are enslaved. Babasaheb made them feel that they were enslaved and incited them to revolt for their freedom. He prodded the untouchables to eradicate the stigma of untouchability; yet he did not allow any conflict to turn violent. During the *satyagraha* at Mahad in March 1927, the *bhojan pandal* (the tent for dinning) was violently attacked by Mahad's upper-caste people, but the *satyagrahis* were able to resist the attack as many of them were army veterans. One *satyagrahi* could have countered at least ten opponents, but they didn't. On the contrary, they suffered injuries because Babasaheb had instructed his followers to avoid violence. He thus showed the people to fight a non-violent social revolution. There was heavy bloodshed in Russia, France, USA during the common man's demand for social change; there was bloodshed in this social struggle of Babasaheb but there was no violence. We attribute the non-violent political struggle to Mahatma Gandhi, but he also could not stop the violence in *satyagraha*. The police station was set to fire by a violent mob during the Chauri-Chaura movement and Gandhiji had to halt the freedom movement after that incident. Babasaheb never allowed any conflict to turn violent and this was a valuable contribution towards nation building. His struggle for social freedom and his contribution to nation building are praiseworthy. This is as important as the fight for political freedom.

Another major reason for the spread of misconceptions about Babasaheb has been his ideological conflict with Mahatma Gandhi, who, as a Hindu, believed in such words can be explained too ideology. He was a supporter of *chaturvarnya* (four-caste system) and was the front face of the freedom struggle against the British. As such he was the only leader of the Congress party since 1920. He was called *Mahatma,* the great soul and his word was considered the final decision of the Congress. He introduced the weapon of *satyagraha* (movement of truth) to fight against the British rulers and initiated this non-violent movement to achieve independence. The essence of Gandhiji's teaching was self-control and this was the principal feature of *satyagraha*. He had said that one shall not attack the opponent but silently tolerate his injustice. Gandhiji taught the common man of Hindu society to become fearless and endure police atrocities in their freedom struggle. He made them strong enough to bear the bullet wounds for the sake of the country. Gandhiji's character was of the highest order and his actions are in tune with his statements. He became the centre of mass faith and hope for the Indian people and was treated as a divine entity. In fact, he forged a unique relationship with poorest of the poor in India; he started wearing the single loin cloth because ordinary poor people of India could not afford to possess enough clothes to cover their bodies. It was like fighting against a large society that believed in Gandhiji and his ideology. Babasaheb did it too–he struggled against Gandhiji. The book, *What did Congress and Gandhiji do for the Untouchables*? has been one of the prime publications. The book was published in 1946 and in it the conflicting issues between Gandhiji and Dr. Ambedkar are described. Babasaheb was an ardent opponent of the *chaturvarna* system. He was of the opinion that the division of society as described in *Purusha Sukta* (a bunch of 16 *shlokas* from the *Rigveda's* tenth chapter) is artificial and unscientific. He criticised the *purusha sukta* in his essay titled '*Jati Nirmulan*' (Eradication of Castes) and in the book, *Who is Shudra?* he described Gandhiji's opinion on this issue as being different. Gandhiji was a supporter of the caste system (*chaturvarna*), but a staunch opponent of untouchability. He was of the opinion that "the caste system is meaningful with its means. There is nothing wrong with people of one caste wanting to learn subjects like knowledge, science, and art of the other caste, but as far as earning their living is concerned, they should choose their own ancestral profession. That means one should continue with the profession of his/her ancestors. The purpose of the caste system is to prevent competition, class-conflict and fights between each other. The caste system determines a person's duties and occupation even before s/he is born. That's why I have faith in the caste system."

Later, Gandhiji changed many of his thoughts; he also endorsed inter-racial marriages.

Babasaheb never accepted the principle of determining caste and class by birth. According to him, the structure of the Hindu society was based on gradual heterogeneity. One cannot change his/her caste; his/her place in society is determined and his/her rights are determined as soon as s/he takes birth. The basis of this system is purity-impurity by birth and that is why this system created a large number of untouchables. Dr. Ambedkar believed that "caste divides workers. The caste system by birth does not relate intelligence to physical labour; a person may not be devoted to his/her work due to this system. The caste system by birth denies human beings the right to develop their core interests, thereby resulting in them becoming lifeless."

Dr. Ambedkar also said that if there was equality in virtues, then caste-based discrimination and untouchability should end over time.

Gandhiji used to say that untouchability was a stigma on Hindu society, while Babasaheb said that it was a stigma on ourselves. Mahatma Gandhi coined a new word like 'Harijan' (for untouchables); Babasaheb also did not like this kind of renaming. He said that changing the name did not change the original spirit. In his own words, "I just can't understand what does it mean for the untouchables of Mumbai to call themselves Hindus? What is wrong with the name *bahishkrut* (excluded) if the goal is to unite all the races belonging to the untouchable class? I doubt if you can give another meaningful name like that. It is like creating an illusion if the purpose of the new concept is to remove untouchability. *Mahar* people call themselves *chokha* (pure) because of social-shame; so the *chamars* call themselves Raidas. But those people are as untouchable by one name as they are by another name. The untouchables in the Madras region call themselves Dravidians, but none can claim that this has removed untouchability." Babasaheb never mentioned Gandhiji as *mahatma*. His opinion was that the *mahatma* was meaning unclear couldn't bring about a fundamental change in society. Babasaheb was also against worship of an individual. He used to say that "no matter how great a person could be, but our conscience should not be devoted to that person.

It may be allowed to worship an individual for spiritual uplift but it should not be allowed in politics; worshipping an individual gives birth to dictatorship." According to him, there was nothing wrong in expressing gratitude to great men who have dedicated their entire lives in the service of the country, "but there should also be some limit to expressing gratitude. Irish patriots, Daniel and Cronell had rightly said," A person cannot express gratitude by sacrificing his self-esteem. No woman can express her gratitude by sacrificing her modesty and no country can express gratitude by sacrificing its independence'."

The biggest conflict between Mahatma Gandhi and Babasaheb came to the surface during the Round Table Conference. Babasaheb demanded a separate region for the untouchables and said that the untouchables, being a part of Hindu society, should be considered a minority and thus be given a separate region in the same way that Muslims are considered as a minority. Gandhiji's opinion was different as he said that the untouchable class was a part of Hindu society. That is why a separate region was not to be given to them. He was not willing to tolerate the attempt to isolate the untouchable society politically from the Hindu society and offered to observe a 'fast unto death' against such a move.

Later, the British government declared the Communal Award in 1932 (division between classes). The untouchable class was given a separate region under this award. Mahatma Gandhi was lodged in Yerawada Jail at that time and yet he refused to accept this award. He launched a fast unto death in Yerawada Jail. Babasaheb was under tremendous pressure as he had to choose between saving the life of Gandhiji or accepting a separate region for the untouchables. He was in a great dilemma. Finally, both of them came to an agreement and the famous Poona Pact came into existence. Separate region for untouchables was abolished according to this pact but reservation came into existence in its place. The untouchables were given 78 seats according to an award, which provided separate regions to untouchables, but the Poona Pact granted 73 additional seats for them, thus giving them a total of 151 seats, as per the newly formed reservation system. Dhananjay Kir's description of who won and who lost this conflict is beautifully described, "Gandhiji is a winner on the diplomatic front in Yerawada, but Mahatma Gandhi has been defeated. Gandhiji made Ambedkar helpless by stripping him off his armour by carving a separate untouchable society. Gandhiji proved to be a great politician, but, Ambedkar became a *mahatma* by saving Gandhiji's life." Babasaheb never collaborated with the National Congress but vehemently opposed Mahatma Gandhi, because of which Babasaheb's contemporaries never considered him a patriot. But was he really pro-British? Did he not understand Gandhiji's position and his importance? Why didn't he join hands with Jinnah, a staunch opponent of Gandhi? Why didn't he inspire all untouchables to be on the side of British Government in order to stabilise their power? Why did he give importance to national interests? Why did he support the democratically-elected government even in the Round Table Conference? Why did he never allow his *satyagrahas* to become violent? Why didn't he convert to Islam or Christianity when he was converting himself from Hinduism to Buddhism? Why did he think of adopting one of these religious means and become a non-national? The answers to many such questions should be considered.

□

2

National Perspective during Movements

Dr. Babasaheb's national perspective is clearly evident, be it a movement for social and religious rights or his role on the path of politics. He could have easily adopted Islam, if the purpose of his life was only to eradicate untouchability; but that was not his only purpose. His goal was to cure Hinduism completely. He wanted an egalitarian Hinduism by demolishing the difference between upper and lower classes. He became established as a national leader by 1930 when he placed his demands at the first Round Table Conference in London. He demanded rights for the untouchables on the one hand and democratic *swarajya* (complete freedom) on the other. This Round Table Conference was to lay the foundation for the future constitution of the country.

Dr. Babasaheb Ambedkar delivered his speech at the first Round Table Conference held on 20 November, 1930. The conference was attended by a representative of the British Prime Minister as he was the one to have convened the conference. Explaining that there was no change in the status of untouchables during the British rule in India, Babasaheb said, "We were in a very bad situation because of untouchability before the arrival of the British. What did the British do to improve the situation? It was forbidden for us to take water from the common well of the village. Did the British government give us the right to draw water from the well? We could not enter the temple before the British came.

Can we enter now? We were not recruited into the police force before the British came. Is the British government now recruiting us into the police force? We were not taken into the Armed Forces before the British came. Does the British government allow us to join the military forces? Are all these areas open to us today? None of these questions can be answered affirmatively."

In the same statement, Babasaheb further added, "It is not that we blame the British for being indifferent to our problems, but we realised that they are completely incapable of solving our problems." He then discussed in detail the reasons for this incapability. He said, "There was a strong pressure on government officials that they were afraid of making any such move (i.e. making a policy for untouchability) as it would have a severe repercussion in Hindu society." He continued, "The lives of the untouchables have been shrouded in darkness for thousands of years and this society of untouchables is being exploited by the landlords of India. The working class is not paid enough by the rich and none of these malpractices have been stopped by the British government. Why didn't the Britishers do it?" He cited the reasons in these words: "They were afraid that if they tried to change this social as well as economic system, they would be strongly opposed by certain people, so, who can really benefit from such a government and how much?" That is why, in that same speech, Babasaheb demanded that the untouchables need a government of the people, by the people and for the people so that we can alleviate our suffering ourselves. "As long as the British government rules in this country, we are not likely to get even a little bit of political rights. This is possible only through *swarajya* (self-rule)."

Is there any need to make any extra comment on this statement of Dr. Babasaheb? He said that untouchables have remained slaves because of the British government and slavery could end through *swarajya*. It should be noted that Dr. Babasaheb was demanding complete freedom in 1930. Not only did he demand, but he also made it clear that there was the need for a democratic State to make *swarajya* complete. It was an expression of his patriotism as he wanted to see the country independent as well as a democratic, self-governed State.

Babasaheb frequently opposed Mahatma Gandhi but he also accepted Gandhiji's qualities within his heart. It was Babasaheb who took the initiative to save Gandhiji's life when the latter launched a fast against the Communal Award. He had said at that time, "If we think of humanity, it is my duty to save Gandhiji's life." Dr. Ambedkar's opposition to Gandhi was not anti-Gandhi.

The basis of independence had been evolving since 1935. Dr. Babasaheb was aware that there was no obstacle to the independence of the country. On the occasion of his 55th birthday on 14 April, 1947, Dr. Babasaheb was honoured to which he responded thus: "We have a dual responsibility of self-determination in political freedom-one for the self and the other for the country. Everyone wants Hindustan to be independent. Although we have been neglected in the Tri-Ministerial Plan, I am of the view that there should not be any obstacle to the independence of the country."

Muhammad Ali Jinnah had joined the Congress for some time. At the Congress convention of 1920 at Nagpur, Jinnah addressed Mahatma Gandhi as 'Mr. Gandhi', at which the audience voiced their anger and demanded, 'say Mahatma Gandhi ... say Mahatma Gandhi' and disrupted Jinnah's speech. Jinnah returned to Mumbai directly from the stage. He was so livid that he never appeared on the Congress stage again. He became an enemy of Mahatma Gandhi as well as the Congress, though Babasaheb never joined hands with Jinnah. Jinnah could not be a friend as he was an opponent of Gandhi. Though Babasaheb supported Jinnah's demand for Pakistan, he however did not support Jinnah. Babasaheb believed that the Muslims could not stay with the Hindus and if forced to stay together, the two would fight, so it was better for them to leave the country. It was Dr. Ambedkar's view that Muslims should not live in this country.

The above-mentioned description shows how Babasaheb was concerned about the country. He said, "This country belongs to the Hindus, not because they are in majority, but because they have lived here since ancient times; so it is their country. Their label may have changed from time to time but identity remains the same. Hindu is the latest label, they are the same people who were known as the people living in Aryavarta in ancient times."

In his article in the 21 December, 1928 issue of *Bahishkrit Bharat*, Babasaheb wrote an article titled 'Hindu Theology, Its Area and Its Functionaries, in which he referred to India as a 'Hindu nation'. He said, "Hindu *rashtra* is one of the most ancient nations. This has been so and no one needs to be reminded about it. It is a fact that other nations which were her contemporaries like Egypt, Syria, Rome as well as Greece became extinct, while Hindu civilisation is still intact. But, that doesn't mean that the Hindu nation is strong. In fact to call it strong is a sign of self-aggrandisement and recklessness. There are many facets of life and not all of them show strength or self-esteem. Defeating the enemy when he invades and maintaining one's own freedom is one facet of life and accepting the enemy's refuge and becoming his slave is another facet of life. We will be alive in both the cases, but a life of independence can never be compared to a life of slavery. Hindu society has survived for so many years but, only as a slave country. There may be some who may think that there is pride and honour in such a life, but I am ashamed of such a life. It is better to say that the invaders kept us alive rather than saying that we survived."

Reviewing the nation's plight as a slave nation, Babasaheb went on to say, "We are alive because the enemy did not kill us. This is not a life of self-respect. The downfall of the Hindu nation was due to its theology. The reason for the failed tradition of the Hindu nation lies in its wrong methodology. The world has come a long way in terms of social reforms." This was his stand during the Mahad *satyagraha* and it has historical significance.

Dr. Ambedkar believed that the caste system could be eliminated only if there was true patriotism; that inequality cannot be eliminated without keeping national interest as the supreme goal.

During the Mahad *satyagraha*, he explained in detail the purpose of his struggle and how people could unite and what would be the organisation of the Hindus. "If the untouchables get freedom, they alone will not make progress but also use their potential, intelligence and industrial skill for the prosperity of the nation. From this point of view, the movement for abolition of untouchability is not only a movement for their upliftment but also a true people's movement. The untouchability movement is, in a sense, a patriotic one. There would be no need for a movement like *satyagraha* if the untouchables only wanted to save themselves for their self-interest because they can easily achieve humanity and equality through conversion, against which they are fighting now. And they can also use the same energy for their own educational as well as economic progress and which they are spending now to eradicate untouchability."

He also wrote in *Bahishkrit Bharat* (3 February 1928): "Inequality based on *chaturvarna* (four-caste system) must first be eliminated if we want to empower the Hindu society. The Constitution of a new society is to be based on two elements–one single caste and equality. Therefore, the path to eradicating untouchability is as much of self-interest as it is of national interest."

In a broad sense, his struggle against untouchability was aimed at reconstructing the Hindu society. It was impossible to reconstruct the Hindu society after segregating the untouchables from Hindu society and he also wanted to remain a Hindu while doing so. He did not want to be separated from the Hindu society culturally or religiously, and this was his ideology until 1935. But, then he felt that providing only religious, cultural and social rights to the untouchables would not solve the issue. "The untouchables should be given equal political rights and active participation in politics as well," he declared and here he made a strategic difference between the untouchable society and Hindu society. He said, "Untouchable society is not a part of Hindu society from a political point of view and they should be considered as a minority and be given the same rights that the minorities get."

Babasaheb was pursuing a two-pronged ideology of being a part of society, both culturally and religiously, but remaining politically separate from the Hindus and so deserved to be granted the minority status. This may seem contradictory, but it also shows how the political views differed. He did not want to weaken the Hindu society by being completely removed from it but, at the same time, he did not want the untouchables to be put under political dominance of the upper-caste Hindu society.

Talking about his views on India's independence movement

and his role in it, he said, "People do not realise that the present controversy is not for acquiring freedom; it's a struggle between the Hindu-Muslim culture. The role of untouchables is crucial because of their numbers. The original culture of Arya Dharma, which is the basis for Hindu society can remain intact only if the untouchables remain in Hinduism, but if they convert to Islam, then the Arya culture of this country will be in danger and the culture of the foreign invaders would become supreme. It is clear that the untouchables have a decisive role to play in this situation. Muslims cannot win without us and Hindus cannot move forward without keeping us together, so much so that our untouchable brethren should realise how important and vital they are."

His public struggle began with the establishment of an organisation called Bahishkrit Hitkarini Sabha. The purpose of this organisation was not to conduct a national movement or take part in the freedom movement; the prime aim was to highlight the issues of untouchables. In 1927, Babasaheb was elected to the provincial legislature and he went to attend the Round Table Conference in 1930-31, 32. The *satyagraha* movement of Chavdar Lake in Mahad had taken place in 1927, followed by the *satyagrahas* demanding entry into the Kalaram temple and Parvati temple. The views expressed by Babasaheb in the provincial legislature on the *satyagraha* reflect his 'nation first' attitude.

Babasaheb's favourite subject was education. He told the students, "Acquire knowledge, be self-respecting and be polite." That was a time when primary education was being discussed in the Mumbai Provincial Assembly where Babasaheb said, "Increasing the scope of primary education is very important from a national point of view. In the present situation, it is certain that a country whose majority people are uneducated cannot survive anywhere. The ubiquitous primary education is the foundation of national progress. It may take several centuries for primary education to reach all if this issue is left to the will of the people; so a law has to be enacted to make primary education compulsory. We can see that all developed countries have eliminated illiteracy by making primary education compulsory. People, who already know about the benefits of education, need not be pushed for the same, but it is necessary to make education compulsory for those who do not know the importance of education and those who are indifferent towards education."

He delivered numerous public lectures as a professor, lecturer, renowned public leader, legislator and member of legislature on his favourite subject as he loved teaching as well as the students. Details on this subject are further covered in Chapter 12 of this book.

Dr. Ambedkar wrote the editorial of *Mooknayak* (Issue 19; 23 October, 1920) calling on the youth to serve the motherland. "Don't be afraid of anyone; fight for your rights. Just as we have to endure obstacles through diseases and disasters, so there are obstacles in the path of upliftment of our society. But, it is not right to lose heart due to such obstacles. So, let the youth be proud of their clan and family for the benefit of the society in which we have been raised and for the salvation and to pay back for the obligation of the motherland, the country in which we were born and raised; make the right use of yourself and immortalise our glory. Only good deeds make the man great; keep this in mind."

Babasaheb's views on national unity were ignored during this period. The All India Depressed Class convened a session at Nagpur on 8-9 August, 1930 to seek the views of the participants on the recommendations of the Simon Commission as well as on the constitution of the State. On the first day, that is, 8 August, Babasaheb delivered the presidential address at the convention. He spoke about the basic issues of the country as well as nationality. The word 'minority' is commonly used in our country today. Babasaheb's views in this regard should be considered and properly implemented: "I would like to raise another issue in this regard. This country is divided into castes as well as sects and the country cannot remain united and self-governing without making provision in the constitution for the protection of all castes and tribes. This is a fact and cannot be challenged. But minorities also need to keep in mind that even though one particular caste dominates us today and we are divided into different castes, our ultimate goal is to establish a united India. Minorities, who want to maintain their dignity, should accept this goal. It will be clear that the minority organisations that are demanding security will have to be careful not to become an obstacle in India's unity while securing their own security. It is true that you have been banned from and deprived of many rights but you should try to secure protection against this. You have to be careful that your protection provisions do not create discrimination in this country and do not become permanent. We should expect a bridge to be built to fill this gap of discrimination. It is the duty of the majority society to allow provisions for the protection of minorities. But at the same time, it is the sacred duty of the minorities not to hinder the work of establishing unity among us. In this regard, it must be acknowledged that a joint constituency as well as a reserved constituency would be a better alternative than an independent constituency."

In 1930, when he was invited to attend the Round Table Conference, Dr. Babasaheb Ambedkar was presented a Certificate of Honour when he said, "I will definitely ask for what we need, but I will support it if there is a proposal for the independence of this country. Like the Congress, I also feel that then this country can make tremendous progress in every way." He was not a political follower of Gandhiji but an ideological opponent of him. However, he said, "If they will propose freedom (of the country), I will support them."

Dr. Ambedkar's pain was evident in his speech when he said, "If everyone in the country had the right to carry arms, the country would not have become a slave to foreigners." In his *Diksha Bhoomi* speech in 1956, Babasaheb said, "The country was enslaved because the weapons were snatched from the hands of the untouchables. Why did foreigners occupy our country? The Kshatriyas died in our country and so we also perished. If we had the right to take up arms, this country would not have been enslaved. No one could have won over this country."

Babasaheb added in 1931, "In the new State-system, the future government of India as well as India's security system should not be governed by the British but by the Indian people to a large extent." This statement meant that regarding the question of defence of India, all the people of the country should be involved and not be limited to just one particular race or caste.

One thing can be distinctively concluded from his statements that his role was at the national level regarding the untouchability movement. He repeatedly said that issues related to untouchables were not confined only to untouchable tribes but had national dimensions. His view was that untouchability hampered the progress of the country, resulting in the country becoming slave to foreigners. His vision was invariably national from the very beginning regarding education, security of the country or issue of religion. With nation first at his heart, he linked everything to the nation and this is something which we fail to take note of. Even when a bill to give maternity leave to women was being debated in the Mumbai Legislative Assembly in 1927, he said, "Giving maternity leave to women is in the interest of the nation and there is no scope for further discussion." His criticism of Hinduism as well as the *varna* (caste) system presents a one-sided image of him to most people, but that is not correct.

The world advanced and moved towards science and technology and industry, but we kept fighting among ourselves and considering the touch of a person from another religion as a sin. Babasaheb wrote thus in an editorial in *Bahishkrit Bharat*: "People over here accept the rule of foreign rulers, but they cannot accept their own countryman to rule over them because they cannot acceptit if the ruler is not from their own caste. As soon as a ruler from one caste came to power, he would become an alien and unreliable for the people of all other castes. In such a scenario, even a good leader was not acceptable to other castes as he belonged to a different caste. Each caste believes that there should be a leader from its own caste; as a result, instead of following a scholar-leader of the other caste, they prefer to follow a foolish leader of their own caste. Every caste thinks that with the advent of *swarajya* (self-rule), power will pass into the hands of another castes and our caste would be in trouble. It is rather better to have power in the hands of foreigners. Caste discrimination increases the malevolence among castes. As a result, hatred among castes runs for generations."

Dr. Babasaheb said that it was essential to eliminate the caste system and sectarianism of Hinduism in order to build a unified Hindu nation. "Many people here have tried to eradicate apartheid but they were not successful" (*Mooknayak*: 28 August, 1920).

Dr. Babasaheb Ambedkar wrote in his treatise *Lord Buddha*

and His Dhamma: "It is most important to eliminate all such rules and regulations from the religion which creates social discrimination, and that is the way to form a true religion–that Brahmins are best and Shudras are worst–the nation cannot stand by such rules. Create harmony in the society with thoughts like 'all are equal: I am just like everyone else-just like us, everyone else... 'Every Indian is my brother.' Brotherhood means national unity' for the progress of the nation. And such ideas must be adopted with an open heart as per the teachings of Lord Buddha."

Dr. Babasaheb believed that the nation could prosper only if there was a spirit of solidarity and sense of ownership in the nation. He wrote in the editorial of Mooknayak (28 August, 1920):

"A lively nation is not an ordinary person. It is just like a single human being who cannot be a family or a home, a society, a village, or a province, or a nation. There cannot be any so-called single caste or a single society in a nation. Many people together form a family; many families together form a society; societies together become a village; many villages together form a province or a country. All individuals in a family have a sense of mutual intimacy and when such a spirit in every society will prevail, only then the nation will be able to survive. There is a possibility of an invasion by outsiders when there is no vitality and unity in the society. We need to eliminate such a possibility. There will be no internal unity if there is no reciprocal sense of ownership. Every city has horse-drawn carriages. The municipality issues licences after examining their wheels and horses. If there is any deficiency in it, the horseman participates in the race only after fixing it. Extra dexterity is required in terms of a nation, which can progress only there and then."

It is necessary to understand some of the traditional terms before understanding Babasaheb's contribution to nation building. The 'nation' and 'State' are technical terms which we consider as synonyms in everyday practice. We never say that India is my nation; instead we say, 'India is my country.' Nation and State are used as synonyms, but we have to understand that they have a specific meaning, especially when we use the word 'nation'.

□

3

People and Land of the Nation

The land of India is described in many ways in our Indian scriptures: "This is the land of God, this is our motherland, this is our conception." In the *Ramayana*, Sri Rama says to Sri Lakshman, अपिस्वर्णमयीलंकानमेलक्ष्मणरोचते, जननीजन्मभूमिश्चस्वर्गादपिगरीयसी। *(Lakshman, I cannot honour Lanka, even if it is made of all gold. Honour of mother and motherland is even higher than Heaven).*

There are two famous *shlokas* describing the land of India:

1. समुद्रवसनेदेविपर्वतस्तनमण्डले।
   विष्णुपत्निनमस्तुभ्यंपादस्पर्शक्षमस्वमे॥

("O Goddess Earth! The sea is your dress. You are adorned with mountain-like breasts and you are the wife of Lord Vishnu. I bow to you and apologise for the touch of my feet on you!"

2. उत्तरंयत्समुद्रस्यहिमाद्रेश्चैवदक्षिणम्।
   वर्षंतत्भारतंनामभारतीयत्रसंततिः॥

This *shloka* defines India as "the land to the north of the sea and south of the Himadari (Himalayas) is called India. The people of this land are called the Indian people."

Apart from this, there is also Sanskrit literature and texts which describe the land of India. It is our ancient tradition to consider the land of India as Mother India, which is the only country in the world to worship the country as 'motherland'. For Indians, India is a holy land, a fatherland. Veer Savarkar once composed the following poem in England, while looking out at the sea:नेमजसीनेपरतमातृभूमीला. सागराप्राणतळमळला. ('O sea, take me back to my motherland, my soul is longing.'

There are some other shlokas (verses) describing and worshipping the land of India thus:

असाधंबध्यतोमानवानांयस्याउद्वत:प्रवत:समंबहु।
नानावीर्याऔषाधीर्याबिभर्तिपृथिवीन:प्रथतांराध्यतांन॥ १॥

(Despite differences in virtues, deeds and temperament among the people of our motherland, there is a great deal of harmony and unity. Our motherland which grows many different herbal antidotes, let it fulfil our desires and augment our glory.)

यस्यांपूर्वेपूर्वजनाविचक्रिरेयस्यांदेवाअसुरानभ्यवर्तयन्।
गवामष्वानांवयसश्चविष्भगंवर्च:पृथिवीनोदधातु॥ २॥

(Our ancient sages have done many miraculous deeds for this land, in which the manly pro-God heroes have waged a crusade against the demonic powers, where cows, horses and animals take special refuge. Such is our motherland; let her raise our knowledge, bravery, brilliance, gallantry and wealth.)

विश्वंभरावसुधानीप्रतिष्ठाहिरणयवक्षाजगतनिवेशनी।
वैष्वानरंबिभ्रतीभूमिरग्निमिन्द्रऋभाद्रविणेनोदधातु॥ ३॥

(This land which nourishes all the living beings of the world, rich in mineral wealth, dignifies all, with golden heartland, shelters all the living beings of the world, nourishes the cosmic fire. May this land provide the leading and mighty Indradev and all of us with various kinds of wealth and prosperity.)

यार्णवेऽधिसलिमममानआसिद्यांमायाभिरन्वचरन्मनीषिण:।
यस्याहृदयंपरमेव्योमन्त्सत्येनावृतममृतंपृथिव्या
सानोभूमिस्त्विर्षिंबलंराष्ट्रेदधातुत्तमे॥ ४॥

(The heart of the land which is always covered with the true nectar flowing from the sovereign sky, the land which intellectuals follow with all their skills, may the land bring radiance and vigour to our best nation.)

Dr. Babasaheb did not mention these *shlokas* (verses) while describing India, but described India in his treatise titled *Ancient Indian Commerce*, thus: 'India's geographical location is perfect for a newly developed culture. Nature has enriched India in such a way that even the primitive humans would be envied in terms of making proper use of the gifts received from nature as a safe haven and to develop themselves to the best of their ability. India is separated from China and Tibet in the north by the Himaliyan ranges, Assam and Burma in the east (Tenasserim mountain range) and Afghanistan (Karakoram/Hindu Kush mountains) in the west. It is also protected due to the mountain ranges in its northwest. Such natural elements are creating their own small world for this peninsula. The natural shield protects it and the remaining borders are being protected by the sea in the form of a bay."

He added, "This inverse triangle contains diverse and abundant natural resources. There is a rich fauna in India (of British era) and there is a remarkable diversity also. India has an abundance of existing animal species and other dependent species. This number surpasses the number of species found in the whole of Europe. But despite the fact that Europe's surface area is more than half that of India, the diversity of flora and fauna has remained conducive to the existence of diverse fauna. The richness of flora has proved to be a boon for India's economic self-sufficiency, which is considered to be the prerogative of only a select few states of the planet' (*Ancient Indian Commerce*)."

This is how Babasaheb described this land so magnificently. Some verses from *Atharvaveda* quoted initially also describe the earth. So, what were the people of this land, rich in nature and rich in natural resources, doing? Babasaheb replies, 'A well-to-do person cannot remain inactive, because economic incentives make him stronger and more active. He immediately starts using the surrounding situation for his own prosperity. Indian ancestors were no exception to this rule. It would be wrong to compare today's Indians with the Indians of that time. Today's Indians may be physically similar to their Indian ancestors but that is not the end of comparison. During a certain period of time, the territory which was in the possession of the ancient Indians made tremendous progress in comparison to other contemporary barbarian people. Although their deeds are not documented and we cannot find their proof, whatever other contemporaries have written about them shows that the ancient Indians made tremendous progress in many areas. However, we will focus on economic trade here" (*Ancient Indian Commerce*).

In this complete thesis, Dr. Babasaheb refers to Indians as 'Hindus'. Babasaheb said, "Many Hindus were eloquent, but weak in financial accounting. The reason was that education had become a monopoly of only a few. The Brahmin class was intelligent and did not engage in any kind of productive work. Therefore, there are no texts available about Hindus' productive works."

Our land was enriched by our ancestors through their hard work. Dr. Babasaheb did not give any figures in his thesis. Maybe not much research had been done on it at that time, but today there are plenty of writings on the economic history of India. Matthew Joseph's *History of Indian Economy* is a very descriptive article available on the Internet. In this article, he presents statistics on the production capacity of ancient India as follows:

"The history of India begins with the emergence of the Indus Valley civilisation, which developed during the period 3500 to 1800 BC. The economy of the Indus Valley civilisation was mainly based on trade. Transportation facilities proved to be convenient for them. The people of this culture farmed, raised domestic animals and made sharp tools and weapons from metals like copper, bronze and tin and utensils made of terracotta, gem, gold and silver, sapphire, metal, flint, stone, shells and pearl, etc. They used to trade colored gems. They used ships to travel to Mesopotamia and sell gold and silver jewellery there. Merchants' guilds also made silver coins in mints around 600 BC. This period was a period of trade and prosperity for the citizens. The Mauryan Empire (321-185 BC) united the Indian peninsula around 300 BC when the Middle East was ruled by the Greeks–Seleucids and Ptolemy. A prosperous economy developed here due to political stability and military security. This led to an increase in agricultural production; businesses and industries also developed in a similar manner. The empire used a lot of money to build and maintain roads across India. With the development of infrastructure came security and universal weight and measurement system, thus increasing trade due to circulation of currency. In the following about 1500 years, India developed a rich culture, including the creation of wealth on a large scale. From the first to the seventeenth century AD, India was a powerful economy (superpower) in the ancient and medieval world and controlled one-third to one-fourth of the world's trade."

Below are figures provided by Angus Maddison, a retired professor at the University of Groningen in the Netherlands and an honorary Fellow at the University of Cambridge. The figures show India's wealth in 1000 AD, 1500 AD and 1700 AD. India's contribution to the world's gross domestic product (GDP) in AD 1000 was more than a quarter, in 1500 AD as well as in 1900 AD, it was less than a quarter.

Gross Domestic Product (GDP) (Figures in US dollars)

Year	1000	1500	1700
India	33,750	60,500	90,750
China	26,550	61,000	82,000
Eastern Europe	10,165	44,345	83,395
Whole World	116,790	247,116	371,361

In the mid-eighteenth-century India, the Marathas conquered and regained much of the territory from the Mughals. Some small territories belonging to Nawabs in the north and Nizam, etc. in the south remained with the Muslims. Almost during the similar period, in the middle of the eighteenth century, the British expanded their power in India. India's trade began to decline from that period onwards.

The thesis titled *Ancient Indian Commerce*, has historical significance because it provides the background for further research. Dr. Babasaheb, in his thesis, elaborated on how rich the Hindus were in ancient India. The main occupation of the people at that time was farming. The Hindus lived in villages with 30 to 1,000 families living in one village. Babasaheb also mentioned a famous pre-traditional saying, "Farming is excellent, trade moderate and jobs are lowest." Though at the same time he didn't forget to mention that Brahmins also worked as shepherds and did farming. The Hindus were more interested in agricultural business as compared to the ancient Greeks.

Babasaheb also expressed his views on cow slaughter. The faith of Hindus towards cows has never been understood by foreigners. Many missionaries even tried to create confusion about the intellect of Hindus by misinterpreting *gaupuja* (cow-worship). Babasaheb further wrote: "The basic aim to encourage cow worship was to bring economic stability of that time. Romans did not offer wine made from such grape vine which was not selected; that was also for economic reasons. Cows are the lifeline of farmers; a cow provides oxen which are essential for farming. Having to eat beef, one needs to kill a cow. That poses a threat to agriculture. Thus, Hindus banned the consumption of beef out of extreme foresight, but human beings do not value only ideals. So, religious beliefs have to be formed around it. Thus many kinds of stories about cows have been created in Hindu religious texts."

He said, "Economic growth requires a variety of products. Production requires raw materials, manpower, machinery and skill and production means creating wealth. Wealth is, in fact, in manufactured goods and not in money. Money only serves trade in terms of an exchange. The value of money depends on the quantity of goods produced. This is a simple rule of economics. Babasaheb gave information about how his ancestors, i.e. the Hindus formed labour organisations, industrial organisations and trade organisations. It was through them that the Hindus made this land prosperous."

Babasaheb said that slavery was not an economic practice of Hindus. "Yes, criminals had to be enslaved for different kinds of crimes, but the Hindu attitude towards criminals was of forgiveness. Therefore, the practice of slavery did not start in India. There were three types of artisan categories involved in manufacturing:

- First, carpenters, shipbuilders, wagon and caravan builders and architects.
- Second, metalworkers; metal work involved making agricultural implements, different weapons, sharp-edged weapons, fine needles and gold and silver items.
- Third, brick and stone workers including craftsmen working on a wide variety of stones and soft gems."

Babasaheb further wrote: "There were different types of organisations in each industry. Some industries were established only in certain regions. They were connected with different cities. A system was created to monitor every essential activity. There were many different types of groups and each group had a president.

There was emphasis on doing traditional work, but it was not until then, that caste-wise occupation became the norm. Trading was done in large groups. The industrial centres were connected by excellent roads. The *Ramayana* describes the routes from Ayodhya to Rajgriha as also roads going north from Hastinapur (a place near present-day Delhi). Babasaheb gave information on many such roads in his treatise. In today's language, all the basic infrastructure required for industry and trade were in place and these were built by our ancestors. Use of money for exchange in trade was also in place."

Economic prosperity results in many different developments. In ancient times, the Hindus started establishing their own colonies in different countries. European historians do not accept this fact. Expressing grief over this, Babasaheb said, "On seeing the current situation of India, the Europeans are not ready to believe that the people here may have gone abroad for trade or colonisation." Babasaheb explained that the ancestors of Indians had crossed the Indian Ocean by overcoming all kinds of natural obstacles. The Hindus were already accepted as influential trading partners of the Indian Ocean before the Arabian Sea emerged as a trading power. They also traded with East Africa. India's trade with Egypt and Roman Empire was largely by water and land. Local culture and ideas were propagated along with trade. There was a lot of cultural exchange along trade routes in ancient times. On this subject, Babasaheb wrote, "Culture always follows trade. It was more applicable in ancient times than in today's perspective. Traders not only carried goods from one country to another but also carried their own culture with them. They also propagated and spread their culture abroad. The exchange of cultures between two countries had the greatest impact on Egyptian architecture." James Ferguson (*History of Architecture*, Part-1, pp. 142-3) mentions, "The original idea of this architecture was from Egypt, though its subtlety or preciseness belongs to the Indians. The Egyptian version of the nine-storey pagoda in Bodh Gaya, India, dates back to the first century AD." Ferguson added, "The connection between India and Egypt was possible because the two cultures were linked by trade. The masterpieces of architecture symbolise this relationship" (*Ancient Indian Trade*, Dr. Babasaheb

Ambedkar, Vinimay Publishers, Mumbai).

There have been many invasions of this ancient land throughout history. Dr. Babasaheb, in his book, *Thoughts on Pakistan*, mentioned the names of the barbaric Islamic rulers who ruled over northern India for 762 years. The Islamic invasion took place for two reasons-to propagate Islam and plunder the wealth of prosperous India.

Regarding the Muslim invasions, Babasaheb wrote: "The first invasion of India took place in 711, under the leadership of Muhammad bin Qasim. The invasion was short-lived; he could not occupy any land. At the same time, the Caliphate of Baghdad began to disintegrate. Mahmud of Ghazni later invaded in the year 1001. He invaded India seventeen times. Then in 1173, Muhammad Ghori came as an invader, who wreaked havoc in northern India. Genghis Khan of the Mongol dynasty, invaded in 1221. He came to the border of India but he did not enter India. After that, in the year 1398, Timur made the worst attack. Babur invaded in 1526. In 1738, Nadir Shah invaded India. In 1761, Ahmad Shah Abdali came to India." Dr. Ambedkar has noted that Qutbuddin Aibak demolished a thousand temples. After providing numerous facts on Mughal invasions till the invasion of Ahmad Shah Abdali in 1761, he wrote: "These Muslim invasions were neither just to plunder India nor to satisfy their hunger for victory; they had another motive also."

Babasaheb said that all these invasions were not just about greed, plundering prosperity or to conquer the land; they wanted to kill the idol worshippers (pagans), destroy their places of worship and convert the people to Islam. Babasaheb has made this clear in his treatise (from page 55-62) by citing examples of many scholars have said of this treatise Idea of Pakistan. One thing to keep in mind is that Babasaheb wrote this treatise to justify why Muslims should be given Pakistan. The Muslim invaders not only changed the geography of India but also made cultural attacks on it, which led to the emergence of two rival factions in India. In his research book entitled *Ancient Indian Commerce*, Babasaheb presented a very detailed portrayal of the undivided India and has used the word 'Hindu' for the people who had become destitutes due to Muslim aggression.

Babasaheb described how the people of this country were torn apart and "how long could a Hindu can claim that North India is only a part of Aryavarta? This part was in our possession, so how long could a Hindu insist that it would remain an undivided part of our nation till the end? Those who are against partition and talk of sentimental attachment to the old historical reality that at one time Afghanistan too was a part of India, where Buddhists and Hindus lived side by side, should be asked if the motive of Muslims and the policies adopted by them like invasion of India be audited or not?" (*Thoughts on Pakistan*, p. 63).

Two different scenarios emerge in Babasaheb's writings–an ancient glorious India and an India humiliated by Islamic Invasion. In his speech at the Nagpur Diksha (initiation) Ceremony, he said: "The main reason for the destruction of Buddhism is the inhuman aggression of Muslims. Muslims destroyed thousands of idols; Buddhist monks were killed. At that time, India's border was as far as up to Afghanistan, whose ancient name was Gandhara. There was an ancient and largest university in Takshashila. That region is not even in India today. Once India was a most prosperous country and along with prosperity, India promoted its culture all over the world. Hindus went abroad with their culture and religion. That religion was also competent enough to be propagated, but later everything was lost. Our ancestors enriched this land with their deeds and converted it into a Golden Land, but, subsequently the same land was converted into a miserable land by their own deeds. The geography is same but the attitudes and thinking of its residents have changed. This change has weakened the nation, enslaved the nation, impoverished the nation. One has to think about the third important component of the nation–the culture of the nation besides thinking about the people and the land (of this nation)."

□

4
Indian Culture

The third and important basic component of a nation is culture. Culture connects people living in a particular region or peninsula. It is difficult to define culture, but different scholars have interpreted it in different ways. Two views are presented here to cut short the entire description: in the words of E. B. Tylor, 'Culture is that complex whole which includes knowledge, belief, art, morals, law, custom and any other capabilities and habits acquired by man as a member of society.'

The second definition says: 'Culture is defined as a social jurisdiction based on practice, rhetoric, materialism, with an emphasis on the expression of consistency and inconsistency in ordinary social life.'

Cambridge English Dictionary states that culture is 'the way of life, especially the general customs and beliefs of a particular group of people at a particular time'.

The word 'culture' is used to denote many things in many ways–food culture, dance culture, literary culture, environment culture, language culture, etc. The word 'culture' may be associated with any other word in general practice, but when we think of the word 'culture' in a technical sense, the word must acquire a definite meaning. It includes the different people with different languages, religions, customs, festivals, values, concepts, dress and costumes which vary from one region to another. A group of people living in a particular region or a country perceive themselves as being different from other groups of people. They harbour the belief of 'we and others' in their mind. When we look at the size of the European continent, almost all countries are smaller than a single state of India in terms of area and population, but, it is not easy to unite all of them to form a single country, named Europe.

It is not so with India. Despite extreme diversities, India is united and a single nation. India is very diverse, not only culturally but geographically too and in terms of atmosphere as well. There are snowy regions, and regions with extreme heat throughout the year. People in India speak many different languages and dialects. They vary in terms of costumes and their food habits. There are white, wheatish, extremely dark and yellow-race people living in India and the beauty lies in their origin–their ancestral homes date back to the prehistoric era and yet they are Indians! India is one nation despite all these diversities, because the culture of India is ONE; their cultural traditions are SAME.

There are numerous different sub-castes (the word *gyati* is normally used for these sub-castes) in India. They perceive themselves as socially different from each other and do not mix with each other; inter-caste marriages are considered as social taboo. Although Hindu deities are accepted by all Indians but some of these different sub-castes accept some and reject other deities. Some groups worship only Krishna, while others are devoted to only Shiva. But, despite all these differences, unity is there in their cultural life. What Dr. Babasaheb has said in this regard is especially important, "Cultural unity is the only factor for the unity of all peoples in terms of ethnography. If this view is accepted, I would like to make a bold statement here that no other country can match India in terms of cultural unity of the people. India is not united only in one sense, but it is united from top to bottom and left to right from the point of view of every other factor of unity one can expect" (*Castes in India*).

Dr. Ambedkar knew that the basis of India's unity was cultural and social and that only cultural and social consciousness could bring about a change. His following statement is very relevant, "Civilisation is a witness to the fact that all political revolutions took place only after social and cultural revolutions; and that determines the success and significance of the political revolution." Giving examples from India, Dr. Ambedkar said, "While the Buddha's cultural and social revolution took place before Chandragupta's political revolution, the success of Shivaji's political revolution was due to the contribution of the saints of Maharashtra, which embarked on cultural and social change." In this context he cited the example of Guru Nanak's cultural-social enlightenment and its influence. One thing is certain–that Dr. Ambedkar's fundamental emphasis was on a cultural and social revolution.

Dr. Ambedkar wrote in his paper '*Castes in India*' presented at Columbia University in 1916: "India has an all-encompassing cultural unity. Although society is divided into innumerable castes and sub-castes, it is bound by one culture." He added, "A nation cannot stand alone through a single culture. Social cohesion along with cultural unity is just as important for the nation to stand firm."

Babasaheb completely rejected the belief that the Aryans came from outside (of India). He also refuted this theory in his paper, '*Castes in India*' presented, in 1916, at Columbia University. He wrote: 'Europeans gave undue importance to apartheid in the caste system (of India). Dr. Kelkar is right when he says that all the kings and maharajas, whether they were of Arya *vansh* (clan) or Dravidian descent, were all Aryans. Foreign scholars came to India and drew a line of distinction (among them)." Babasaheb further wrote: "My study reveals four points of the riddle of caste. One, although the structure of the Hindu people is mixed, they have a deep cultural unity. Two, caste is the division of a large cultural unit into smaller fractions. Three, originally, only one caste existed. Four, classes turned into castes through imitation and social exclusion."

Dr. Babasaheb was conscious of the unity of Indian culture and had often criticised the followers of Brahminism, *chaturvarna* and the *Manusmriti* in very harsh words. His critique was against the distortions in the original Hindu culture, "Recognition to *chaturvarna* is the main cause for the destruction and decline of the Hindu nation. This practice of *chaturvarna* (which is not an original element of Hinduism, according to him) has been prevailing since centuries. Its roots are very deep and that is one of the principal causes why Hindustan has suffered many setbacks...Untouchability is the worst form of inequality. Such a strong living example of inequality is not found anywhere else than in Hinduism. No one can find the practice where one person is not allowed to touch another person and to call that person a degenerate or a sinner other than in Hinduism or Hindu society. When someone considers that a touch of another human being can turn the water impure or even turns the God impure, then it is a nadir of humanity. This is a stigma on your body, on your words; someone says that untouchability is a stigma on Hinduism, but not a single Hindu believes that Hinduism itself is stigmatised. Instead they believe that you are stigmatised"(*Yanche Vichardhan* by Babasaheb Ambedkar, pp. 17).

The culture of a nation includes same values, same traditions, same outlook on life, same concepts about nature and animals and respect for men and women who have sacrificed or dedicated their lives to establish the values of life. It would be more appropriate to quote what Babasaheb said, "The birth of Hinduism is based on *chaturvarna* system and the blueprint for the Hindu society contrasts with the blueprint of the rest of the world." He described the Hindu society as a four-storeyed building, where the Brahmins lived on the topmost floor, Kshatriyas thereafter, Vaishyas on the third floor and Shudras on the lowest floor. There was no stairway connecting all these four storeys. No matter how worthless the resident of the upper floor was, s/he could not go down and no matter how learned the lower floor person was, s/he had no right to go upstairs. The Hindu society suffered from such inequality. He said that the scenario of Hinduism and other religions was completely in contrast. One's importance increased when s/he entered any other religion, but one's respect did not increase unless one was expelled from Hinduism. "Hinduism has two distict parts: (1) philosophy and (2) conduct. Philosophically untouchables here are the same as touchables, but in terms of conduct they are not only unequal, but also impure. That means that dealing with them is unrighteous." He further added that the ethical values in any religion should be based on the philosophy of that religion. It was such views of his that made him more and more bitter about Hinduism.

He was critical of the Brahmins, about whom he said, 'My

point of view about the word 'Brahminism' is not about the power, rights and interests of the Brahmin caste; I never use this word in that sense. My point of view about the word 'Brahminism' is against the lack of liberty, equality and fraternity; Brahminism has created havoc in all these matters. Although the Brahmins are creators of such an havoc, this situation is not confined to Brahmins alone. Such malpractices have controlled the thinking and conduct of all the castes." Brahmanism is a mindset, which affects all castes. He also believed that all the castes suffered from the belief in casteism.

His views on Hinduism were based on his experiences in life. His biography describes many incidents of his struggles against the practice of untouchability because of which he had to suffer as a child, be humiliated during his student life and on many more occasions. As a result, he organised the Mahad *satyagraha* to be allowed entry into the Kalaram temple and establish harmony, equality and fraternity. Unfortunately, these *satyagrahas* did not fuflfil the results he expected. He then decided to agitate politically. He termed the Congress as the 'Hindu Congress' and said, "It is pointless to say that the Congress is not a Hindu organisation." He expected the Congress and its leaders, particularly Mahatma Gandhi to be the medium of change among the Hindus, but they did not come up to his expectations. Such a callous attitude made him more bitter towards the upper-caste Hindus.

Addressing the Berar Province Untouchable Conference in Amravati (on 13 November, 1927), he said, "From time to time many scholars have advised the *Savarnas* (upper caste people) to remove the stigma of untouchability, but their prejudice is so strong that they are not bothered about doing anything."

Did this mean that Babasaheb was anti-religious? Was he a heretic? Was he apostate? No, he actually considered religion to be an integral part of life. He was a great religious scholar of modern India. In this context, he should be placed on par with great religious personalities like Swami Vivekananda and Swami Dayanand Saraswati. His statement clarifies how strong his faith was in religion, "it seems to me that you like politics most (addressing his own volunteers); you like politics more than anything else. It's not so with me; I'm more interested in religion.

I'm going to use my strength for that."

In his speech on 28 October, 1954, he said, "I have three *gurus*. My prime and best *guru* is the Buddha because Buddhism has had a lasting influence on my mind and I am convinced that only Buddhism can bring welfare to the world. I would always say that Hindus must convert to Buddhism, if they want to keep their nation alive." His second guru was Kabir as his father was a believer of Kabirpanth (Kabir sect). Poet Kabir's thoughts had a profound effect on his mind right since childhood. As the third *guru* was Jyotiba Phule, as he was the real *guru* of the non-Brahmin caste. It was Jyotiba Phule who taught a lesson in humanity to all lower-caste people like tailors, potters, barber, fisherman, janitors, skin flayers, weavers, etc.

In a speech delivered at Deekshabhoomi at Nagpur on accepting Buddhism (15 October, 1956), Babasaheb said, "Religion is a very important thing for the uplift of all the human beings. I know that a cult (Marxism) has emerged due to Karl Marx's teachings. According to them, there is no such thing as religion; there is no importance of religion to them. They are satisfied if they get their breakfast of bread, butter, cream, chicken and eggs and a full meal in the day followed by a peaceful sleep at night. Their life revolves around going to the cinema and they get what they need. This is their philosophy. I do not agree with them. I do believe that there should be economic progress and this process of economic development is essential for human beings, but they forget that man has also got a mind along with the body. Both should be considered; the mind should also be developed. In fact the mind should be cultured."

It should be noted that Babasaheb's emphasis was more on making human beings civilised. His discourse at a Buddhist monastery in Worli (on 19 September, 1950) is no less relevant even today. He said, "Purity does not come in a person's mind as long as abusive treatment and horrible disrespect for moral value in everyday life. It is to be understood that if it is not taken into account how one human being should behave with another human being, then India will never rise."

Religion gives 'culture' the 'form of culture', for which he used the word 'Dhamma' instead of 'Dharma' (religion). Babasaheb said,

"It is said that religion is a personal matter; it should be confined to oneself and should not be given importance in public life.

- In contrast Dhamma is social, primarily and in principle, it is social.
- Dhamma is linked with virtue. This means that one person should treat another person appropriately in every sphere of life.
- Dhamma is not needed if a person is alone.

Whether one feels good or not, Dhamma is necessary when two persons get together in any relationship. It is impossible to do without it. In other words, there can be no society without Dhamma.* The society may decide not to choose Dhamma as a tool of governance, but Dhamma is not separate from the tool of governance.

- A society which does not accept Dhamma in governance will end in anarchy. Else, the other option for the society is to choose the rule of force, i.e. dictatorship.
- Or the society has to accept Dhamma for governance and punish those who violate the rules of Dhamma.

*Anarchy and dictatorship knock down one's freedom. Feedom can be maintained only with the third option."

In a nutshell, Babasaheb considered Dhamma to be most important in life.

What kind of values of life did Babasaheb present through Dhamma? First and foremost was purification of the mind. He considered character development to be the most important thing in life and a person without character was akin to an animal.

Keeping the mind pure and always have good thoughts in mind was an important characteristic for him. He described in his book, *Gautam Buddha and His Dhamma* :

- "The mind is the creator of all thoughts and deeds, thus it is the lord and the cause.
- If there are evil thoughts in the mind, man's words and deeds also become evil. '*Papad bhav dukhe* –that is, the way the wheels of the chariot follow the horse, in the same way *karma* follows the mind.
- The mind is the cause of all suffering. The mind commands and causes action to take place.

- If there is a good thought in the mind, then both words and deeds of a human being are good. Happiness comes from virtue and follows a person like a shadow of the deed."

Our words and actions should synchronise. Principles sound good but such principles have to be acted upon. One should act according to the principle as it is an important aspect of Indian culture. On page 220 of the book, *Gautam Buddha and His Dhamma*, Babasaheb mentioned the Sallekha *sutta* of Lord Buddha. Here are some excerpts:

"* You shall not commit any harmful act even when other people behave in a harmful manner. You shall purify your mind with determination.

* You shall not kill even if other people kill.

* Even if other people steal, you shall not steal.

* Even if other people's lives is not the best, your life should be the best.

* You shall not follow those who tell lies, slander or misbehave.

* You shall not be greedy even if the other people are greedy.

* You shall not hate even if other people hate you.

* You shall not get distracted from the path of right vision, right resolution, right speech, right action, right livelihood, right exercise, right memory and right meditation, even if other people harbour a false vision, false determination, false speech, false action, false meditation.

* If others make a mistake on the path of truth and *nirvana*, you shall not get distracted from that path.

* When other people are lazy and slovenly, you shall not suffer from such traits.

* You shall be humble, even if other people are arrogant.

* You must be convinced if other people are sceptical.

* Let other people harbour bad traits like anger, hatred, jealousy, miserliness, greed, hypocrisy, deceit, stupidity, arrogance, bad company, laziness, disbelief, shamelessness, lack of conscience of truth-false, awkwardness, inaction, turmoil, lack of wisdom, etc., you shall remain detached and away from their company."

Babasaheb gave importance to good conduct in life. He believed that knowledge becomes dangerous if not accompanied with good conduct. Knowledge is like a double-edge sword, which protects, if the person is good, but kills if in the hand of the person with bad conduct. Babasaheb said, "Good conduct is ultimate; there is nothing like it in this world. It is the beginning and it is an end. It is the source of one's happiness and best in all kinds of situations. So one must purify one's conduct."

Attitude towards women is also an aspect of one's cultural values, 'You should realise that the female gender is an embellishment to society. Every society respects the character of a woman, and expect their wife to be of excellent lineage. Today thousands of women marry poor men and live with them in poverty. She willingly goes hungry along with her children, but she does not take to prostitution just because she finds happiness in it." He cited the example of Draupadi to clarify the subject in detail.

Babasaheb not only preached, but adopted and followed all that he preached. He was a man of good conduct and kept away from immoral deeds in his personal life. He never misused public money, nor did he use it for his own benefit; he never cheated nor trapped anyone in life. Maisaheb writes, "Saheb never ever touched a drop of alcohol even while living in Western countries. He was a true ideal of modesty, character, morale and gentleness. Despite the doctors' advice, he made it clear that 'no matter what happens to me, I will not take a drop of alcohol.' Since he was needed to be given at least a spoonful of brandy as a medicine, I ordered a small bottle of brandy. As Saheb would not consume alcohol directly, we decided to give him a glass of Coca-Cola or lemon juice with a spoonful of brandy in it. But, that didn't work as he could smell the alcohol even from a distance. So he moved the glass away from his mouth every time we tried to trick him with it. At last we had to give up trying anymore and Saheb didn't surrender to our tricks. He never drank even a drop of alcohol in his whole life, not even as a medicine. Saheb's immaculate demeanour and character was pure and white like washed rice" (*Dr. Babasaheb Ambedkar-Mahanirvana by Conversion*, p. 43; Prof. P. V. Sukhdeve).

He was very careful even when accepting donations. He accepted contributions only from people of good character and refused to accept any contribution from a famous film actor like Dilip Kumar. Babasaheb had been staying in a hotel in

Aurangabad. Incidentally, Dilip Kumar too happened to be staying in the same hotel. Balu Kabir and Bhalchandra Karal arranged the actor's meeting with Babasaheb. Dilip Kumar expressed his wish to donate to Dr. Ambedkar's educational institution. During the conversation, Babasaheb said, "I hate some people in the film world for being unprincipled and bad characters." Dilip Kumar replied, "Not all people are same." After that Babasaheb started talking about one scandal (of Dilip Kumar) after another, which made him upset and he said, "I do not agree with you." Babasaheb said, "I understand that because I told you the truth and the truth is always bitter." Dilip Kumar became angry at this candid and bold reply and walked away from the meeting. The atmosphere became strange and heavy. Balu Kabir said to Babasaheb, "You should not have made such a bold statement. Our organisation would have received a huge donation from him and his wish to help was genuine." At this, Babasaheb became more angry and shouted, "What the hell are you talking about? Are you a fool? I have never taken and will never take any money collected unjustly and corruptly and sell my character. I don't care if my institutions close down, but I will not continue with the sacred work of disseminating knowledge through unethical money" (*Dr. Babasaheb Ambedkar-Mahanirvana by Conversion*, p. 56; Prof. P. V. Sukhdeve).

Babasaheb's cultural values were based on the teachings of Lord Gautam Buddha. The Buddha had said, "Just as human beings need food, so does everyone need knowledge." In a speech to students of Milind College at Aurangabad on 22 December, 1955, he talked of wisdom, modesty, compassion and friendship. He said, "All of you have come for education, but in my opinion education alone cannot be sacred and sufficient. One should possess four important characteristics as preached by Lord Buddha along with knowledge; they are *pragya* which means wisdom, *sheel* means virtuous conduct, *karuna* (compassion) means love for the entire human race and *maitri* or feeling friendship for all living beings as this will give value to your intellect. In my opinion, a person with intelligence but without compassion is like a butcher. Compassion means humane love for all human beings! We, humans shall go even beyond that and develop intimacy (with all human beings) and this ideology was presented only by Lord Buddha."

Babasaheb believed that education constituted the foundation of civilisation and culture. "There is an inseparable link between education and a civilised society. Social change is an ongoing process, but the path to social change is enlightened only through education. Education awakens the dormant powers within a person and converts him from an animal to a human being."

Dr. Ambedkar said, "The purpose of education is to moralise and socialise the individual. Transformational thinking must be firmly entrenched in the mind of the society in order to accelerate the process of continuous social change. This thinking can only be inculcated in the minds of the society through comprehensive and universal education. The concept of universal education is based on the idea of 'learn and teach'. There will be no awareness in any society without education and there is no progress if there is no awareness. It is also to be noted that the inequalities existing in the society will never be removed without education." He asserted firmly, "There is no other tool like education for building an egalitarian society. Education is essential for equality." As a professor, he was familiar with the mindsets of students and said, "Education should develop the mind, vision, power to think and problem-solving skills." Emphasising on value-based education, he said. "Students should assimilate knowledge, modesty, good conduct and strict discipline to boost self-confidence." Explaining the reason, he said, "There is no divine power like self-confidence and one should not lose one's self-confidence under any circumstances."

'*Ahimsa paramo dharma*' (non-violence is the prime religion) has been the principal feature of Indian culture. In his book entitled, *Lord Buddha and His Dhamma*, Babasaheb referred to a misconception about Lord Buddha's philosophy of non-violence which he felt had destroyed India. He carried out all his agitations in a non-violent manner and within the framework of law. However, society has to face both violence as well as non-violence and the State cannot survive without violence. So the State has to have a police force and the armed forces. The army fights when there is an external attack while the police takes action when there is an internal agitation leading to violence.

What are the situations when violence is justified and when non-violence should be observed? Babasaheb has described these in detail in his book, *Lord Buddha and His Dhamma*, citing the example of King Bimbisara (p. 381), many soldiers of Bimbisara fled and became monks to avoid bloodshed. When King Bimbisara heard of this, he went and met Tathagata (Lord Buddha). At that time Tathagata advised him, "It was never my intention for soldiers to renounce their allegiance or patriotism in the name of non-violence or under the guise of non-violence. Dear followers, do not support such State-servants! Anyone who supports such people would be guilty of wrongdoing."

Another example was that of a General, who was not sure of punishing a criminal for committing a heinous crime. Should tyrants be punished or not? He asked Tathagata for advice. Tathagata replied, "Those who are punishable must be punished and those who deserve mercy should be given mercy. At the same time, never harm anyone but show love and compassion towards them." Punishment has to be inflicted on a criminal for his misdeeds and a murderer has to be sentenced to death for his act. "Being punished purifies one's soul. When one understands this, he is happy, , instead of grieving over his plight."

Babasaheb wanted to learn Sanskrit right from his childhood, but he couldn't because the so-called guardians of religion forbade him because of the belief that' teaching Sanskrit to untouchable students would corrupt the religion'. Ultimately, he opted to learn Persian as a second language. Later, at an older age, he learned Sanskrit by himself through hard work just as the legendary Eklavya had done. He expressed his love for Sanskrit thus: "Even though I was learning Persian and I got 95 marks out of a hundred, I would say that Persian literature is nothing in comparison to Sanskrit literature. Sanskrit has everything like poetry, poetics, study of allegory, drama, the *Ramayana*, the *Mahabharata*, philosophy, logic, mathematics, etc. Persian has nothing of these. I was proud of Sanskrit and I was constantly thinking that I should acquire a thorough knowledge of Sanskrit language, but I was deprived from studying Sanskrit due to the orthodox beliefs of teachers."

Despite being deprived of learning Sanskrit because he was

an untouchable, Babasaheb Ambedkar proposed that 'Sanskrit should be the national language of India' in the Constituent Assembly. It was Dr. Ambedkar who signed the resolution for approval.

When the issue of national language was being discussed in the Constituent Assembly, Dr. Babasaheb and Pandit Laxmikant Maitra began talking to each other in Sanskrit. The news was published in the Hindi newspaper *Aaj* on 15 September, 1949 under the title '*Ambedkar ka Sanskrit me Vartalap*' (Ambedakar's conversation in Sanskrit). The front page article was also published on 13 September, 1948 by the English newspaper called *The Leader* which was published from Allahabad. [such important news published in magazines and newspapers are stored in the National Archives of Delhi]

During the discussion on the national language of India, there were mainly three options–Hindi, English or Sanskrit. Some regional leaders insisted on their regional language as the national language, but most members were supporters of Hindi or English language. Finally, the Munshi-Iyengar committee proposed Hindi as the national language while English was to be kept as the national language for 15 years for the ease in dealing. On 5 August, 1949, the Congress Working Committee decided to adopt two languages under the chairmanship of Dr. Rajendra Prasad. There was an in-depth discussion among the national leaders on the language policy in September 1949, when Babasaheb on behalf of the Indian Scheduled Caste Federation pressed for Sanskrit, but young activists like B.P. Maurya protested strongly and even announced a walk-out from the meeting. Ultimately, Dr. Ambedkar had to withdraw his proposal but he called a press conference to express his views on the subject. The Congress leaders discussed the language policy from September 21 to 25, 1949 in the Constituent Assembly, where voting was conducted on the last day of discussion. Both the Congress party and the opposition won equal number of 77 votes.

According to an article published in *Hindustan* magazine, President Satyanarayana did not cast his final vote at the time of polling. Prof. Nijamuddin Mohammad also gave a speech in favour of Sanskrit in the Constituent Assembly. Most of the signatories who were in favour of the resolution to make Sanskrit as the national language were Tamilians from the state of Tamil Nadu.

According to an article published in the English newspaper, *The Statesman* on 25 September, 1949, the All India Meeting of Sanskrit Scholars, chaired by Dr. Saraswat, requested for Sanskrit being declared the national language. Since Sanskrit was included in the Eighth Schedule of the Constitution, it was decided to use Sanskrit words mainly for the purpose of dissemination of the national language Hindi and the slogans of various departments, ministries and institutions of the Central and State Governments had to be in Sanskrit. Thus, the credit goes to Dr. Ambedkar for Sanskrit language acquiring a little more importance at the national level in an independent India.

Babasaheb was a protector of culture; not a destroyer. He tried to establish the best Indian culture by eradicating the perversions like *chaturvarna*, considering heterogeneity as most valuable, contrary to creating differences between human brethrens. Babasaheb was the embodiment of cultural values like wisdom, modesty, compassion and friendship. He believed in '*sarve bhavantu sukhinah*' (let all be happy) for which he strived throughout his lifetime.

People, land and culture constitute a nation. Next, we shall see how Babasaheb visualised the prosperity of this nation.

□

5

Natural Resources and Prosperity

Dr. Ambedkar advocated rapid industrialisation of the country if it wanted to keep apace with the world. He wanted India to come out of the mindset that it was an agricultural country. India was a vast country covering Afghanistan, Pakistan and East Pakistan (Bangladesh) which are now different nations. Even today its territory covers a large land area.

India is an agrarian country, with nearly 70 per cent of the population dependent on agriculture as per the records of 1920-30. It is obvious that agriculture is not only the main source of employment but also a principal source of wealth creation. Despite it all. The farmer of this country has remained backward and oppressed religiously, socially and educationally. This has been portrayed very well by Jyotirao Phule in his Marathi books, *Shetakyacha Asud* (Farmers' Whip) and *Gulamgiri* (Slavery). Babasaheb too had focused on the atrocities committed on farmers. This shows that he was concerned not only about the untouchables in terms of social justice, but the country at large.

It is a pity that Babasaheb's contribution as an economist was never emphasised by his countrymen. In fact, this multifaceted man was a 'visionary economist'. It was only in 2016 that it came to one's notice that Babasaheb, in his thesis in 1916, had said that the Indian currency should be changed from time to time to control corruption and black money. When Prime Minister Modi withdrew the currency notes of Rs. 500 and Rs. 1000 from circulation, such a hue and cry was raised by the people. Babasaheb's understanding and passion for economics was so deep that he planned to write several books on this favourite subject of his. He authored *Studies in History, Economics and Public Law,* wherein he reveals his thorough knowledge of economic theories and views on various economic problems. He was not only a leader of his time but one who could give statistical data on matters relating to the Indian money and banking system. In 1915, he presented a thesis on the subject 'Trade of Ancient India' at Columbia University in America and this earned him a post-graduation degree. In this book, he discussed the administration of the East India Company from 1792 to 1857, presenting the statistical analysis of how the East India Company destroyed the Indian economy by 1858 and plunged it into a mountain of debt. In 1916, Columbia University accepted the dissertation titled *National Dividend of India-A Historical and Analytical Study: The Distribution of India's National Income* and awarded him a doctorate. Eight years later, a London publisher published the same dissertation, entitled *The Provincial Economic Evolution of British India* in which he attacked the British bureaucracy, imperialism and the social status quo in India. Babasaheb very lucidly exposed how the British rulers had served the business interests of Britain. He obtained his M.Sc. degree from the London School of Economics in 1921 for his dissertation on '*Provincial Decentralisation of Imperial Finance in British India*'. In 1922, he wrote a dissertation on *'The Problem of the Rupee: Its Origin and Its Solution*' and submitted it to the University of London for obtaining the degree of Doctor of Science. On the advice of Edwin Cannon, he presented the revised treatise titled *The Problem of Rupee*–on returning to Mumbai. The same was accepted by the London School of Economics and he was awarded the degree of DSc. Since Dr. Ambedkar spent most of his time in law and politics, the country and the world could not derive benefit from his views on economics.

The focus of his thinking was the heritage of Indian culture and his economic *mantra* was: *bahujana sukhaya, bahujana hitaya* (Welfare of the Masses, Benefit of the Masses). He authored the book, *The Problem of Rupee* in 1923, at the age of 32 and it became so popular that the first edition sold out in a short span of two years. During this period, the British Government of India set up a Royal Commission on Indian Currency and Finance, which invited Dr. Ambedkar to present his views on the subject in 1925. The Hilton Young Commission came to India in 1926 to study the overall financial system in British India. Surprisingly, every member of this commission carried a copy of his book, *The Problem of Rupee: Its Origin and Its Solution* during their visit to India! Dr. Ambedkar spoke of the flawed British system for finance and suggested that money should not be regulated by the government but by an autonomous body. This was when the foundation of the Reserve Bank was laid and the Reserve Bank of India came into being under the Reserve Bank Act 1934.

Dr. Ambedkar's views on inflation in India and the measures to control it, the norms on gold policy and the devaluation of the rupee, as well as the import of gold, are relevant even today.

Dr. Ambedkar suggested a four-point programme in 1925 regarding India's currency system: one, stop minting rupee coins by the government; two, give gold coins to those who bring gold to the mint; three, let the money in circulation remain and not issue new money; and four, the government shall not convert money into gold or gold into money.

He was insistent on adoption of a gold policy under which he ordained that gold should be used not only as a reserve but also as a currency. If people bring gold to the mint and ask for a gold certificate instead of a coin, the gold certificate should be given so that it can also be used as a currency.

Dr. Ambedkar even pointed out the reason for the decline in our exports and increase in imports. He said it was due to internal inflation, which had led to a deficit in the international trade balance and the current account deficit. He showed that there were three alternative ways of implementing economic democracy: one, individualism through more economical independence and free-market system of the individual; two, establishment of political democracy and economical power by the State; and three, control of economic power by the State.

According to him, the outline of State administration and development was as follows: "1. the State should own and operate the key industries; 2. basic industries should also be owned and managed by the State; 3. agriculture should remain a State-owned industry; and 4. organisation of agro-industries on the following basis:

- The State will divide the land into farms of a certain size and give these to the villagers for cultivation on lease.
- This land should be distributed among the people of the village without any discrimination of caste or creed and in such a way that there would be no landlord, lessee or farm labourer.
- It will be the responsibility of the State to help these collective farms financially by providing the required amount of water, livestock, equipment, fertiliser, seeds, etc.
- There would be a State monopoly in the field of insurance and the State would make it mandatory for every adult citizen of the country to accept a life insurance policy as determined by the legislature as per the individual's salary."

In terms of public financial management, Dr. Ambedkar makes excellent presentation through his book *Problem of Rupee* on the evolution of the Indian currency as a medium of exchange and its equivalence in terms of precious metals, like gold and silver. Similarly, in terms of public money, his dissertation entitled "The Evolution of Provincial Finance in British India" is a major contribution to Indian public finance. In this book, he refers to the period (1833 to 1921) of British India and the relations between the Centre and the states. Dr. Ambedkar said that the role of the government was to generate more revenue through taxes, but, there were limits to increasing tax revenue in a poor country like India. So there should be equitable distribution of wealth between the various levels of the government, i.e. between the Central, state and local bodies.

He categorically stated that caste was a major obstacle to economic growth and development in India. Caste does not allow people to learn inherited skills from anyone other than their own caste. This inevitably reduces the mobility of labour. The caste system also reduces the mobility of capital as the profession is caste-related and inherited. Reduction in the mobility of labour as well as capital leads to production inefficiency, thus hindering economic growth.

Dr. Ambedkar wrote in *What Congress and Gandhi Have Done to Untouchables* that the caste system as an economic system allowed exploitation without any obligation. Untouchability was not just an inevitable system of economic exploitation, but a system of uncontrolled economic exploitation. He emphasised that India's economic development strategy should focus on poverty alleviation, elimination of inequality and end exploitation of the people.

In his book, *States and Minorities*, he suggested that the State should be entrusted the responsibility of organising the economic life of the people, thereby ensuring highest productivity and equitable distribution of wealth without closing every possibility of private venture.

He said that the agriculture sector should not be neglected when concentrating on the growth of industrialisation. Agriculture would play an important role, both in meeting the food needs of the growing population and in providing raw materials for industries in India. Agriculture had to be made a strong foundation for rapid industrialisation of the country, on which the sovereignty of modern India could be built. He wanted nationalisation of all land holdings, but was against confiscation of land. Nationalisation of land should be done by providing compensation in the form of debentures equal to the value of the land to land owners.

The roadmap for India's development as per Dr. Ambedkar's economic views included the Damodar Valley Project. In 1942, he was a member of the Executive Council of the British Viceroy (Labour, Irrigation & Power) (*Dr. Ambedkar's Role on Economic Planning Water Policy* by Sukhdev Thorat). It was a ministerial-level post. He addressed a total of five conferences during his tenure, out of which two were for the Damodar Valley Project, one for the Mahanadi river and two for generation of electric power. He undertook the multi-purpose Damodar Valley Project which was to provide water to deprived Bihar and Bengal during his tenure. The main objectives of the project were flood control, irrigation, provision of drinking water and power generation on the Damodar river. The Damodar Valley Bill was introduced in the

Constituent Assembly in December 1947 and passed in February 1948. Babasaheb coordinated between the state governments of both the states as well as the Central Government. The result was that the project was completed in less than four years and the River Damodar, which was known as the 'River of Sorrow', became a blessing for Bihar and West Bengal.

The other project was Babasaheb's economic model. The financial system of any country should be evaluated in terms of the country's expenditure on developmental public works, like railways, roads, canals, etc. Dr. Ambedkar exposed the blatant injustice done to Indians. He referred to the public expenditure by the British on the water system in Manchester, England and which was higher than all the public expenditure incurred by East India Company in India between 1834 and 1848.

Babasaheb expressed his ideas on the economy of agriculture, farmers, farming conditions, employment as well as industrialisation. During his tenure as a member of the Mumbai Legislature, he introduced a Bill to demolish the *vatan* system with respect to Mahars (untouchables) and *vatan* (alienated land). Similarly, he introduced another Bill to abolish the Konkan's *khot* system. On 3 May, 1929, he wrote an editorial in the issue of *Bahishkrit Bharat* titled '*Khot* System Means the Slavery of the Peasants'. He wrote, as such the condition of the farmers in India was very bad and what was worse was the condition of the farmers in Ratnagiri district which had been ignored for many generations due to the special situation.

The *khoti* practice prevailed only in Ratnagiri and Colaba districts. It was one way by which the government collected tax from farmers. There were two systems in practice for tax collection (1) *ryotwari* practice and (2) *khoti* practice. Government representatives collected tax from farmers under the *ryotwari* system, while in the other practice a private person was appointed to collect taxes on behalf of the government. This person is known as *khot*. Unfortunately this *khoti* practice was continued as per the lineage of the *khot*. The *khoti* system was an exploitative system for farmers, who kept on paying *khoti* despite paying regular taxes to the government. Dr. Babasaheb asked, 'Why are farmers being looted? Why is there such tyranny? in his above-mentioned editorial article.

The atrocities perpetrated on the farmers due to the practice of *khoti* did not stop at taxes and the *khot's* share; farmers were harassed under the guise of different manipulations with the *khots* extorting money from farmers under various pretexts. Babasaheb wrote, "If the *khot* was a Brahmin, there would be no fruit left on the tree grown in the yard of the farmer for himself and the family members of the farmer would not be able to eat it even though he was growing the vegetables on his farm. That is, the farmer had no ownership of any kind. Everything that was produced in his home and arm belonged to the *khot*.

He listed the forms of deceit committed against the farmers:

- "False accusations against farmers.
- Holding farmers' livestock hostage.
- Getting free labour from the farmers on their own land.
- Robbing farmers by lending them money.
- Commiting social atrocities and forcing farmers to wear torn clothes."

Babasaheb said that it was a shame for the Indian society to practice slavery of this kind and which is continuing even in the 20th century.

The khoti was not actually the landowner, but was getting some honorarium in return for collecting the tax. In a way he was a government employee who abused the rights he received as a *khot,* who fraudulently snatched the land of thousands of farmers and, unfortunately, this practice is still going on. Farmers have lost their rights. Human rights of the farmers in the areas of *khoti* practice had to be restored. Babasaheb wanted an end to the practice of *khoti*. He raised all the issues in a speech delivered at the Mumbai Legislative Assembly on 17 September, 1937, while introducing a Bill to end the practice of *khoti*. The Bill proposed:

- The *khoti* practice should be eradicated and direct contact established between the farmers and government officials.
- *Khots* should be properly compensated in return for the loss of their rights as *khots*.
- Farmers should be given the right to the land and be brought under the Land Revenue Act.

Dr. Babasaheb fought tenaciously for the eradication of the

practice of *khoti* in Ratnagiri and Colaba districts. As a result the *khoti* practice was eventually abolished. That shows his struggle was not only to impart economic justice to the untouchables, but also bring justice to all the peasants.

Babasaheb's views on Indian agriculture and farmers were in line with the economic theory. He discussed agriculture, farming, rural poverty, declining income in agriculture, rural employment, agriculture dependent population, industrialisation, etc. on the basis of economic principles. Agriculture in our country was evaluated on the basis of fudged economic criteria and it was another reason for the exploitation of farmers.

A Bill was introduced in the Mumbai Legislature in 1927 to protect the interests of small landowners. During the discussion on this bill, Babasaheb presented his views on agriculture as well as on the condition of farmers in India. He also wrote a detailed article in the *Journal of the Indian Economic Society* under the title 'Small Holdings in India and their Remedies'.

At that time, the government was finding farming an unprofitable venture due to the fragmentation of land. The family once dependent on agriculture was now no longer able to meet its needs through agriculture. The central point of discussion was that the fragmented farmland fell in different belts and was scattered for even a single family. Therefore it was not profitable to gain sufficient produce from these scattered pieces of farmland. Another issue of discussion was whether the divided farmland could be united or not? And the third issue was whether it was possible to prevent division of land after a certain limit? In a nutshell, the subject of discussion was how to unite the scattered land and divided land. The committee called Vadodara Samiti was formed to study and resolve this issue. It presented a report also and it was published in public domain as well.

The legislature, however, discussed the following pertinent points:

- Small pieces of land become an obstacle in agricultural development.
- Farming divided into small pieces is not profitable.
- Extensive farming in large farmland is beneficial.

Participating in the discussion, while presenting his economic points of view, Babasaheb said, "I do not agree that small-scale farming is not profitable or economically not viable." Whether farming is economically viable or not, does not depend on the size of the farmland; it depends on whether farming is profitable over other means of production or not. Agricultural productivity depends on labor as well as capital. We can always say that farming is not profitable even though the farmer has enough labour and sufficient capital but the farm production is low. He said that the reality was something different–farmers were not only short of labour but the shortage of capital is even more severe.

Whether farming is beneficial or detrimental depends on how many labourers are employed and how much is invested in agriculture. It was argued that the size of the farm should be stipulated for a family to have enough food and income to subsist. But Babasaheb did not accept this argument as he said that there could be no measure of consumption and capacity to make economic decisions in terms of agriculture. He rejected associating the size of the farm with the size of the farmer's family. The financial principle says that one has to review the financial investment made in a project (which includes capital, labour and other resources) and the income earned out of that investment. If income is more than investment, then the business is said to be profitable; the same principle applies to agriculture as well.

According to Babasaheb, the number of dependent people on agriculture was very high in India. This number was many times higher in 1927 than it was today. If there was a need for only five labourers to work on a farm of particular size and 20 unemployed people were present in the family, then all of them would have to work on the farm. This is known as 'disguised employment' in terms of economics. It seemed that all 20 people worked on the farm but in reality, only five worked on the farm. This placed an additional burden of 15 people on the land as they were not nurtured from farming. This was why it was not fair to say that farming was not profitable. If we want to increase the productivity of agriculture, we have to reduce the burden of additional people who are not working on the farm. Now how is that possible?

Babasaheb suggested rapid industrialisation in answer to this question as it would eradicate rural poverty and unemployment.

The burden on agriculture would reduce by employing additional workers in the industry. This would be beneficial in two ways: first, the additional labourers working in the industry would reduce the burden on the agriculture sector; second, the industrial labourers would make an additional income, part of which would go into their savings. They would thus be able to raise funds and the capital raised this way could be used in farming. This was how Babasaheb presented his views on the economy. "It may seem strange, but industrialisation is the best solution to India's agriculture problem. Industrialisation will have a manifold effect, i.e. the pressure on farmland would reduce and the amount of capital would increase, leading to the growth of the economy. Not only that, industrialisation would also reduce the chances fragmentation of farmland. Industrialisation is a natural and powerful solution and so we should think of this solution instead of the half-hearted solutions we thought of earlier in this article."

"Adoption of industrialisation can pave the path for reunification of agricultural land divided into small pieces and there would be no need for artificial effort." The solution suggested in the Bill and debated in the Mumbai Legislature was more dangerous than the original problem. The solution was to assemble a small piece of land and hand over the ownership of the land to one person. At that same time, discussion on the inheritance rights of Hindus and Muslims was also going on. According to the Inheritance Rights Act, after the death of the head of the family, his heirs inherit a portion of his property. Immovable and movable property gets divided. In this order, naturally the agricultural land gets divided among the heirs. One view was that such a process should be stopped. It was easy to ask for a change in law, but its implementation was no less difficult.

Babasaheb strongly opposed it and said that despite the flaws in Hindu Law at many places, there was a strong basis for protection of public interest in Hindu Law on inheritance. Due to social and economic inequality created in Hinduism, a large number of people had been enslaved. But the reason that they were in a good position even in slavery was because of the Hindu Inheritance Rights Act, which had brought the bourgeoisie under control. "We do not want to associate economic slavery with social slavery. Socially they may not be independent, but economically they should be allowed to be independent and therefore I strongly oppose making unnecessary changes in the Inheritance Rights Act."

Water Crisis Prevention Plan

Water crisis is a serious problem and because of which frequent drought situations have to be faced. The problem had to be addressed nationally and that required a comprehensive national approach. Babasaheb suggested a comprehensive solution to this problem. It is unfortunate that Babasaheb has been recognised only as a builder of Indian Constitution and proponent of eradiction of untouchability but very few know about his contribution to solving the national water crisis.

Dr. Ambedkar was in the Viceroy's cabinet from 1942 to 1946, holding portfolios of labour, irrigation and energy. The river-valley project along with the multi-purpose project was started during his period in office. Three major projects, namely, Damodar river-valley, Hirakud river-valley and Son river project were started during his tenure. Frequent Damodar and Mahanadi floods during the monsoon season caused severe damage to agriculture, properties and livestock. Public life was largely affected by these floods. Experts were highly confused on how the flood water of these rivers could be stored for future use.

Babasaheb addressed five different conventions on 15 November, 1943 and 8 November, 1945 on this subject. Commenting on the recommendations of various committees on river development in Odisha, Babasaheb said, "I am saddened to say that the honourable members of various committees have not come up with a proper approach to solving this problem. According to them, excess water is a problem for us. I am of the opinion that when a large amount of water flows in the rivers, our efforts should be made to ensure that these flood waters reach the sea properly."

He added, "People are more affected by the problem of lack of water than by the problem of excess water. The fact is that water is an asset and cannot be altered. Water is a public resource and should be properly distributed." Thus he not only looked at the problem of heavy floods and excess water from a different perspective, but also focused on the constructive and important aspects of the water problem.

Babasaheb had a plan to develop all the river valleys of the country. The various objectives of his scheme were to control excess water-flow, construct lakes, generate electricity, use for irrigation in agriculture, water transportation as well as for conservation of forests. That was his multipurpose plan, which was similar to the Tennessee River-Valley project in the United States. Babasaheb had done an in-depth study of the Tennessee river-valley scheme and introduced the idea in India on a similar basis.

He addressed government officials in Kolkata on 3 January, 1945, "Waterways by rail–the objective of our waterways policy is limited to canals and irrigation. We have not yet noticed the difference between a railway and a waterway. Just as there are no territorial boundaries for railways, there should be no territorial boundaries for waterways as well. But our constitution has differentiated between railways and waterways." This is a mistake and the damage will be enormous. For example, if one state wants to use its water resources for power generation, but the location of the dam is in a different state or suppose the state is agricultural does not need power generation or does not have enough funds to implement the scheme, that state will not allow another needy state to use its land. Even if there are complaints about this, the state will hold its right in the name of regional autonomy. Consideration to amend the constitution for use of water resources by the railways is suitable, but it is not necessary for the government to wait for constitutional amendment. Similarly, constitutional difficulties cannot be barring if each state is willing to cooperate in joint projects for the use of water resources."

He continued, "Joint multi-purpose plans like the US Tennessee Valley Plan can be implemented in India as well, if the states cooperate with the Centre and allow regional border crossings. The Government of India has set up a Central Technical Electricity Board for this purpose and is also considering setting up a Central Waterways, Canals and Water-transportation Commission, which would be responsible for advising states on how water sources can be used other than canals for irrigation. The first project on Damodar river will be planned on this basis. There will also be a canal to control floods in the Damodar river as well as to provide irrigation, water-transportation and power generation. Apart from the Centre, Bihar and Bengal will jointly manage the scheme. Not only Bihar, but Bengal will also express its views on this plan because the location of the dam will be the primary issue in this scheme. Whatever both of them will decide on the issue of location, the final decision would be made on the basis of expert advice. This is a multi-purpose plan and the Commission will be responsible to make all arrangements to complete this project. The project is expected to pave the path for a new policy on our waterways and will also lay the foundation for a system to improve the living conditions of the people living in poverty in the country."

Babasaheb was serious about power generation issues also. Uninterrupted supply of electricity for industry was the only way for India to achieve rapid economic growth. According to him, "It is possible to commence big power projects by building dams on India's rivers." His views on the matter were clear. In 1943, in his address to the 'Power Policy Determining Committee', he said, "Before concluding my speech, I would like to present to you some observations on the need for and importance of important objectives for development of power generation in India. It is obvious that the person who is holding the position of president should be aware of the importance of the subject and the current state of the objective. This can be cleared with the answer to a simple question–Why do we need cheap and sufficient electricity in India? The answer is, India cannot move faster on the path of industrialisation without having sufficient and affordable electricity. That leads to another question, what is the need for industrialisation? Answer to this question is that industrialisation is highly required to curb poverty in the country."

The department headed by Babasaheb proposed the formation of a Commission for Waterways, Irrigation and Water-transportation. It was finally approved with A.N. Khosla appointed as Chairman of that Commission. He was an internationally renowned engineer and was regarded as an international expert on dam construction. There is an interesting story regarding his appointment. Babasaheb wanted an Indian to chair this

Commission, but since there was British rule in the country, the British wanted an Englishman to be appointed at that position. Khosla, when approached, was not ready to take on the responsibility. Later Babasaheb called him to his office and explained to him how he was suitable for the position in place of any Englishman. He also added, "Pressure is mounting on me to appoint an Englishman to chair this Commission, but I want this to be done by an Indian, and I am sure you can do it." Khosla was finally appointed on Babasaheb's recommendation and request.

The Damodar river-valley project, the Mahanadi valley project as well as Son river project were commenced just before Independence and were finally completed after the country achieved Independence. The credit was given to Nehru, but historically that was wrong. Shri Sukhdev Thorat has written, "On one occasion, in the presence of Jawaharlal Nehru in Cuttack, a ceremony was held under the chairmanship of Dr. Khosla. Babasaheb had already left the cabinet at that time. Nehru made that very popular statement at the ceremony, "This dam is the modern temple of India," but while giving his presidential speech, Dr. Khosla humbly clarified that it was Dr. Ambedkar who had made a big contribution to these projects. Addressing the people, he said that the foundation of what Nehru called the modern temple of India was laid by Dr. Ambedkar in 1942-46.

Babasaheb's contribution to the development of electricity as well as waterways in India is significant as he had made an ambitious plan to eradicate poverty in the country. Along with agriculture, it was also necessary to develop the industrial sector so as to eradicate poverty in India. And water is an important component in the development of both.

Babasaheb also expressed his views on the mineral deposits of the country, "There is a lot of ignorance and many misconceptions about India's mineral policy. The mineral policy of any government is basically based on its industrial policy. We didn't do any geological survey in our country. That is why the Indian Geological Survey needs to be restructured." He suggested that the survey should cover topics, such as (1) mechanical geology, (2) mineral use in industries, (3) central mineral development, (4) geophysical operations and (5) fossil fuel development. It is necessary to control the mineral resources as well as to legislate accordingly. In this regard, he said, "First, minerals are important in terms of nationwide mineral development and security; second, the technical form of the mineral; three, the purpose of the mineral usage; four, the value of minerals or products made out of them. Minerals are divided into two categories or you can say that there are two categories of minerals according to our legal provisions. Both categories will be generally under control of government and we will have limited rights to approve excavation or provisional licences as per the control system and to determine the terms and conditions of such licences as well as to revoke these licences. There are 28 other minerals that require more elaborate control. Elaborate control includes the right to approve licences as well as the right to direct the excavation method, process, classification of grades, to point out improvements to excavation operations and control over the procurement process, as well as the right to initiate research for cultivated usage."

On one occasion, Babasaheb said, "The basic question in the context of the issue raised by Mr. Niyogi is whether we can stop the export of minerals altogether? The answer to this question depends on whether we can import minerals, if we do not have our own sources. India is short of important minerals like oil, copper, lead, zinc, tin and sulphur. The way to control the export of such scarce minerals seems safe to the government and another, the minerals should not be exported in raw form but for that, it is beneficial to set up a related industry in our own country. Approval of drilling and possible licences for oil drilling is currently on hold. The reason is that the government does not want various oil companies to hire technical staff for their own benefit. There is a dearth of such employees. The ban will remain in place until and after the end of the war. The right to grant licences rests with the regional governments, but the regional governments still adhere to the rules of the 1919 Act prohibiting non-English individuals. In companies seeking such licences, the employee must be Indian or have a predominantly British member on its Board of Directors. Coal will be included in the new law, which includes issues such as coal mining, segregation, sale as well as use of low-grade coal. The cooperation of the mine owner as well as all the departments involved in his business is required for the implementation of this law. Thus an all-inclusive permanent mineral policy will be based on three things. A more stringent mineral policy will be needed when industrialisation kicks off in the country. The success and usefulness of the mineral policy also depend on the constitutional provisions, the division of powers between the region and the Centre, and the role of the government."

This is how Babasaheb envisioned our land and its natural resources and it was all inclusive as well as beneficial for all. In other words, there was a definite national vision behind it; there was the spirit of making this country prosperous and a poverty-free India.

Building prosperity is very important for the nation but that is not the only aspect to make the nation flourish. Internal security of the nation should also be considered seriously to make the nation safe and secure. He envisioned a caste-free, exploitation-free, egalitarian, fraternal and economically prosperous India. In Babasaheb's view, overall development was possible only through united India, where all Indians contribute their part.

□

6

Challenges to the Nation and Security

Dr. Babasaheb is well known for his fight against untouchability but very little is known about his concern for the country's security. In an article published in *Bahishkrit Bharat* 18 January, 1929 titled "Nehru Committee's Plan and the Future of Hindustan," Babasaheb expressed his concern thus, "The way the Congress people are fighting for Independence leads to the fear that the country will return to slavery once again. When we examine the map of Asia, we can see that we are trapped between completely different cultures. On one hand we are under siege of the people of China and Japan, while on the other hand, there is a siege by three Muslim countries like Turkey, Persia and Afghanistan (Pakistan had not yet separated). I believe this country, which is trapped from both sides, has to be very careful. In this situation, if either China or Japan were to attack the country, it is not clear who will be the winner, but one thing is sure that it will be fought back unitedly. On the other side, if independent Hindustan is attacked by three Muslim countries, like Turkey, Persia or Afghanistan, then can anyone guarantee that all will unite and will cope under such circumstances? I can't."

Dr. Babasaheb opposed the formation of provinces on the basis of language, in 1929. Why did he oppose it? What was the primary need for the country in 1929? The need was for a strong spirit of nationalism. Babasaheb wrote, "If there is one thing that is lacking in this country, it is the spirit of nationalism. Apart from many other reasons for lack of nationalism, the main reason is the diversity of languages. It is not possible to create a sense of national unity until this issue is not fixed, i.e. there is one language as a national language for the whole country. Such regionalisation on the basis of languages nurtures more of a regional spirit and that diminishes the spirit of nationalism. So such a type of regionalisation would tantamount to attacking the spirit of unity at its roots. It is a fact that such a regional structure does not lead to a national spirit; it can never create a national spirit. I think it is more in the national interest to try to have one language in the whole country than to create a linguistic province."

Most of our fellow countrymen are not aware about the history of the Partition of the country, but if one were to look at the whole series of incidents during that period and the political moves made, then one can realise that politics by Muslims was directed towards Partition. Babasaheb has given an accurate review of this politics in his above-mentioned article of 1929. Muslims, at that time, demanded that three regions–Sindh, Balochistan and the border region should be separated and given the status of independent territories. Sindh was part of Mumbai province at that time and the majority of Muslims were confined to Punjab and Bengal. If Sindh, Balochistan and the North-West Frontier regions were separated and made independent provinces, then Muslim domination would have been established in five out of the nine to ten provinces in India. It clearly showed that Muslims were demanding Muslim domination and the pity was that it was also approved by the Nehru Committee. As per Babasaheb's point of view, such political moves were dangerous for Hindus and also for Hindustan.

In *Bahishkrit Bharat* of 18 January, 1929, he wrote: "Muslims in India have a penchant for Muslim culture. This tendency is so strong that their goal is to spread Muslim culture and form a Union of Muslim nations and bring non-Muslim (infidel) nations back under their dominion. I think it is a mistake to think that Muslims who are not proud of Hindustan as their own country will defend Hindustan during foreign invasions."

Dr. Ambedkar also discussed the Islamic views on Dar-ul-

Harb (abode of war) and Dar-ul-Islam (abode of Islam). For Muslims, concepts of Dar-ul-Harb and Dar-ul-Islam served to differentiate between non-Muslim areas from Muslim areas. Dar-ul-Islam designated the territory as Muslim where Islamic law was implemented, whereas Dar-ul-Harb represented the land ruled by non-believers. He believed that Muslims wanted to convert the whole of India into Dar-ul-Islam. The idea of Pakistan originated from the same mentality.

He discussed in detail issues like Muslim mentality, Muslim attitude, reason for their enmity with Hindus, lack of reforms in Muslim society, religious fundamentalism, the status of women in Muslim society in his book, *Pakistan or Partition of India*. He clearly stated that Muslims should be given Pakistan if we wanted to protect India. The number of Muslims in the Indian Army was very high around 1945-46. Babasaheb expressed concern over the numbers, saying, "Looking at the current structure of the Indian Army, the number of Muslims seems to be higher and the fact is that all these Muslims are from Punjab or the North-West Frontier area; which implies that Muslims of the Punjab and the North-West Frontier Province are the people who will save us from foreign aggression. The Muslims are aware about their recruitment by the British and know that they are the gatekeepers of India. This is the reality and in view of that, Hindus should seriously consider protecting India's borders." More about this subject is given in the seventh chapter of this book and it shows how Babasaheb envisioned the internal security problem of India due to the fundamentalist *jehadi* mentality and Islamic terrorism 75 years before it showed its face on the surface.

Kashmir has always been a sensitive issue in India-Pakistan relations since Partition. Pakistan invaded Kashmir in 1948 and occupied one-third of Kashmir, calling it Azad Kashmir. The Indian Army was sent to counter the invasion of Pakistan at the time of the tribal attack. Dr. Babasaheb was insistent on sending the Mahar Battalion to Kashmir and the fight put up by the Mahar Battalion in Kashmir under the leadership of Major General Kulwant Singh is unmatched. The full story was published in the *Times of India* on 26 October, 1952. It said, "The bravery and conscientiousness shown by the battalion of the Mahar Regiment in the December

1947 war has earned them everlasting honour. The history of the battle of Zangar and the contribution of the Mahar Battalion to it will be written in golden letters in the history of the Indian Army."

Pakistani troops attacked our outpost near Zangar on 24 December, 1947. It was a tactical attack with cannons as well as other deadly weapons. It seemed that the attack would be extremely difficult to thwart, but the Mahar soldiers fought back and did not leave their post. Showing extraordinary courage, they killed hundreds of enemy soldiers. They even fought with bayonets of their guns and took to hand-to-hand fight when their ammunition got exhausted. The brave among them were awarded one Mahavir Chakra and five Veer Chakras. The then Army chief, General Thimmaiah said, "The name of your battalion will forever resonate in these hills as well as in the surrounding countryside." The soldiers of Mahar Battalion justified Babasaheb's faith in them.

Pakistan has been eyeing Kashmir since the day the country became independent on 15 August, 1947. Pakistan has not been ready to accept that Kashmir is an integral part of India. Dr. Babasaheb was a staunch opponent of Article 370 which gave special status to Kashmir right from the beginning. It was added to the Constitution at a later stage at the instance of Pandit Nehru. Dr. Ambedkar had handed over the report of the Drafting Committee of the Constitutional Assembly to the president of the Constituent Assembly, Dr. Rajendra Prasad on 21 February, 1948. The draft did not mention about any special status to Kashmir. Dr. Ambedkar could have never agreed to the stipulation and moreover he was concerned about the future of thousands of people from Valmiki society who had taken refuge in Kashmir. His fears proved correct as the Valmiki brethren were deprived of all their rights for 70 long years. They had no right to vote, to get a government job or run for an election and were even denied the benefits of reservation. It was because of Prime Minister Narendra Modi, who repealed this unjust and treacherous clause after 70 long years that these people started securing their rights.

If Dr. Ambedkar had not been in favour of Article 370, then how was it added to the Constitution? Mr. Sheikh Abdullah, the then Chief Minister of Jammu & Kashmir, approached Pandit

Nehru for earning special rights for Kashmir. Pandit Nehru heard him out and asked him to meet the Chairman, Dr. Ambedkar, of the Drafting Committee. Dr. Ambedkar even refused to listen to Sheikh Abdullah's such anti-constitutional and anti-national proposals. He clearly told Sheikh Abdullah: "Do you want India to protect Kashmir, deliver food to the people of Kashmir and give the people of Kashmir a special status over the whole of India and even after doing so, do you want the people of India to have no rights in Kashmir? I am the Law Minister of India; I cannot be a party to any such thing in the interest of the nation."

Pt. Jawaharlal Nehru, the then Prime Minister of India, instructed his confidant N. Gopalaswamy Iyenger (Minister without Portfolio in the interim government) to work out a new draft with the Diwan of Maharaja Hari Singh of Kashmir due to Dr Ambekdar's non-compliance. It was basically due to the mysterious brother-like relationship between Sheikh Abdullah and Jawaharlal Nehru that Kashmir was given a different flag, a different constitution and a different Prime Minister, which was completely anti-national and anti-constitutional.

Dr. Ambedkar's opposition to such a special provision was so strong that he even refused to attend the meeting on the day the resolutions were to be passed.

There were only two non-Congress ministers in the cabinet during the period 1947-1952–they were Dr. Syama Prasad Mookerjee and Dr. Ambedkar, both were opposed to granting such a special status to Kashmir.

5 August, 2019 proved a historic day for the country. Kashmir truly became an integral part of India, for which the government of Prime Minister Narendra Modi would have received many blessings from the late Sardar Vallabhbhai Patel, late Dr. Babasaheb Ambedkar and late Dr. Syama Prasad Mookerjee had they been alive.

Dr. Ambedkar strongly opposed the Article 370, which gave special status to Kashmir and which was forcibly added to the Constitution. He was opposed because his heart was beating for the interest of the Scheduled Caste people and the nation. He even admitted that Article 370 was an obstacle to the unity of the nation and that was why he did not participate in the discussion on this clause in the Constituent Assembly. He had taken the same position at the time of Partition of the country. He was of the view that Muslims of Pakistan could not be trusted and that the Scheduled Caste should migrate to India as soon as possible.

His visionary views proved true when this Article 370 not only harmed the nation but also the Valmiki people who migrated from Pakistan and took refuge in Jammu & Kashmir. They did not get any government job for 70 years because of it and nor did they derive the benefits of reservation. They suffered for 70 long years but got everything only when the Article 370 was repealed.

In spite of that, a group of so-called Dalit (Scheduled Caste) leaders protested against the repeal of Article 370 to appease the Kashmiri Muslims!

Just as the repeal of Article 370 has proved beneficial for Valmikis in Jammu & Kashmir, similarly the introduction of a new legislature, known as CAA, by the Modi government will be in the interests of the Valmiki and Maheshwari societies who had faced terror and atrocities in Pakistan. The CAA is meant to provide them rights of citizenship and all other facilities which every Indian citizen gets. Yet, it was unfortunate that the so-called Dalit leaders came out in support of the Muslims to serve their own political interests and machinations. We, as citizens of this country, are enjoying all the rights provided by the Constitution and so could the Valmiki, Meghwal and Maheshwari communities who migrated from Pakistan to India. They are settled now in large numbers in the Kutch and Ahmedabad regions of Gujarat. One such refugee, Ramsang Sodha had been an MLA in Tharparkar district of Pakistan. He said, "The biggest beneficiaries of CAA have been the Hindu refugees from Pakistan. Although the law came in late, many people would have survived if it had come earlier. Hindus are in a minority in Pakistan and the condition of minorities in Pakistan is pitiable and beyond our imagination. They are tortured unto death and there is no one to listen to them. Currently only 2 per cent Hindu population is left behind in Pakistan and it won't be a surprise if it becomes zero in a short period of time." His son said that the Ahir, Valmiki, Bhil, Maheshwari, Meghwal, Rabari communities were taking refuge in India and will benefit a lot from this new law. Harjivanbhai Wankar, a social worker from

Bhuj, said, "The Indian government has done great benefit to the people fleeing from Pakistan to India, by enacting this law. Ninety per cent of Hindus are leading a life of slavery in Pakistan, and most of them are from Scheduled Castes. Minorities, especially the Scheduled Caste Hindus are not safe there; frequent incidents of atrocities, conversions and rapes come to the fore. These people want to come to India. They will benefit most from this law."

Even during the Partition, Dr. Ambedkar had appealed to the Scheduled Caste people who had remained behind in Pakistan to come to India.

In the biography of Dr. Ambedkar, written by Dhananjay Kir, entitled, *Dr. Ambedkar–Life and Work,* Kir said, "The situation was aggravated on both sides by the Partition of India. There were riots everywhere. Dr. Ambedkar wrote a letter to his friend Kamalakant Chitre at that time. He wrote, 'it is not just a common riot, it is a huge protest; there is a large number of casualties and deaths. Daily life in Delhi has come to a standstill for the past few days'."

Dr. Babasaheb had suggested the relocation of Muslims and Hindus to Pakistan and India respectively well before the Partition simply to avoid a situation like the civil war and genocide in both India and the newly formed Pakistan. But the Congress, which had repeatedly avowed to keep the country intact, accepted both the Partition and the ensuing violence. The way the Congress fell to the argument for the formation of Pakistan worsened the situation in the country. Once again, Dr. Ambedkar's fears had come true!

About two lakh people were killed in the widespread massacres, leaving millions homeless, women abducted, forced conversions. Dr. Ambedkar saddened at the situation had issued a statement condemning the Pakistani government for the killings. He also complained against the Pakistan government's refusal to allow the untouchables to come to India and converting them forcibly to Islam. Dr. Ambedkar appealed to the untouchables trapped in a difficult situation in Pakistan to come to India and said, "You will surely be deceived if you trust Pakistan or the Nizam of Hyderabad and the Muslim League. The Scheduled Caste people may hate the Hindu society, but it is a mistake to think that the Muslims are their friends. Islam should not be accepted just to save your life."

Dr. Ambedkar gave an assurance to those who were forcibly converted to Islam that the same treatment would be meted out to them as it was before their conversion. The Nizam openly opposed India and considered India as an enemy. He told the Scheduled Caste members to never support the Nizam and demanded from Jawaharlal Nehru to bring the Dalits to India as soon as possible. Two years later, when India launched a military operation against the Nizam's Hyderabad. Dr. Ambedkar supported Sardar Patel who had directed the action. (*Dr. Ambedkar: Life and Work*, p. 398-399). When Kashmir was invaded in 1947 and the Indian Army made the Pakistanis to bite the dust, Nehru called a ceasefire and took the Kashmir issue to the UN which passed a referendum on Kashmir. Dr. Ambedkar's views on Kashmir were: "We are fighting over Kashmir and in my opinion, the issue is not as to who is right or who is wrong, but I think Kashmir should be divided." Babasaheb said that the Hindu and Buddhist areas of Kashmir should be merged with India and the Muslim areas should be given to Pakistan. The issue is between Kashmiri Muslims and Pakistan, so let them solve it on their own. And if you don't want to divide it into three parts, the referendum should be held only in the Kashmir Valley (where the Muslim population is high). I am afraid that the idea of holding a proposed referendum is about holding a referendum all over Kashmir. If this happens, then Hindus and Buddhists will be pushed into Pakistan against their will. This will be same as the situation that had arisen in East Bengal earlier." Babasaheb's views on Kashmir were crystal clear.

Babasaheb strongly opposed Nehru's plan to build a tunnel in the mountains to connect Kashmir with the country. (Today this tunnel is called 'Jawahar Tunnel'). He said, "The Prime Minister thinks that he can use this tunnel, but he does not understand that if the enemy invades Kashmir and occupies it, the enemy will reach Pathankot directly through this tunnel. Not only that, the enemy may reach the door of the Prime Minister directly. The decision to build a tunnel under the English Channel was long opposed as England feared that enemy troops might enter England from France in the same way that France could be reached by that route. If either China, Pakistan or Russia attacks tomorrow and occupies Kashmir, the enemy will be able to enter our courtyard."

Four issues are important in terms of national security: (1) the country's foreign policy, (2) the internal economic system, (3) social cohesion, and (4) the military. Among them, military situation is very often discussed. The situation of India during Nehru's tenure was unique because of his foreign policy. The basic premise of any foreign policy should be patriotism as well as pragmatism; under no circumstances does idealism find a place in it. Idealism is good as long as one talks about it, or delivers lectures across the world, but one cannot sacrifice national interest for idealism. Babasaheb was a fierce critic of Nehru's foreign policy and said, "We had friendly relations with almost all countries in the world when India got Independence; all of them were well-wishers of our country. The situation today is quite the opposite; India has no true friend. Not that all of them are India's enemies, yet they are annoyed with India. All this is due to the ambiguous foreign policy of the Congress government. Many countries have become unfriendly and turned their backs on India because of India's a) Kashmir policy, b) haste in persuading Communist China to join the UN [for a permanent seat in UNSC] and c) immature policy towards the Korean war. By emphasising on idealism, Pt. Nehru has made two big mistakes: (1) he gave Tibet to China on a plate and (2) made an agreement with China on the basis of Panchsheel. India will have to pay a heavy price for these two big mistakes." Babasaheb expressed his views boldly, regardless of anyone's resentment. Nehru worked hard to take up the issue of China's promotion in the UN. This was completely ridiculous! Babasaheb questioned, "Why do we need to fight for China's problem? China is able to fight its own battle. Why are we at enmity with America in favour of Communist China?" Regarding national security, India had no reason to spoil its relations with America.

Dr. Babasaheb used to tell Pandit Nehru, "One should be discern between capitalism and parliamentary democracy while determining the country's foreign policy. One may oppose capitalism and that is not bad, but it does not mean that you become a supporter of dictatorship while opposing capitalism." Babasaheb was clearly pointing towards China, which still has dictatorship under a communist party. "India should try to become a permanent member of the United Nations Security Council) rather than trying to persuade China to do the same." Babasaheb expressed these views in 1951 and India is still not a permanent member of the Security Council at UN. "The policy adopted to save the world would be an axe to grind at India's own feet. This suicidal policy should be cast aside as soon as possible," said Dr. Babasaheb when commenting on India's foreign policy.

On account of Nehru's China policy, he said, "Pt. Nehru says that Mao has accepted the Panchsheel. (Buddha's Panchsheel means five virtues: not to kill, not to steal, not to commit adultery, not to lie and,not to drink alcohol) but China will certainly not follow Panchsheel. China is a dictatorship country and is a threat to India." He further said, "It is surprising that Nehru took Mao's acceptance of Panchsheel seriously. Panchsheel is an important part of Buddhism. If Mao believes in Panchsheel, should he treat his country's Buddhist community differently? Panchsheel has no role in politics and not at all in communist politics. All communist countries believe in only two things-one, morality is unstable and another, there is no such thing as ethics in the world. Today's values are not tomorrow's values." Dr. Babasaheb meant that any statement made by China should not be trusted. Babasaheb was adamant that China could not be trusted at all and his statement proved true when China invaded India in 1962.

Many international events took place during this period and some of them influenced or may influence India in future. They were: the Suez Canal conflict, the Korean war, the Vietnam war and the SEATO and CENTO agreements. Let's take a look at Babasaheb's views on these events. A sea canal constructed at Suez in Egypt connects Mediterranean Sea and Red Sea. Known as the Suez Canal, its length is 165 kms and the width is 48 m. The canal was constructed by a French engineer in 1859 to reduce the distance of the sea route between Asia and Europe. Earlier, all sea vessels had to travel all the way around the African continent to reach Europe, but the distance was reduced by four and a half thousand miles. This canal was nationalised by President Nasser in 1956. England, France and America opposed it and attacked Egypt. Nehru immediately announced support for Nasser. Babasaheb opposed Nehru, "The Suez Canal should be under the control of the international community, not Egypt. India's foreign trade runs through the same canal. What will happen to India's trade if Egypt becomes India's enemy tomorrow? Egypt and Pakistan, both are Muslim countries and they are friends also."

Other events were the Korean and Vietnam wars. Communist attacks were on the rise in Korea and Vietnam at that time. North Korea was already occupied by the communists who also tried to occupy Vietnam. Babasaheb was a staunch opponent of the communists as the economic ideology of communism was not acceptable to him; he considered the communists as dictatorial and chaotic and found them violent and avoid adhering to any policy-values. He believed that if communism were to spread in the world, it would be deadly and dangerous for mankind.

The United States formed an organisation of Southeast Asian countries to stop the spread of communism. This organisation was named as Southeast Asian Treaty Organisation or SEATO and it was formed for collective defence in Southeast Asia and was also known as the Manila Pact. It was signed in September 1954. The purpose of this organisation was to defend each member of SEATO if invaded. Another similar organisation was formed under the Baghdad Pact. This Central Treaty Organisation or CENTO was a military alliance to prevent the Cold War. India somehow was not a part of any of these pacts. The reason was Nehru's hatred for democratic America and his love for communist Russia. Babasaheb favoured signing such treaties for maintenance of our security. Babasaheb quoted one of the famous quotes of Bernard Shaw, 'Good ideas are good, but one should not forget that it is dangerous to be overly good.'

Babasaheb categorically believed that some religious traditions not only harmed the Hindu society but also the nation. India was not only thrown out of the race to be the best but also became slave to foreigners. The nation was always first for him. When Karnataka province was being separated, he quoted in the Mumbai Legislative Assembly in 1938, "For me, the nation is always first and last is also the nation."

India had been facing internal aggression for centuries. Babasaheb Ambedkar was aware of this anti-national mentality and knew that the threat to the nation was more from internal vulnerabilities than external ones. That is why he mentioned traitors like Jaichand in the Constituent Assembly. In a speech given on 25 November, 1949, while introducing the final draft of the Indian Constitution in the Constituent Assembly, he said "From 26 January, 1950, India will become a democratic country. *(Applause)* But what about her freedom? Will she retain or lose her freedom? This is the first thought that comes to my mind. It is not that India has never been an independent country. The point is, she has lost her freedom once; will she lose it again? This very thought makes me extremely worried for the future of the country. Not only has India lost its independence once before, but the fact that it has lost its independence due to the betrayal and treachery of some of its own people makes me very upset." He went on to say: "It is certain that if the (political) parties put the cult (or caste) above the country, our freedom will be endangered a second time and that freedom will be lost forever. The country should be strongly protected against any such possible incident. We must be determined to defend our freedom to the last drop of our blood."

Babasaheb insisted, "India needs another capital and it should be in South India. There should be a sub-capital in South India for military security as well as equal power-share in the country. The best option for the sub-capital could be the region of Hyderabad, Secunderabad and Bolarum; it should be taken over by the Central Government to establish a sub-capital. The idea of running a government sitting there in Delhi is ridiculous. It is essential to establish another capital in South India in terms of security; that will make us strong in military power as well and people of South India will also get a chance to be involved in governance."

Army is not sufficient to strengthen the security of the country; the country's economy should also be extremely strong. Communist Russia was a superpower until 1990, but, its economy collapsed In 1990 and states forcefully occupied by Russian military started becoming independent countries. The Soviet Union (USSR) collapsed and many new countries formed while the remaining part is now known as Russia. Babasaheb had often expressed his views on democratic and economic equality and said, "Due to our social and economical system, everyone doesn't get an equal social and economic opportunity. Our democracy could be in jeopardy if we continue with such denial."

He believed that the other biggest issue in terms of national security was social cohesion, "It is necessary to build social democracy to build social unity. Social democracy means forming the society based on three principles–liberty, equality and fraternity, out of which brotherhood is most important... Every citizen should love the other like a brethren; that is the basic need of social cohesion. United society will never tolerate any foreign aggression and will thwart such aggression. The history of England, Russia, Japan, France and Germany is a good example."

The issue of national security should be more comprehensive than being limited to the military. Ranging from terrorism to NGOs, all are a challenge to the country's security today. "No one is above the country," said Ambedkar, who believed that rulers who think only of the interest of the country can keep the country safe.

□

7

Jehadi Mentality and Identity of Pakistan

It becomes clear to us when we think comprehensively that the focus of Babasaheb's entire life was on empowering the Hindu society by eliminating social inequality and spreading equality, love and harmony. He expressed his devotion and patriotism in one sentence: "Nation is first... and the last is also nation. The nation is always greater than the individual. No matter how big the individual becomes, he is always smaller than the nation and I am ready to give my all for the service of the nation." Fake secularists, hypocritical Ambedkarites and Marxists knew that the closer they got to these ideas of Babasaheb, the more they would be pricked.

Dr. Babasaheb had already discerned global Muslim terrorism 75 years back and this has proved true when we see what the world is experiencing today. While opposing fanatical orthodoxy and perverted untouchability pervading in the Hindu society, he criticised the religious fundamentalism-inspired politics of Muslim society. The so-called intellectuals of the country deliberately suppressed these bold ideas of Babasaheb for many years after Independence. His book, *Thoughts on Pakistan* is worth reading as it reveals the real mentality of the people (especially the Muslims) of that time and it was this that was responsible for the creation of Pakistan. Many other issues are also discussed at length and with historical evidence, like why the famous Somnath temple was demolished, what were the motives behind the Muslim invaders for invading this country for centuries and destroying it, why do Hindu-Muslim riots occur, why did the country's leadership kneel down to Islamic fundamentalism; why *jehadi* fundamentalism is spreading in India and in the world today. The answers to all these questions can be found in his book.

Even today, when Islamic fundamentalism and Muslims denote the same, it becomes necessary to comprehend Babasaheb's views. His point of view on Islamic fundamentalism was very clear and at a time when the country's leadership was appeasing the Muslims under the guise of Hindu-Muslim unity, Babasaheb wrote an editorial in *Bahishkrit Bharat* of 18 January, 1929: "It is natural that their (Muslim) inclination is towards the Islamic States, but this inclination has gone too far. Their sole objective has been to spread Muslim culture and form a union of Muslim nations and dominate as many infidel countries as possible. Due to this mentality, even if their feet are in Hindustan, their eyes are always fixed on Turkey or Afghanistan. As per my view, it is dangerous to think that the Muslims, who have no pride in being Hindustani and who have no sense of intimacy towards their Hindu brethren, are capable of defending Hindustan against Islamic aggression."

Babasaheb further wrote: "We know that it is not good for us to be against the Muslim community at a time when the Hindu community is not happy with us, but we should also be concerned about the welfare of our country. That is our feeling and that is why we have taken this risk."

Babasaheb's *Thoughts on Pakistan* was the first book of its kind when it was published and shed light on Islamic fundamentalism, its roots and its results in future. He expressed his views on Islamic fundamentalism, intolerance, aggression and religious bigotry which had led to the Partition of India and the emergence of a country called Pakistan on Indian soil. This book establishes the veracity of Babasaheb's future political vision. When the Muslim League proposed the idea of a separate Pakistan under the leadership of Muhammad Ali Jinnah at its Lahore convention in 1940, all the top leaders of the country called it an illusion, a mere nonsense, but Babasaheb knew that no one could stop it. He had minutely studied Muslim fundamentalism and the political nature of Islam. He was already aware of the activity that had given birth to Pakistan and written in the preface to the book: "I believe that the demand of Pakistan is not the one which will be forgotten over time; it is not the result of a momentary political inconsistency. As far as my study goes, the demand for Pakistan is getting stronger along with the political development of the Muslim masses in the same way that character development takes place along with physical development."

Babasaheb himself was distressed at the idea of forming Pakistan, "The problem of Pakistan, which is a headache for all, has bothered me the most."

He knew the Islamic ideology as well as the diplomacy of the British government. He said, "It is undeniable that we have to look at the plan for Pakistan. Muslims will force authorities to consider this plan, in the wake of which, before transferring political power, Britain will insist on some kind of agreement between Hindus and Muslims...The hope of Hindus that Britain will use force to suppress Pakistan's demand is foolishness; that is impossible."

Babasaheb's view of Muslim ideology was that Pakistan had been created due to intolerance, aggression and religious bigotry of the Muslim psyche. This he has presented in his book, *Thoughts on Pakistan* (1941), which was reprinted as *Pakistan or Partition of India* in 1945.

Babasaheb was of the view that Hindu-Muslim unity was an illusion and that talking about secularism was utterly futile. He said, "My logical statements have been addressed mostly to Hindus. There is a clear reason for this, which is easily understood by anyone. As Hindus are in a majority, their point of view must be important. It is impossible to find a peaceful solution to the problem (of Hindu-Muslim animosity) without solving their (Hindus') problems, whether rational or emotional. Apart from that, there are some special reasons behind my reasoning mainly addressing Hindus, which is not clear to others."

"I think that the Hindu leaders who are guiding the destiny of their brethren, their 'seeing eye' (as Carlyle says) has vanished and they are wandering in vain, the result of which, I fear, will prove fatal for Hindus. Hindus do not seem to know this, but it is clear from experience that Hindus and Muslims are neither one in nature, nor in their spiritual practices, nor in their political will and for a while, when they moved towards cordial relations, even at that time there was a tense situation between them."

"Yet Hindus will gladly embrace the illusion that going beyond the bitter experiences of the past, there is still something left for a broad and real unity of goals, sentiments and policies between the two communities to enhance intimacy between Hindus and Muslims."

The Congress leadership of the time called the idea of Pakistan a product of Jinnah's mind, but Babasaheb was not under any such illusion. According to him, "...Hindus are under the illusion that Pakistan is just Jinnah's madness and has no support from the Muslim masses or other Muslim leaders. They are clinging to the illusion that Sir Sikandar Hayat Khan and Mr Fazlul Haq are not openly supporting Jinnah. If the Hindus will not play their role properly, they too will be in a condition on which they are laughing at Europe today, and will be destroyed like Europe."

Hindus were speechless on the demand to split the land, which was considered as their holy land for centuries, and create two nations–Muslim nation and non-Muslim nation. They were offended by the attitude of Muslims of India that they were a separate nation from Hindus. Hindus have always felt that certain features of Indian social life served to unite the two communities, but, was that enough (for unity)?

Dr. Ambedkar said, "It is undeniable that most Muslims in India do belong to one or the other Hindu caste. It is also true that every Muslim does not speak the same language, and most speak the language that Hindus speak. Certain rituals are also common between the two communities and it is also true that some religious practices are similar in both communities. But the question is whether all these will make Hindus and Muslims one nation, or whether they have a desire to harmonise with each other?" (*Pakistan or Partition of India* by Dr. Babasaheb; p. 15).

"...First of all, it must be understood that the similarities between them are not the result of any conscious effort to adopt social customs or to establish unity between the two communities. The reality is that these similarities are results of several other reasons. Some similarities are due to incomplete conversion processes. In a large country like India, where most of the Muslims are made up of savarna or Dalit Hindus by converting to Islam, the people have not been fully Islamised and the conversion may not have been effective. This may be due to the fear of revolt by the converts or a way to persuade them to convert or the lack of religious teaching due to insufficient Islamic clerics. So it is no surprise that a large number of Indian Muslims reveal their Hindu origins in their religious and social life. And one reason may be that they have lived in the same environment for centuries. It is natural for living in the same environment to react similarly, and it is also natural for individuals to become similar by reacting to the same environment in the same way."

"Is there any historical event that Hindus and Muslims alike remember with pride or distress? This is the question at the root of the problem. If Hindus consider themselves and Muslims as part of the same nation, then they need to answer this question: When it comes to the historical relationship between the two communities, the only thing that comes to mind is that the two communities have always been like armies at war with each other. There has never been a concerted effort for common achievement between the two."

As Bhai Parmanand has stated in his book, *Hindu Nationalist Movement'*: "Hindus in their history have a reverence for Prithviraj, Rana Pratap, Shivaji and Banda Vairagi who fought against Muslims to protect this land and for its honour, while the Muslims consider invaders like Muhammad bin Qasim and rulers like Aurangzeb as their national heroes. In the religious field, Hindus derive their inspiration from the *Ramayana*, the *Mahabharata* and the *Gita*, while Muslims derive their inspiration from the *Qur'an* and *Hadith*. The factors that separate them from each other are more powerful than the factors that bind them together. Hindus are making the mistake by relying on some peculiarities of social life of Hindus and Muslims, for example, same caste, language and country. These are only coincidental and superficial. The political and communal animosity of Hindus and Muslims separates them more than what makes them unite. Prospects may be different, if the two communities can forget their past" (*Pakistan or Partition of India* by Dr. Babasaheb; pp. 17-18).

Dr. Ambedkar believed that it was also necessary to know the history, which has been responsible for the bitter truth of today's Hindu-Muslim relations. He believed that the constant incursions of Muslim armies, which began with Muhammad bin Qasim's invasion of Sindh in 711, and the methods adopted by the invaders, had created a bitterness between Hindus and Muslims which could not be removed even after a century of joint political activities.

Dr. Babasaheb wrote, "The temples were also demolished along with the attacks. Forced conversions were made; wealth was plundered; men, women and children were severely humiliated or enslaved. So it is not surprising that the memories of these attacks have remained forever and the Muslims have been remembering these with pride while the Hindus have been remembering this with shame and disgrace till date."

"It is certain that the Muslim invaders came to destroy India with hatred in their hearts towards the Hindus, but, they did not go back simply by spreading hatred and knocking down temples along the way–it would have been a blessing, if that had happened. They were not satisfied with the temporary results of their invading expeditions. They also did something which was permanent-to sow the seeds of Islam. The plant has now spread in an enormous way" (pp. 47-48).

Dr. Ambedkar gave the following excerpt from Titus's book, *Indian Islam* and Lane Poole's book *Medieval India* (pp. 36-46):

"The first Muslim invasion (of Muhammad bin Qasim in AD 711) did not allow them to occupy the region permanently. As the Caliph of Baghdad, the one who ordered the invasion, was forced to relinquish control of the remote region like Sindh in the middle of the ninth century. Shortly after this retreat, Mahmud of Gazani's fierce attacks began from AD 1001 and continued. Mahmud of Ghazni died in AD 1030, but, he invaded India 17 times in his short reign of 30 years. Then came Muhammad Ghori, who started his barbaric attacks in AD 1173. He too was killed in 1206. Mahmud wreaked havoc in the country for 30 years followed by Muhammad Ghori also ravaged the country for 30 years thereafter. Genghis Khan and his Mughal army then launched attacks which started in 1221. It was a cold season at that time, so they stayed on the border of India and could not enter India. Twenty years later, he attacked and plundered Lahore. The most terrible attack of the Mughals was led by Timur in AD 1368. Then came a new attacker in the form of Babur in AD 1526. The invasions of India did not stop even after Babur; there were two more attacks. In the year AD 1738, Nadir Shah invaded Punjab. It is said that his attack was like a terrible flood of a river or a roaring sea. Then in the same year, Ahmed Shah Abdali invaded and defeated the Marathas in the battle of Panipat, permanently eliminating the possibility of the Hindus regaining their land which had been usurped by the Muslims."

"These Muslim invasions were not only carried out with the intention of plundering and conquering the land; they had a clear purpose behind it. The invasion of Muhammad bin Qasim was a punitive campaign. He came to punish Dahir, the King of Sindh. This was because Dahir refused to pay compensation after seizing an Arabian ship at Dewal port in Sindh. But, of course, one of the aims of his campaign was to establish Islam in India by cracking down on Hindus who believed in idolatry and in many deities. The essence of the letter that Muhammad bin Qasim wrote to Hajjaj was thus:

"King Dahir's nephew, his warriors and other high-ranking officials have been killed and the infidels have either been converted to Islam or have been killed. Temples with idols have been desecrated and mosques as well as other places of worship have been built in their place, where religious teachings are given; prayer calls (*azaan*) are regularly made to offer *namaz*. Every morning and evening (religious) meetings are held and slogans of '*Allah-o-Akbar*' are shouted" (*Indian Islam* by Titus, p. 10).

"Upon receiving this message with the severed head of King Dahir, Hajjaj sent a reply to his General:

'.... God's command is, infidels should not get any refuge; just cut their necks. Believe that this is God's will...' " (*Indian Islam* by Titus, p. 10).

Dr. Babasaheb further wrote: "Mahmud of Ghazni also saw many of his attacks on India as *jehad*. Al-Ulbi, a historian under Mahmud Ghazni, describes the attacks as follows:

"He demolished the temples with idols and established Islam.

He captured towns, wiped out vile people with corrupt minds, killed the idolaters, and appeased the Muslims. He then returned home and declared his victory for Islam and swore that he would wage *jehad* against the Hindus every year"(*Indian Islam* by Titus, p. 11).

Muhammad Ghori also carried out attacks, motivated by bigotry. Historian Hassan Nizami describes his actions as follows:

"He wiped out the filth of infidelity and wickedness from the land of India with the force of his sword and liberated the whole region from the injustice of polytheism and idolatry, and not a single temple is left by his royal pomp and fearless bravery."

In his memoirs, Timur shows the reason for his attacks on India: "The purpose of my attacks on Hindustan was to campaign against the infidels and to renounce their infidelity and make them accept the true faith according to the command of Muhammad (PBUH), and to cleanse the filth of polytheism from that land and make it a holy land, as well as to uproot temples and idols, so that we, in the sight of God, will become the *Mujahids* and *Ghazi*, who is a believer in faith and fights for it" (*Medieval India* by Lane Poole; p. 155).

"From the very beginning, Mahmud of Ghazni adopted war rituals that created terror in the hearts of Hindus. After the defeat of Raja Jaipal in AD 1001, Mahmud ordered that Raja Jaipal be put in bondage and paraded in streets so that his sons as well as other chiefs would see him in a state of shame, bondage and humiliation and the fear of Islam would spread in the land of the infidels."

"Minhaj-us-Siraj further tells how Mahmud became widely known for having destroyed as many as a thousand temples, and of his great feat in destroying the temple of Somnath and carrying off its idol, which he asserts was broken into four parts. One part he deposited in the Jami Masjid of Ghazni, one he placed at the entrance of the royal palace, the third he sent to Mecca, and the fourth to Medina" (Dr. Titus: *Indian Islam*, p. 22-23).

It is said by Lane Poole that Mahmud of Ghazni "who had vowed that every year should see him wage a holy war against the infidels of Hindustan' could not rest from his idol-breaking campaign so long as the temple of Somnath remained inviolate. It was for this specific purpose that he, at the very close of his career, undertook his arduous march across the desert from Multan to Anhalwara on the coast, fighting as he went, until he saw at last the famous temple." There were a hundred thousand pilgrims who wanted to assemble, a thousand Brahmins served the temple and guarded its treasures, and hundreds of dancers and singers played before its gates. Within stood the famous *linga*, a crude pillar stone adorned with gems and lighted by jewelled candelabra which were reflected in rich hangings, embroidered with precious stones like stars that decked the shrine...Its ramparts were swarmed with incredulous Brahmins, mocking the vain arrogance of foreign infidels whom the Lord of Somnath would assuredly consume. The foreigners, not daunted, scaled the walls; the God remained dumb to the urgent appeals of his servants. Fifty thousand Hindus suffered for their faith and the sacred shrine was sacked to the joy of the true believers. The great stone was cast down and its fragments were carried off to grace the conqueror's palace. The temple gates were set up at Ghazni and a million pounds worth of treasure was rewarded to the iconoclast' (Lane Poole: *Medieval India*, p. 26).

"The work done by Mahmud of Ghazni became a pious tradition and was faithfully followed by those who came after him."

"It seems that Mahmud of Ghazni was especially happy with the genocide of the infidels. During the invasion of Chandraya in AD 1019, many infidels were cut off or taken prisoner and the Muslims did not even look at the booty until they were satisfied with killing the infidels as well as those who worshipped the sun and fire.' The historian then writes ridiculously that 'the elephants of the Hindu armies automatically abandoned the idols and went to Mahmud on their own, believing the devotion to Islam to be the best" (*Indian Islam*; p. 22).

Describing the cruelty of the Muslim invaders, Dr. Babasaheb further said: "It is said that Qutbuddin Aibak also demolished a thousand temples and built mosques in their place. He built the Jama Masjid in Delhi on which he inlaid stones and gold found in temples demolished by elephants, and engraved on it the divine commandments (of the *Qur'an*). Evidence of the planned use of this terrorist method can be found in the inscription carved on the eastern gate of this mosque, stating that the mosque was built from the stones of the twenty-seven demolished temples" (*Indian Islam*).

Amir Khusrau says that Alauddin, in his zeal to build another minaret similar to the one built by Qutbuddin, not only dug a mountain and took stones but also got it by demolishing the temples of the infidels. During his southern conquest, Alauddin carried out a campaign to demolish temples in the same way as his predecessors had done in northern India.

Sultan Feroze Shah, in his (*Futuhat-e-Firoz Shahi*) victory story, beautifully illustrates the whole story of what he did to the Hindus who dared to (again) build new temples for themselves. "When the Hindus in and around the town (Delhi) did this (rebuilding the temple) which was against the law of the Prophet which says not to tolerate it, I demolished those temples under the guidance of God and slaughtered the leaders of the infidels, and the rest punished by whipping. This was done until this evil was completely eradicated. Where idol-worshipers used to worship idols, today, by the grace of God, Muslims are worshipping the true God."

We can also see the description of the demolition of the temples which were renovated by Hindus, even during the reign of Shah Jahan. Direct attacks on Hindu holy places are very proudly described in the *Badshah-nama*:

The historian says, "The emperor was informed that during the time of the late emperor (Akbar), many Hindu temples were started to be built in the infidel stronghold of Benares, but they could not be completed. The *kafirs* now want to complete those temples. The emperor, the custodian of the faith, ordered that all the temples which had begun to be built in Benares and in all the territories under his sultanate, be demolished. The Allahabad sub-division has received information that seventy-six temples have been demolished in Benaras district" (*Indian Islam*).

A final attempt was made by Aurangzeb to abolish idolatry altogether. The author of *Maasir-e-Alamgiri* proudly describes Aurangzeb's attempts to destroy the temples in order to stop religious teachings of the Hindus in these words:

"In April 1669, Aurangzeb learned that in the Thatta, Multan and Benaras sub-provinces, especially in Benaras, foolish

Brahmins were studying useless *Shastras* in their schools, and that Muslims and Hindus came from far and wide to study. The 'custodian of faith' (the king) ordered the governors of the provinces to completely destroy all the schools and temples of the infidels; he ordered ban on the teaching and practice of idolatry altogether. The emperor was later informed that the Vishwanath temple in Benaras had been demolished."

As Dr. Titus wrote, "Invaders like Mahmoud Ghazni and Timur were more interested in breaking idols, plundering them, enslaving Hindus or making their lives hell with the sword of Islam. But, when the Muslim monarchy was permanently established, it became a primary requirement to convert as many Hindus as possible to Islam. Making Islam the religion of the whole of India has become an important part of State policy."

"Qutbuddin, whose reputation for demolishing temples was almost as great as that of Mahmud of Ghazni, must have resorted to repeated attempts to convert in the late twelfth and early thirteenth centuries. This example is enough for him–when he reached near Koil (Aligarh) in AD 1194, all the intelligent and wise people in the fort were converted to Islam and the rest were cut down with the sword."

Mahmud not only demolished the temples but also pursued a policy of enslaving the conquered Hindus. In the words of Dr. Titus,

"In the early days of Islam in India, not only was the slaughter of infidels and the demolition of temples carried out, but as we have seen, many defeated Hindus were enslaved. A special attraction for the invading chiefs and common soldiers in these invasions was the distribution of booty. It seems that Mahmud made the genocide of the infidels, the destruction of their temples, the capture and enslavement of them, and especially the looting of the temples as well as the property of the priests his main objectives. It is said that at the time of his first invasion, he had seized a large quantity of booty and had enslaved about five lakh beautiful Hindu men and women and taken them to Ghazni."

"When Mahmud looted Kannauj in AD 1017, he had taken away so much wealth and so many people as captives that the fingers of those who counted must be tired.' Describing how Hindu slavery became so common in Ghazni and Central Asia after the invasion of 1019, the historian writes:

"The Hindu could neither keep a horse for riding, nor carry a weapon (for self-defence), nor could he wear any good clothes, nor could he enjoy any luxury of life."

Historians of the time say, "These orders were so strictly obeyed that small servants like watchmen, porters or *muqadams* (because they were Hindus) could not ride horses, they could not keep weapons, they could not wear good clothes and even could not eat *paan*. No Hindu could roam around with his head held high. There were all sorts of ways to get fines, such as beatings, shackles and imprisonment."

So that was the story of 762 years–since the arrival of Mahmud of Ghazni (AD 1001) to the return of Ahmed Shah Abdali (AD 1763) (*Pakistan or Partition of India*, pp. 36-46).

Regarding the basic political motivations of Islam, Dr. Babasaheb Ambedkar wrote: "...According to Muslim law, the world is divided into two sections–*Dar-al-Islam* (the abode of Islam) and *Dar-al-Harb* (the country of conflict). Countries in which political power is in the hands of Islamic rulers and ruled according to Islamic law are called *Dar-al-Islam*, and *Dar-al-Harb* means countries with Muslim populations but political rulers are not Muslims. According to Islamic law, India cannot be the homeland of both Hindus and Muslims. It may be the land of Muslims, but it can never be the 'land of Hindus and Muslims alike'. And this land is said to belong to the Muslims only when it is ruled by the Muslims. The moment this land is ruled by a non-Muslim, it does not remain the land of Muslims. Instead of *Dar-al-Islam*, it becomes *Dar-al-Harb*."

"Don't think that these are just bookish things, because this idea has the power to be an influential force in influencing the behaviour of Muslims. This concept had a great impact on the behaviour of Muslims even when the British occupied India. Hindu minds were not affected and questions were not raised by the advent of the British Raj, but the Muslims immediately started thinking whether Hindustan is now a habitable place for the Muslims or not. The debate took momentum within the Muslim community and according to Titus, it lasted for about 50 years–whether India is *Dar-al-Harb* or *Dar-al-Islam*. Some more zealous elements even declared *jehad* under the leadership of Syed Ahmed Shahid, who taught the Muslims to migrate from here to the countries with Muslim Raj and run his own movement all over Hindustan."

Dr. Babasaheb also exposed the sectarian face of Sir Syed Ahmed, the founder of Aligarh Muslim University. Dr. Babasaheb wrote: "Sir Syed Ahmed, the founder of the Aligarh movement, used all his strength and influence to persuade the Muslims that Hindustan should not be considered as a *Dar-al-Harb* just because there is no Muslim rule in India. He urged the Muslims to consider Hindustan as *Dar-al-Islam* as they have complete freedom to follow the customs of their religion. The migration movement ceased for some time, but they were still sticking to the principle that Hindustan is *Dar-al-Harb*. During the Khilafat movement, in 1920-21, the flag-bearers of the Muslim nation again propagated the whole thing vigorously and the Muslim community also gave favourable reactions to this propaganda. Many Muslims not only agreed to emigrate under Islamic law, but actually left their homes in India and moved to Afghanistan."

It is also worth mentioning here that migration is not the only way to free oneself from *Dar-al-Harb*. There is another commandment under Islamic law, to wage *jehad*, according to which "a Muslim ruler spreads the rule of Islam (through war) until the whole world comes under the rule of Islam–for which every Muslim ruler is obliged." When the whole world is divided into *Dar-al-Islam* and *Dar-al-Harb*, it is natural that each country will fall into either one of the two divisions. This means that in principle it is the duty of every Muslim ruler who is capable of converting *Dar-al-Harb* to *Dar-al-Islam*.

In 1857, the Muslims revolted and tried to turn India into *Dar-al-Islam* once again (even if it was a country's freedom struggle for Hindus!).

Dr. Babasaheb went on to say: "Not only can they wage *jihad* but they can also call on other foreign Muslim countries to help in the success of the *jihad*. And in the same way, if any other foreign Muslim power wants to wage *jihad* against India, Muslims can help it for the success of its efforts."

A third principle that needs to be discussed here is that Islam does not believe in geographical borders. Its relations are on social and religious grounds, so they do not consider the borders of countries. This is the basic premise of pan-Islamism. Inspired by this, every Muslim in Hindustan says that he is a Muslim first and then an Indian. It is this spirit of Muslims that explains why Muslims have played such a small role in India's progress. On the other hand, they will use all their power to support the Muslim countries. This also explains why for them the place of Muslim countries comes first and India comes second.

"... the possibility cannot be ruled out, if the form of this religious fundamentalism of pan-Islamism moves towards the adoption of a pan-Islamic political form"(*Pakistan or Partition of India*, pp. 287-91).

Thus influenced by their own ideological motivation, "To what extent do Muslims accept a government that is to be created and run by Hindus?" asked Babasaheb. In this context, he described how Muslims view Hindus against them.

"....Hindu is a *kafir*–infidel–from the Muslim point of view and any *kafir* is not honourable. He is a low-born and disreputable person. That is why the country under the rule of *kafir* is *Dar-al-Harb* for Muslims" (*Pakistan or Partition of India*, p. 3).

Dr. Ambedkar also cited some examples: "....Muslims never forget to believe that the Hindus are of lower grade than them even when Hindus were supporting from all the ways at the time of the Khilafat movement of Indian Muslims."

A Muslim wrote in the pro-Khilafah newspaper, *Insaf*:

"What do '*swami*' and '*mahatma*' mean? Can Muslims use such words for non-Muslims in their speeches or articles?"

He further wrote: *swami* means master and *mahatma* means 'one with the best spiritual powers' and it is like '*Ruh-e-Azam*' and 'Supreme Soul'. He asked Muslim clerics to issue an official *fatwa* stating whether it was permissible in Islamic law for Muslims to use such words of honour for non-Muslims."

"Details of a unique incident that took place at a function organised to celebrate the release of Mr. Gandhi from prison in 1924 was printed in the press. The ceremony was held at Unani Tibbia College, run by Hakim Ajmal Khan. According to the news, a Hindu student compared Gandhiji with Hazrat Isa Masih (Jesus Christ). All the Muslim students were outraged at this matter as it hurt their sentiments, and they threatened the Hindu students to be ready for violent consequences. It is said that Muslim professors also joined in the demonstration with the students of their community for hurting their sentiments" (pp. 294-5).

"Maulana Muhammad Ali, the leader of the Khilafat movement and a close associate of Gandhiji, used devotional words like '*mahatma*' for Gandhiji when he presided over the Congress session in 1923 and compared him to Jesus Christ. Speaking in Aligarh and Ajmer a year later, Muhammad Ali said: "Gandhi's character, no matter how pure, but religiously, he is descending from any Muslim, even if that Muslim is characterless."

"His utterances caused a great deal of controversy. Many people did not believe that Muhammad Ali, who had shown so much respect and faith for Gandhiji, could have such a low and insulting attitude towards him. When Muhammad Ali was once speaking at a meeting at Aminabad Park in Lucknow, he was asked if it was said that the sentiments you expressed against Gandhi were true. Muhammad Ali replied without hesitation, 'Yes, according to my religion and opinion, I consider any adulterous and immoral Muslim to be better than Gandhi' (p. 296).

Dr. Ambedkar has discussed at length the efforts of Hindus to establish Hindu-Muslim unity and the reasons for its failure. He wrote:

"Britain's conquest of India brought about a complete political revolution in the comparative situation between Hindus and Muslims. Muslims have been ruling over Hindus for 600 years. When the power passed into the hands of the British, they were brought up on par with the Hindus. To descend from the level of a ruler to a state of co-ruled or co-slavery was a sufficient insult to them. But it would be even more embarrassing to come down from the co-slavery situation and become a slave to the Hindus (Muslims thought they would have to live under Hindu rule in an undivided independent India). That is why Muslims say that; isn't it natural that they want to avoid such an unbearable situation by creating an independent nation in which they can live happily and the conflict between the rulers of another community and the people under their rule cannot become an epidemic and ruin their lives?: (pp. 31-2).

After giving this short preamble, Dr. Babasaheb Ambedkar also described the efforts of unity made by Hindus:

"...It can be said that the history of these efforts (to win the hearts of Muslims) started in 1909. (In 1909, a Muslim delegation led by Aga Khan met Viceroy Minto at Shimla and presented to him the demands of the Muslims. These were mainly two– separate electorate in each legislative body and the predominance of Muslims in all constituencies). The demand for this delegation of Muslims was enforced by the British rulers on the one hand (1909) and on the other hand, many Hindus, including prominent figures like Gopal Krishna Gokhale, agreed to the demands. Many Hindus are blaming Gokhaleji for accepting the principle of separate electorate, but they forget that it would have been foolish not to do so" (p. 298).

"However, Hindu-Muslim unity could not be achieved despite the consensus reached in 1909 in favour of a separate electorate. Then in 1916, the Lucknow Agreement was signed. In that agreement, the Hindus satisfied every demand of the Muslims, but there was no unity between the two" (p. 299).

"Mr. Gandhi has always said that *swarajya* cannot be achieved without Hindu-Muslim unity. Mr. Gandhi not only popularized this slogan in Indian politics but also made untiring efforts to make it a reality" (p. 135).

"The Muslims started the Khilafat movement in 1919, with the aim of pressurising the British government to keep the Turkish Empire intact and its caliphate (where the Caliph rules) safe. Gandhiji declared his active support to this movement. There were many people who doubted the morality of the Khilafat movement and tried to keep Mr. Gandhi away from participating in a movement whose moral basis was questionable. But Mr. Gandhi convinced himself so strongly that the Khilafat movement was justified that he was ready to kneel down to any opposition. He repeatedly argued that the movement was just and that it was his duty to take part in it" (p. 136).

"...but unfortunately, Mr. Gandhi's hope that 'no government can quell the non-violent protests of the people of the whole country' was thwarted. Within a year of starting the non-cooperation movement, he had to accept that Muslims had become impatient."

"Gandhiji worked so diligently for Hindu-Muslim unity that for him everything else became secondary. "...It is a notorious fact that some fanatical Muslims have killed many prominent Hindus who hurt the religious sentiments of Muslims through their articles or by participating in the purification movement" (p. 12).

Dr. Babasaheb Ambedkar criticised Gandhiji for not condemning Muslims for these killings, and that too because of the fear that doing so may hurt the efforts of Hindu-Muslim unity. Dr. Ambedkar was also a critic of the act of forgiving Muslims for their every mistake.

Dr. Babasaheb believed that the efforts for Hindu-Muslim unity were delusionary, and the Congress and Gandhiji did not find them guilty despite clear evidence of Muslim involvement in the riots. Babasaheb said, "Even though Muslims committed heinous crimes against Hindus, Gandhiji did not ask them the reason."

What was the result of Gandhiji's efforts to establish Hindu-Muslim unity? From Dr. Ambedkar's point of view, "it is necessary to get the information about the relationship between the two communities during the 20 years' period between AD 1920 to AD 1940, which was the period of Mr. Gandhi's best efforts for Hindu-Muslim unity. These details of the relationship are contained in the annual reports of the Government of India to the Parliament of India on the status of India" (p. 153). There reports describe the bloody riots that took place between the two communities. "One such riots is the Moplah riot in 1920–a heart-wrenching story of atrocities committed by the Moplahs (Muslims) in the Malabar region of Kerala on Hindus (p. 147) – mass killings, forced conversions, desecration of temples, disgusting insults to women, looting, arson, destruction. In short, the Moplahs carried out all acts of brutality and sheer barbarism against Hindus"(p. 153).

"If these descriptions of violence are evaluated along with the efforts of Hindu-Muslim unity made by Shri Gandhi, it will be a very painful and heart-breaking affair. It is no exaggeration to say that this description is like a record of 20 years of civil war between

Hindus and Muslims; In between, there was an occasional peace like an armed ceasefire" (p. 175).

Regarding Muslims' insistence on making Urdu the national language of India and insistence of *gauvadha* (cow sacrifice) as well as ban on singing and playing near mosques, Babasaheb said: "Their demand to make Urdu the national language of India is irrational. Out of 6.8 crore Muslims, only 2.8 crore Muslims speak Urdu"(p. 268)..."...Another interesting thing is that the spirit of Muslims is to take advantage of the weaknesses of Hindus. Proof of such unfair exploitation is the right of Muslims to *gauvadha* (cow sacrifice) as well as their demand for a ban on dancing and singing near mosques. There is no emphasis in Islam on sacrificing cows for religious reasons and they do not sacrifice cows when they go for Hajj to Mecca and Medina. But in India they are not satisfied with sacrificing any other animal. The third thing is that criminal tactics are adopted by Muslims in politics" (p. 269).

"From the observation of these 30 years of history, it is natural to ask the question whether Hindu-Muslim unity has come true? Has there been no effort to establish it? Or is there still something left to do? The history of the last 30 years says that Hindu-Muslim unity could not be established. On the contrary, today it is the greatest animosity between the two. True and sustained efforts have been made for the unity of the two, and now there is nothing more to be done, except that one party surrenders completely to the other. Now when someone who is not in the habit of being unnecessarily optimistic says that the efforts for Hindu-Muslim unity are like a mirage and that idea should be rejected now, no one will dare to say that the person is pessimistic or overly idealistic. It is now up to the Hindus to decide whether, despite the unfortunate end of all their previous efforts, they will continue to pursue the goal or to abandon the efforts of unity and try to reconcile with the Muslim allies on another issue (meaning a separate nation for Muslims–Pakistan)" (p. 307).

What is the reason for the failure of these unity efforts?

"The real definition of the failure of Hindu-Muslim unity is that no one understands that the problem between the two communities is not just a wall of differences and there are no physical reasons behind the enmity between the two. This enmity is of a spiritual nature. This is a problem arising from reasons that have their roots in historical, sectarian, cultural and social enmity, and political enmity is only a shadow of it. These factors have created a river of hatred that is constantly overflowing with more and more water from its own sources."

"One of the things that raises doubts among Hindus about the intentions of Muslims is the desire of Muslims to convert the oppressed class of Hindus to Islam."

"Muslims have always lured the Dalit and oppressed class of Hindu society to convert them in Islam. Major animosity between Hindus and Muslims stems from the idea that Hindu society will become more powerful by assimilating its own oppressed class" (p. 235).

In his book, *Thoughts on Pakistan*, Dr. Babasaheb Ambedkar elaborated on the religious basis of Muslim politics. According to this description, Muslim politics had two dimensions–aggression and separatism.

"A cursory glance also suggests that aggressiveness is the basis of the attitude of Muslims towards Hindus and vice-a-versa. This aggression of Hindus is a newly developed instinct and it is started just now. While the aggression of Muslims is their innate nature and it is much older than that of Hindus. It may be possible that Hindus can leave Muslims behind in the display of aggression over time, but in the current situation, the Muslims have left Hindus far behind in their display of aggression."

"A little description of the political aggression of the Muslims is necessary because this political aggression has given birth to a disease which cannot be ignored."

"Three things deserve special attention in the context of this Muslim aggression: the first is the ever-increasing political aspirations of Muslims and which started in 1932" (p. 236).

Describing how difficult it is to satisfy the desire of Muslims to gain more and more political facilities, Dr. Ambedkar has said something like this: "Looking at the demands made by the Muslims in the Round Table Conference and what was given to them, one would think that these would be the last demands of the Muslims and this agreement of 1932 would be final. But it can be seen that Muslims are not satisfied with that either. And a new list seems to have been drawn up to protect Muslim interests."

"The second thing to understand is the spirit of Muslims to take undue advantage of the weaknesses of Hindus. If Hindus object to something, then Muslims start making their own policy by insisting on the same thing, and they give up their undue demand only when Hindus are willing to pay the price in the form of some other facility instead" (p. 256).

"The third thing to understand is the use of violent methods by Muslims in politics. Violent harassment is a testament to the fact that bullying has become a permanent part of their strategy in politics. It seems that they are deliberately using the same policy which was adopted by the Sudeten-Germans against the Czechs" (p. 5-20).

Dr. Babasaheb Ambedkar said, "The Congress has adopted a policy of keeping Muslims happy by giving them political and other facilities, because they understand that they cannot achieve their desired goal of independence without the support of Muslims. I think the Congress does not know two things. The first is that there is a difference between appeasement and agreement, and this difference is important. To appease means to pay an aggressor or an aggressive community a price for oneself, and that value is to turn a blind eye to atrocities committed by the aggressor against innocent people, for which he is offended for some reason, such as murder, plundering, and arson; while an agreement means drawing some boundaries between the two parties which neither party can violate. Appeasement does not control the demands and expectations of the oppressor, while agreement seems to control them."

"Another thing that the Congress did not understand was that the adoption of such a policy of concessions has increased the aggression of the Muslims and what is worse is that the Muslims have come to understand from all these concessions that these Hindus have a mentality of defeat and there is a lack of the will to face Muslims. This policy of appeasement will put the Hindus in a dire situation in the same way that the allies (Britain, France, etc. in World War II) used to put themselves by appeasing Hitler."

Referring to an interview of Rabindranath Tagore in his book, Babasaheb wrote: "In 1924, a Bengali newspaper editor interviewed the poet Rabindranath Tagore. He said: "Another important reason in the poet's thought, which makes Hindu-Muslim unity impossible in its true sense is, Muslims cannot limit their patriotism to any one country." The poet said that he directly asked many Muslims–will they fight against the invader, hand-in-hand with Hindus, to defend their united motherland, if a Muslim country invades India? He (Rabindranath Tagorer) could not be satisfied with their answer. The poet said that he could say with certainty that people like Muhammad Ali have made it clear that in any situation, any Muslim, no matter what country he belongs to, is not allowed to stand up against any other Muslim" (pp. 262-266).

If Dr. Babasaheb Ambedkar accuses the Congress leadership of appeasing Muslims, the accusations are being made to express concern that Muslims are allowed to pursue their own fundamentalist objectives in the name of religious freedom. Ambedkar wrote, "Muslim political leaders will not base their politics on the secular materialistic needs of life, as they feel that doing so will weaken the Muslim community in their struggle against Hindus" (p. 226).

"Democracy is not the main concern of Muslims. Their main concern is what effect will a majority-ruled democracy have on the struggle of Muslims against Hindus? Will it increase their power or will it weaken them? (In their fight against Hindus) if they are going to be weak, they will oppose democracy" (p. 227).

Dr. Babasaheb Ambedkar was very much concerned about the impending animosity between Hindus and Muslims, as it was leading to communal riots at any time. He believed that it was necessary to remove this communal enmity which would give people the opportunity to develop multifold. But he had doubts about that also. He believed that Muslims would not be satisfied even after the demand of separate Pakistan was met.

Accepting the demand for Pakistan, he wrote: "The question is, what about the Muslims who remained in India after Pakistan was formed?" Such a question is quite natural, as it seems that Pakistan's plan is for Muslim-majority areas, where they may need security. But the question is, who will raise this question? It is certain that Hindus will not raise it. Only the Muslims of

Hindustan or Pakistan will raise that question. The same question was asked to Rehmat Ali, a supporter of Pakistan's demand. He answered, "The truth is that their worries are not just like the pain of separation for me. They are a part of our body. Nor will we ever forget them; or they will forget us. Their condition today and their safety in the future will be important to us. As per today's situation, creation of Pakistan will not have any negative impact on the condition of the Muslims of Hindustan. Looking at the proportion of the population (one Muslim for every four Hindus), they will keep on getting as much participation in Legislative Assemblies as they are getting today. And as far as their security is concerned, we can only guarantee one thing–tit for tat."

Dr. Babasaheb was clear that the creation of Pakistan would not solve the communal problem in India: "Whatever it was, the Hindus had nothing to do with the question. The question that should bother the Hindus is to what extent will the communal problem in India be solved by creation of Pakistan? This question is perfectly appropriate and must be considered. It has to be believed that creation of Pakistan will not solve India's communal problem. While redrawing the border will allow Pakistan to become uniform in terms of the form of the people, but Hindustan will remain a mixed country. In Hindustan, Muslims are spread all over the country and most of them are settled in cities and towns. No demarcation of any kind can unite Hindustan in terms of community of people. The only way to unify Hindustan is-population exchange. Until that happens, we have to assume that even with the creation of Pakistan, the problem of minority-majority in India will remain the same, and will continue to cause the same conflict in Hindustani politics as before" (pp. 102-8).

"Those who are doubtful of population swaps need to study the history of the problem of minorities that has arisen between Turkey, Greece and Bulgaria. They will understand that these countries understood that the best solution to the problem of minorities is to exchange the population. What these three countries did was not a simple task. In this work, they had to relocate 20 million people. But with patience, the three countries worked together successfully because they felt that communal peace was more important than anything else."

According to Dr. Babasaheb, the solution to the communal problem was possible only when all the Muslims of India migrated to Pakistan. Babasaheb said, "I would choose to divide the people of India into Muslim and non-Muslim, because this is the surest and most secure way to protect both."

The demand to create Pakistan was widely opposed by Hindus. Dr. Ambedkar analysed various aspects of the subject in detail and then gave his firm opinion that it would be in the interest of millions of Hindus in Hindustan to divide India into two separate nations, one part being Muslim Pakistan and the other part being non-Muslim Hindustan. According to him, Hindus will have to face two serious consequences if the plan to create Pakistan is not implemented.

"(1) There will be a crisis on India's security.

(2) The problem of communal conflict in the country will become serious."

Dr. Ambedkar studied the mixed communal composition of the Indian Army after World War I and came to the conclusion that the number of Muslims in the Indian Army was the highest and that the ratio could not change even in undivided independent India. He questioned whether the Indian Army's Muslim community could be relied upon to defend India in the event of a Muslim country–such as Afghanistan–invading it.

In this regard, Dr. Babasaheb Ambedkar wrote: "It cannot be overlooked that gaining independence is not only important for any country, it is equally necessary to ensure that it can be kept intact. The guarantee of independence of any country can be found only by its brave army–an army that can be relied upon to fight for the country in every crisis. In India, such an army will definitely be a mixed army of Hindus and Muslims. If India is invaded, can the Muslim part of the army be trusted to fight to defend the country? Assuming that the attacker is also a Muslim, will the Muslims support the attackers or will they defend India by fighting against them? This is a very crucial question. It is clear that the answer to this question depends on how much the Muslims in the army have been affected by the two-nation principle, which is the basis of Pakistan's ideology. If they have come under the influence of this principle, the Indian army cannot be called clean. Such an army, instead of being a defender of India's independence, will itself remain a crisis and a potential disaster."

"The question is, will Indians be able to defend an independent India? The answer, I repeat, is that the only way an Indian can defend (independent) India is if the Indian army remains apolitical and untouched by the idea of Pakistan."

"Will the government be able to convince Muslims enlisted in the army that they will shoot at rebel Muslims? The answer also depends on how much the two-nation principle has affected Muslims in the military. If they are affected, India cannot have a safe and secure government"(pp. 360-61).

A description of the mixed sectarian formation figures in the Indian Army during the time interval between the two world wars was presented by Dr. Babasaheb. He expressed his views on the possible impact of this combination on India's security readiness as follows:

'...This survey reveals two obvious facts. The first is that even today (in pre-independence India) the Indian army is a Muslim majority army. Secondly, most of these Muslim soldiers are from the Punjab and the North-West Frontier Province. The formation of the Indian army could mean that only the Muslims of the Punjab and the border areas are India's protectors against foreign aggression. This truth is so clear that the Muslims of those regions are fully aware of this glorious position given to them by the British for any reason, as they have often been referred to themselves as "gatekeepers of India". With this important truth, Hindus should think about India's security problem.'

'To what extent can the Hindus of India depend on these "gatekeepers" for India's freedom and independence? The answer lies in who will try to break in by forcibly opening India's border. Clearly, a possible invasion from India's northwestern border could only come from two countries–Afghanistan and Russia, whose borders are touching India's borders. It is not sure who will invade when. If such an invasion takes place through Russia, it can be hoped that these (Muslim) "gatekeepers" will fight with determination and sincerity and keep the invaders out. But suppose Afghanistan invades India alone or along with other Muslim countries, will these "gatekeepers" keep these invaders out or open the border and let them in? This is a question that no Hindu can ignore. It is necessary to convince the Hindus in this matter as this is a very crucial question."

"Considering all these factors, it must be some 'adventurous' Hindu who will say that the Muslims in the Indian army will remain loyal even in the event of an invasion of India by Muslim countries and there is no doubt that they will side with the invaders."

"...The Hindus of India are faced with a difficult decision – either to have a clean and honest army (which is possible only by Partition) or a secure boundary line (which is possible if Partition is not possible). Which of these difficult paths is best for Hindus? There is no doubt that Muslims in the region have a grudge against Hindus. So what is the best situation for Hindus–to be anti-Muslim by staying apart or to be anti-Muslim by staying together? The only answer to this question can be found by any sensible person that if you want to remain an opponent of Muslims, it is better to be an opponent by being opposed to them than by being with them. In fact, we should pray in our minds that Muslims stay out. This is the only way to liberate the Indian army from Muslim dominance."

"But how is that possible? There is only one way for it and that is to agree to the plan of Pakistan. With the creation of Pakistan, India's security will definitely become stronger rather than weaker."

"If we want to stop the Indian army from being Muslim-dominated, the most certain way for that is to let their plan to create Pakistan be implemented. Opposition to this plan means sharpening an infallible weapon of own destruction with own money. Certainly a clean and honest army is more beneficial than a safe frontier" (pp. 81-87).

Dr. Babasaheb also had a clear view that even if Pakistan was not created, India would be harmed and India's problems would increase. He said, "The question to consider is–is it worthwhile to fight to keep India intact? The first thing is, it cannot be unified India like one body-one soul, even if India remains undivided. Though India may be considered as a single country, in reality two countries–Hindustan and Pakistan–which are tied in an artificial and forcibly stifled unity. The way this epidemic of separatism spreads in political life will sometimes invite a horrible life-and-death struggle to reject this forcibly stumbled unity. Even if some great power stops this disintegration, one thing is certain: this stumbling block will continue to suck India's vitality, erode its harmony, erode the love and confidence of its citizens towards the country, and it will hinder the application of its moral and material resources, if not in their development. India will remain a pale and diseased State...." (pp. 334-5).

Dr. Babasaheb Ambedkar had great doubts about the power and legitimacy of the so-called 'nationalist Muslims' to turn the Muslim community of India away from the mindset of two nations. He wrote:

"It is difficult to find any real difference between communal Muslims, who are part of Muslim society, and nationalist Muslims. It is doubtful that the nationalist Muslims have any real closeness to the Congress party in terms of sentiments, goals and policies which would distinguish them from the Muslim League. The truth is that many Congressmen themselves believe that there is no difference between the two and that nationalist Muslims are like a frontier of communal Muslims. This concept is also not entirely different from the truth; proof of this is that the leader of the nationalist Muslims, Dr. Ansari has refused to oppose the 'communal award', which provides a separate electorate for Muslims, although Congress and nationalist Muslims have passed a resolution opposing it" (pp. 406-7).

Dr. Ambedkar did not rule out the possibility of intense communal strife in independent India. That is why he not only supported the creation of Pakistan, but also the exchange of population between the two countries to end communal animosity between the two countries. However, he wrote that even after Partition, the problem may not be completely resolved in India:

"If we accept that the communal problem of Hindustan will not be fully solved even after the creation of Pakistan, does it lead to the conclusion that Hindus should reject the demand for a separate Pakistan?" (p. 104).

"No, he said firmly. The first reason is that the number of Muslims will be much less than the number of Hindus due to the creation of Pakistan...It seems that the creation of Pakistan may not solve Hindustan's communal problem, but it will certainly reduce its size and make its peaceful solution easier by making it less important" (p. 105).

Dr. Babasaheb Ambedkar's nationalist heart wanted Hindu society to be reformed, Hindu society to be one. He was always saddened by the fact that Hindu society was unorganised due to caste system and that was why the country fell prey to foreign invaders. He said: "There is no enthusiasm for unity among Indians, there is no desire in coordinating with each other, no wish for a single dress or language. There is no enthusiasm to embrace things that are common and national-level by leaving things that are local and of lower-pride."

Today the whole world is troubled by communal fundamentalism. India has been tolerating this fundamentalism for a thousand years. In such circumstances, every single word of Dr. Babasaheb is one hundred per cent true even today. Dr. Babasaheb went to the root of the Hindu-Muslim problem and concluded something that is still useful. He categorically opposed the bigwigs of secularism. His nationalist conscience was so steeped in devotion to India that he fearlessly expressed these views. *Jehadi* mentality and religious fundamentalism are a threat to all mankind and the world. The ideas expressed by Dr. Babasaheb Ambedkar about 75 years ago are useful for all mankind even today.

□

8

Foreign Policy in the National Interest

Babasaheb was not only dissatisfied with the direction of independent India's then foreign policy but expressed actual anxiety at it.

Foreign policy making is a critical aspect for a newly born nation and in the case of India there are still tendencies to vouch in the name of Nehru as the architect of independent India's foreign policy. If somebody had posed the greatest visionary challenge to that foreign policy presumptions right during the Nehruvian period of non-alignment policy towards immediate neighbourhood defence preparedness or the problem of dealing with Islamic countries, he was Dr. Ambedkar who provided visionary insights which are relevant even today. No doubt Ambedkar's contribution for ensuring upliftment and dignified life to the suppressed classes is unparalleled in the Indian context, but if the foreign policy means ensuring protection of national interest while engaging with other nations, then the vision of Dr. Ambedkar provides us with alternative ideas which were counter to the idealist premise of Nehru.

Babasaheb was critical of Nehru's foreign policies on many counts. While resigning from his ministry, he made the most vehement criticism of Nehru's foreign policy. He said, "Anyone, who has followed the course of our foreign policy and along with it the attitude of other countries towards India, could not fail to realise the sudden change that has taken place in their attitude towards us. On 15th of August, 1947 when we began our life as an independent country, there was no country which wished us ill. Every country in the world was our friend. Today, after four years, all our friends have deserted us. We have no friends left; we have alienated ourselves. We are pursuing a lonely furrow with no one even to second our resolutions in the UNO. When I think of our foreign policy, I am reminded of what Bismark and Bernard Shaw have said. Bismark has said that 'politics is not a game of realising the ideal; politics is the game of the possible.' Bernard Shaw, not very long ago, said that 'good ideals are good but one must not forget that it is often dangerous to be too good.' Our foreign policy is in complete opposition to these words of wisdom uttered by two of the world's greatest men."

This clearly reflects that Dr. Ambedkar was looking for a more realistic foreign policy based on the foundation of protecting national interest and was of the firm opinion that the idealist policy propounded by Nehru will not yield results.

There are more instances when he criticised the foreign policy of Nehru. He found fallacies in the three props on which independent India's foreign policy was constructed–one was peace; the second was co-existence between communism and free democracy, and the third was opposition to SEATO.

While criticising the rhetoric of peace, he believed that in foreign relations, use of force is inevitable; therefore, India should not neglect the defence preparedness. He said, "The root of evil is not in the use of force but in the misuse of victory." Even during World War II, he insisted that Britain should prepare India for the defence of their own. Speaking to students of Lucknow University in November 1951, he said: "The government's foreign policy failed to make India stronger. Why should not India get a permanent seat in the UN Security Council? Why has the Prime Minister not tried for it? India must choose between parliamentary democracy and the communist way of dictatorship and come to a final conclusion."

Nehru's tilt towards the communist bloc while pronouncing the policy of non-alignment is well known. Ambedkar believed that it would prove fatal to India in the long run and against the democratic spirit of the Constitution. Referring to communist

Russia's expansionist policy, Ambedkar observed: "Here you have a vast country endlessly occupied in destroying other people; absorbing them within its fold on the theory that it is liberating them." He opined, "Communism is like a forest fire; it goes on burning and consuming anything and everything that comes in its way." Countries living in the vicinity of the forest fire stood in danger. Therefore he believed that the principle of non-alignment was absurd as it was based on the premise that communism and democracy could coexist.

Today, when India's relationship with the US has significantly improved, in the post-Cold War, it was appropriate that India should favour the democratic bloc then led by the US. Dr. Ambedkar believed that Russia and China couldn't be ruled out from making further aggression and occupying any further part of the free world. Nehru's reservation about the US and fears about what Russia would reason for India's non-alignment policy did not allow him to take some firm and principled stand. Dr. Ambedkar felt that 'natural affinity of democracies' should be the guiding principle of India's foreign policy and also closer Indo-US relations. He also expressed the desirability of a league of democracies in Asia and Far East.

Babasaheb's geostrategic understanding of foreign policy was like a true statesman. He considered that the geographical factor was one of the most important factors in a country's foreign policy. Each country had to form its own foreign policy based on its geographical location–this was his firm conviction. While speaking in the Parliament, he drew the attention of the house to the fact that "India had been completely encircled on the one side by Pakistan and the other Muslim countries; and on the other side, by allowing China to take possession of Lhasa."

"The Prime Minister," Ambedkar continued, "has practically helped the Chinese to bring their border down to the Indian border. Looking at all these things, it seems to me that it would be an act of levity not to believe that India, if it is not exposed to aggression right now, is exposed to aggression in future and that aggression might well be committed by people who always are in the habit of committing aggression. The Prime Minister" Ambedkar proceeded, "should not depend upon the Panchsheel accepted by Mao and recorded in the Tibet treaty of non-aggression." He added that if "Mao had any faith in the Panchsheel, which was the essential part of Buddhist religion, he certainly would treat the Buddhists in his own country in a very different way. There is no room for Panchsheel in politics and certainly not in the politics of the communist country." These cautionary words reflect how visionary he was when it comes to India's China policy.

When the whole world is facing the menace of Islamic terrorism and Pakistan is regarded as the fountainhead of such terrorist activities, it was Ambedkar who had warned of such pan-Islamic brotherhood along with Savarkar. His book, *Pakistan or the Partition of India* and his resignation speech in the parliament on 10 October, 1951 present a clear picture about his assessment. His historic book harshly criticises the anti-reformist tendency of the Muslims. He observed, "The dominating influence with the Muslims is not democracy. The predominant interest of Muslims is religion, their politics being essentially clerical..." To the Muslim," the book states–"Islam is a world religion, suitable for all people for all times and for all conditions. The brotherhood of Islam is not the universal brotherhood of human kind; it is the brotherhood of Muslims for Muslims only. For non-Muslims, there is nothing but contempt and enmity. The Muslim has allegiance to a nation, which is ruled by a Muslim; a land not ruled by a Muslim is his enemy land.' The book, therefore, concludes that 'Islam can never allow true Muslims to adopt India as their motherland and to regard a Hindu as their kith and kin. The spirit of aggression is a Muslim's natural endowment. He takes advantage of the weakness of the Hindus and follows gangsterism." Does this assessment make Ambedkar anti-Muslim or communal? He described the problem of Islam which was visible even before the Partition and warned about the possible consequences.

While focusing towards Pakistan, he said, "Your fight with Pakistan is a part of our foreign policy about which I feel deeply dissatisfied. There are two grounds which have disturbed our relations with Pakistan–one is Kashmir, and the other is the condition of our people in East Bengal. I felt that we should be more deeply concerned with East Bengal where the condition of our people seems intolerable from all the newspapers than with

Kashmir. Notwithstanding this, we have been staking our all on the Kashmir issue. Even then I feel we have been fighting on an unreal issue. The real issue to my mind is not which is right but what is right." On this ground, he believed that "there should be complete transfer of the population of Hindus and Muslims, if the Partition takes place."

Ambedkar's vision of foreign policy was problem-solving–democracy, enhancing developmental and strategic options were the founding principles of his foreign policy considerations. His understanding of world politics was realistic and based purely on a premise–'protecting national interest'. It is true that due to his commitment as a Labour and Law Minister and drafting of the Indian Constitution consumed much of his energies, he could not pay much attention to the issue pertaining to foreign policy, which he was worried about, still, the insights he provided about the making of foreign policy and its founding principles are relevant even today.

Today, in 2021, when we experience that our foreign policy has been completely changed by the present Modi government and it is unlike what was stated by Dr. Ambedkar after four years of Independence, almost all nations of the world are friends of India. We have also changed our decade-old policies towards our immediate neighbours–Pakistan and China–from defensive to offensive. Although we have never attacked and we are not attacking anyone's land, we are not now in a defensive position. We are also not appeasing or pleasing anyone; national interest is at the highest priority while making our foreign policy. Today, we are neither non-aligned nor inclined to communism; we are a parliamentary democratic nation and we are aligned with everyone alike. Today, we are part of many helpful international pacts and treaties which are beneficial to the nation. In short, the foreign policy of the current government reflects the very thoughts of Babasaheb Ambedkar, who had expressed it with great worry about 70 years ago.

□

9

Religion: Revival Mantra of Life

Babasaheb declared in 1935, "I was born a Hindu, but I will not die a Hindu. I will convert my religion." He was initiated into Buddhism at Nagpur in 1956 along with millions of his followers. One can analyse his conversion from a religious point of view, but since that is not the subject of our discussion, we will discuss the importance of conversion in the sense of nationalism.

The idea of conversion was coined and discussed by him way before 1924. He gave a speech at the provincial conference of *Bahishkrit Bharat* at Barshi in 1924. He said, "The other way is conversion; any religion should be viewed from both a philosophical as well as a practical point of view. Hinduism is second to none from a philosophical point of view. Not only that, I would say it is the best of any religion in the world. Hinduism vows for a '*sarvan bhuti ek atma*' (Omnipotence is one soul) as the basic element. If the society is behaving according to this noble element, then the way an earthen lamp gives light to all without any bias, the way a tree provides shadow to everyone, whether someone waters it or someone cuts it, the way the river water quenches the thirst of a cow but doesn't become a poison for the lion to kill it–have the Hindus behaved the same unbiased way?! Just look at them; how bad has the practical form of the Hindu society become? Do we find any match between their conduct and their philosophy? Isn't it surprising that the same society which keeps on chanting 'omnipotence is one soul' announces that its own brethren are impure and untouchable? Even more annoying is the fact that those who do not believe in Hinduism are given the equal status as upper-caste Hindus. Christians, for them, are neither untouchable nor unholy for them. It is surprising that the upper-caste Hindus are not defiled by their touch and they have no hesitation in working under them. In a sense Muslims should be lower than the lowest caste of Hindus. They should be even more untouchable and unholy compared to even the lowest caste of Hindus because no Hindu (even the lower caste) makes a living by slaughtering cows and selling beef, but Christians and Muslims have no hesitation in doing so. Surprisingly, they are yet considered more sacred than the castes like Mahar, Mang, Dhed, etc. The upper-caste Hindus behave normally with them (Christians and Muslims); their children study in the same schools and the same classes. They share the same paths (which they don't do with untouchables); share the same well for drinking water; and they deal with them in a normal way in all other cases, but the pity is that those who believe in the supremacy of the Vedic religion and those who follow the Hindu way of thinking and living are being targeted with hatred by the upper-caste Hindus. More pitiable fact is that they are treated even worse than animals. The question naturally arises as to whether we will prosper by living in a religion whose philosophy is highest among all but the practice is lowest ever" (*Speeches of Dr. Ambedkar: 1920 to 1936*, vol. 1, pp. 15-16).

His views at the time of his announcement of conversion were: "The stigma we have been carrying due to being born as Hindu has been an obstacle in our progress. Why do we need a seal of that religion when the upper-caste Hindus disrepute us and treat us as insignificant just because we are born in these castes? Why should we ruin our lives by being a part of the religion that has forced us to live like animals? Wouldn't it be appropriate to get out of this religion and accept any religion where we do not have to suffer insults and do not need to live low and vile lives? It depends on the will of an individual that which religion you accept after leaving Hinduism, but, accept only that religion who gives the right to equality."

Babasaheb announced his conversion in 1935, but he did not

mention which religion the untouchable Hindus would accept after conversion. He discussed many questions, like casteism, sectarianism, treatment of the untouchables, the mentality of the upper-caste Hindus to not give any rights to the untouchables, the pervasive fear that what will happen to their position if the untouchables were given equal rights. He said that conversion should not be rushed and all people should think about it collectively. However, an obvious question to ask was that what would have happened if Babasaheb had converted to either Islam or Christianity? Apart from that, he was also thinking of Sikhism. He mentioned his ideas why he would not convert to either Isalm or to Christianity in a statement he sent to Dr. Munje. Dr. Ambedkar said,

"Obviously Sikhism is the best option. If the backward-class people join Islam or Christianity, they will be expelled not only from Hinduism but also from Hindu culture; but they can still remain in the Hindu culture by converting to Sikhism–that will be an important benefit to Hindus. Consideration should also be given to the effect of conversion of Hindus on our nation. Converting to Islam or Christianity means to become non-nationals. If they (untouchables) become Muslim, the number of Muslims would double–that would increase the Muslim dominance. And if they become Christians, their number would be five to six crore, which would tighten Britain's hold over our nation. But there is no danger for India if the untouchables convert to Sikhism; above that, it will also help in shaping the future of our country. Keeping the interests of the country in priority, the backward class people should go to Sikhism. Aren't these words from the true and noble minded son of a Mother India?: (*Dr. Ambedkar: Life and Work*, Dhananjay Keer).

Acharya Atre quotes Babasaheb as saying, "I say with confidence that our community could have collected crores of rupees, if I and my followers had become Muslims. The country could have been destroyed in just five years, if I had such hatred and feelings of revenge in my mind, but I have no desire to be known as a destroyer in the history of this country" (*Baba of Dalits*, p. 8, Acharya Atre).

On 13 October, 1935, Babasaheb announced his conversion

at Thevala. Christian and Muslim institutions lured him to convert him into their respective religions and they raised a lot of money to convert him. Mr. Godfrey, a priest in London, raised thousands of pounds for this mission. He even published a book, *The Untouchables Quest*, appealing to Christian missionaries to help him through his book. He said, "Millions of untouchables will convert to Christianity if they use Babasaheb's movement." This way, many Christian clergy and Muslim clerics as well as mullahs contacted Dr. Babasaheb, but he rejected all such alluring offers because his heart was full of love for India. While accepting Buddhism, Dr. Babasaheb kept in mind that "this country is mine; India is the land of Gautama Buddha. Lord Buddha was born in this country and the devotion of my followers remains attached to the land of India." The nation was more near to his heart. He said openly, "Possibility was that, if we converted to Islam, each of us would have become a nawab or if we had become a Christian, all of us could become 'Pope', and if we had become Sikhs, all would have become 'Sardars'. We are fully aware of the fact that we have to fight for our welfare. We cannot adopt a religion that distracts us from our patriotism; we cannot accept any religion that would drag away loyalty to foreign lands."

And that is why these patriots embraced Buddhism, which was born on the soil of this country. They took refuge in Buddhism which is like a subsidiary of an Indian culture. His idea of converting to Buddhism was clearly patriotic and humane.

Dr. Ambedkar knew that it would not end the problems in becoming a Christian or a Muslim; he never thought of that.

Babasaheb presented the pain of the untouchables who had become Christians in the fifth volume of *Speeches of Dr. Ambedkar*. The untouchables of South India converted to Christianity and submitted a report to the Simon Commission. Dr. Babasaheb presented some extracts of this report: "We are Christians by religion, our castes were Pallas, Parihas, Malas, Bhadias, etc. Even though we are all equal according to Christianity, we are treated the same as before because we became Christians from backward castes. The upper-class Christians do not allow us to approach them; they are mocking at us. Our Christian brethren consider us untouchable even in church."

Dr. Babasaheb wrote: "This is a very frightening allegation. Being a Christian did not make any difference to the social status of the untouchables. Christianity has not proved itself in eradicating casteism."

Merely ending untouchability was not the real task of Dr. Babasaheb. His life's goal was to reconstruct the Hindu society and it was impossible without eradicating untouchability. He wanted to restructure the society on the basis of the principles of liberty, equality, fraternity and justice. The old system was based on heterogeneity, the basis of which were beliefs mentioned in different religious texts. Babasaheb wanted to eradicate this inequality; he wanted to create a society of only one caste. He wanted social democracy along with political democracy. His life's aim was not to take revenge on the Hindu society. He didn't want to cripple the Hindu society.

In a speech prepared by Dr. Ambedkar for the Jat Pat Todak Sammelan [Convention on Breaking Casteism] (Dr. Ambedkar did not address the Sammelan but published a book entitled *Jati Vichchedan* on the speech prepared for this convention), he suggested, "Hindutva should be saved by destroying Brahminism." The central message of Ambedkar's book was that it was very important to uplift the morality of Hindu society. Not only this, it was dangerous to keep lingering on that issue. This meant that a new philosophical foundation had to be laid for Hindu society, which should be based on democratic values, such as liberty, equality and fraternity. The basic concept, values and outlook of Hindu society had to be changed.

Dr. Ambedkar concluded that Hinduism had became diseased. Based on his findings, he also suggested that the Hindu society could gain strength for its own defence by becoming a monolithic society and warned that Hindus may not sustain for long if freedom was gained without such power.

It was not only Dr. Ambedkar who thought of eradicating castes to restructure the Hindu society, other leaders like Swami Shraddhanand, Lala Lajpat Rai, Raja Rammohan Rai, Bhai Parmanand, Jyotirao Phule, Acharya Prafulla Chandra Rai, Ramesh Chandra Dutt, Bipin Chandra Pal, Jadunath Sarkar, Lala Hardayal, Veer Savarkar, and others gave the same message.

Well-known historian, Jadunath Sarkar opined that the spirit of nationalism had been destroyed due to the spirit of casteism. The spirit of racism is in stark contrast to the spirit of national unity. Well-known revolutionary leader, Lala Hardayal said that the caste system was a curse for India. "Neither Islam nor England destroyed India; casteism within us has become our enemy. Brahminism and casteism have destroyed us." India's great historians, sociologists, thinkers and social reformers have blamed casteism for the destruction of Hindus. It will be difficult to save India's independence as long as we will preserve casteism.

India's experience is that religious conversion leads to conversion of loyalty to nation and that's why conversion is a very sensitive issue. Almost all the Muslims living in India are of Hindu origin. Even they have continued their identity through respective castes after converting to Islam, they have ultimately claimed Pakistan. They think that as Muslims they are an independent nation, their culture is different, their language is different, their history is different, their ideals are different, their religious thought is different–they have found various such bases for separation. When an Indian becomes a Christian, Indian names are replaced with European names like Mary, Margaret, John, Dimelo, Robert, etc. Everything changes, like their dress, language, cultural customs and such things. Faith in each other's festivals vanishes and foreign festivals seem their own. As a result, the spirit that Christians and Muslims are not among us but belong to an alien religion arises in the minds of Hindus. This is a very dangerous issue for national unity. Therefore, conversion is a very serious issue in India and will change the future of the country.

Conversion is at the root of India's greater fragmentation when we realize that India spread as far as Afghanistan. Foreign Islamic invaders and Christian missionaries, following the same path, chose to disintegrate the country through is conversion. That is why conversion is called transnationalism; loyalty to the nation completely changes. Dr. Ambedkar did not convert to Christianity or Islam just because of such fears; he was devoted to India and did not want this nation to be harmed.

Dr. Babasaheb did not desire any further fragmentation of India and wanted to strengthen the sense of nationalism in the minds of the people of this country. Had he adopted Christianity, a sizable chunk of the Hindu population may have become Christian and strengthened the British in India. Even Christian missionaries would also have gained greater strength, who were engaged in conversion under the guise of service.

Babasaheb never thought of converting to Isalm or Christianity. He said, on 1 May, 1936, "I have not asked anyone to convert to Islam or Christianity. If anyone converts to Islam or another religion, that is at his/her own risk. I am not responsible for any consequences. I just needed your declaration for conversion from Hinduism; the target religion is not yet specified by me. And when I specify the same, we 70 million untouchables will convert at once."

Here are some excerpts from Babasaheb's discussion with G.T. Mandkholkar, the editor of *Tarun Bharat*, in Nagpur, "This is not a new idea that I am presenting before the world. All I understand is that I have had this fortune to re-establish the Dhamma *chakra* (wheel of Buddhist religion) that has been installed in this country for thousands of years. You Hindus have deported a rational and great religion like Buddhism which flourished on this land and on the contrary, you let Christianity and Islam to enter this country as your own suicidal act, and even let them flourish to such an extent that it eventually led to the Partition of the country. I am proud that I let Buddhism come back to its own home. It seemed to you Hindus that by declaring conversion I have axed your religion, your culture and the country, but now you will know that my conversion is purely Indian and it is bound to increase the pride of Indian culture. You scolded me with all possible bad words when I announced my conversion in October 1935, but now, 20 years later, you must have realised that I am no less than your people in terms of loyalty to India. Perhaps my devotion to the country is something more because you Hindus have foolishly rejected the unparalleled legacy of philosophy that this country has given to the whole world in the form of Buddhism. I gave that legacy back to the country, I am proud and happy about it" (*Dr. Ambedkar–Conversion to Mahanirvana*, pp. 133-134).

Babasaheb's conversion was not intended to acquire any materialistic benefit. Muslims and Christian clergy had already offered crores of rupees to convert him to their religion, but Babasaheb's intention was purely to regain human rights. He did not want to stay in a religion that discriminated between human beings and which despised them. Hinduism, of which they were a part, degraded them and kept them in social slavery–he wanted to break that slavery. He was not ready to accept (holy) scriptures as the ultimate truth; he was not even ready to believe that there was a power like God which governed this world. He was not ready to accept even the concept of sin and the notion that man is a sinner. Religion in his view was a bonding tool for human beings, to keep them together with each other.

Lord Gautama Buddha presented a different idea from the above. Dr. Babasaheb explained how he was influenced by the ideas of Gautama Buddha, "Buddhism influenced me when I was then just 14-years old. Shri Dadasaheb Keluskar gave me a book, *The Character of Lord Gautam Buddha* as a prize in a competition.' Babasaheb then studied the character of Lord Buddha deeply and his favourite book was *Buddha Dharma ka Sar* (Abstracts of Buddhism) written by Prof. P. Lakshmi Narsu. The book depicts Lord Buddha as a human being, a rationalist and a philosopher who believed only in cause and effect. In a speech on 6 May, 1955, he said, 'Buddhism is unique from any other religion in the world. The followers of every religion and their scriptures say that their religion is ordained by God. Jesus, the founder of Christianity, Moses, the pioneer of Judaism, and Mohammed, the spokesman for Islam, all of them called themselves 'messengers of God'. The words or promises that came out of their mouth were considered beyond doubt. In a way, the possibility of cogitation over the divine promises made by the angels was completely blocked."

Once upon a time Buddhism was very influential in India but eventually it was eroded and almost disappeared from India. There are many reasons for this erosion. One of the major reasons was the rule of believers in Brahminism as they created many obstacles for Buddhists over various issues. Buddhism flourished mostly under the Mauryan rulers but it was destroyed by Pushyamitra through a political revolution when the empire ws brought under the flag of Sunga dynasty. "This Brahminism-believer ruler did a great deal of damage to Buddhism. He heinously restored Brahminism and that has been one of the most influenced historical events that led to the disappearance of Buddhism from India."

Dr. Ambedkar said, "Foreign invasions are also to be blamed for the disappearance of Buddhism from India, with the exception of Greek invasion. On the contrary, there is historical evidence for their financial support for the propagation of Buddhism. The Huns invaded India during the Gupta period, but settled in India after being defeated by the Gupta king. They did no harm to Buddhism. In contrast, Kanishka, the Saka king of Peshawar, accepted Buddhism and became a Buddhist. He built a huge Buddhist university in Takshshila and organised the fourth Dharma Sangeeti (religious conference) on Buddhism. The Mahayana sect emerged, during this Dharma Sangeeti, and Buddhist literature began to be written in revised Sanskrit. Muslim invaders did most damage to Buddhism. Muslims were against the worship of idols, so they smashed the Buddha statues and killed the monks. They mistook the huge Buddhist University of Nalanda as a fort of the army and massacred the Buddhists present. The monks who survived the horrific genocide fled to Nepal, Tibet and other countries."

Dr. Ambedkar said, "The vast library of Nalanda contained two lakh books written on palm leaves and birch leaves and contained thousands of years of knowledge. Bakhtiyar Khilji set it on fire and killed six thousand students studying there and left some of them, who converted to Islam. Wherever the Muslim invaders went, they either killed the Buddhists or converted them to Islam, or demolished Buddhist statues, burned libraries, and destroyed monasteries."

In his speech at the World Buddhist Fellowship International Conference (6 June, 1950) in Colombo, Babasaheb described how Nalanda University had become extinct: "Foreign aggression is also responsible for the decline of Buddhism in India. Buddhism suffered the most from Muslim invaders. They smashed Buddhist statues and killed monks. They mistook Nalanda University to be a fort of Buddhists and massacred a large number of monks considering them as soldiers."

Babasaheb's statements on what he said during the restoration of Buddhism in India, became historical. The influence of communism was growing in India at that time. Communism is an ideology that does not believe in religion and does not believe in moral values; instead it believes in chaos and violence. Babasaheb was in opposition to communism on the basis of its principles. He said on 15 February, 1953 at Delhi, "There are only two options available in the world today, especially in Asia–either the path of the Buddha or the path of Marx. In a course, if the world does not accept the path of the Buddha, the victory of communist ideology is certain. The vision of the Buddha is the only basis left for the world today."

Elsewhere, he said, "How did communism survive? How was communism able to exist? They are (communists) just relying on muscle power; communism has survived only by force and coercion. Communists just want wealth and property. What is happening now in Russia? They are just fighting for wealth. As soon as the landlords who maintain strict discipline in Russia disappear, people will start raising their voice and there will be complete chaos and the behaviour of people will become autocratic. In a way, Buddhism is true communism. Like true communists, Buddhist monks have the right to own only limited necessities. They are allowed to keep only three things–a vessel, a cloth to filter the water and a razor."

Dr. Babasaheb Ambedkar had said 80 years ago that communist ideology was fatal for the country as the communists are violent. He also warned that "the anarchist communist will benefit if our democracy fails. Communist ideology is unconstitutional."

- He considered communism anti-national ideology and said in the Constituent Assembly: The Constitution is often criticised by two parties: the Communist Party and the Socialist Party. The Communist Party wants a constitution based on the principle of proletarian dictatorship. Communists criticise the constitution because our constitution is based on parliamentary democracy. (25 November, 1949).
- I warn you to beware of the communists. They are working against the interests of the workers and I believe that the communists are the enemy of the workers. (At the election meeting in Nagpur; 4 December, 1945) The Communists have perpetually exploited the workers. I

am a staunch enemy of the communists (*Bahishkrit Zilla Sammelan*-District Convention of the Excluded, Masur, District Satara, September 1937).

- Any religion that does not respond against communism will not survive. In my view, if there is one religion that can counter communism, it is Buddhism(In the programme of 5 February, 1956 organised by the Indian Mahabodhi Society, New Delhi).
- Buddhism is the true way of life for everyone. Buddhism will survive only when it is explained how Buddhism is better than communism. Communism will take you to the jungle, to chaos; they are not hesitant to kill opponents to establish themselves. Communists are chaotic; they love violence (20 November, 1956. World Buddhist Conference, Kathmandu, Nepal).

Babasaheb was well aware of the fact that India is a land of religion and religion is its soul. He said, "Dealing in the world is done on the basis of religion. If you tell a woman who has delivered a baby that 'this baby is your enemy, don't feed that baby, it will weaken you, your beauty will be compromised', will the mother of this baby accept it? No matter how difficult it is, even if the mother becomes sick, she will continue to breastfeed. Raising a child is her religious *karma*. All the affairs of the world are run by religion."

"The dabbawalas of Pune deliver food tiffins to others, even if they themselves go hungry. Tiffins contain meals like *biryani*, *pulao*, etc., but they honestly deliver them as per their duty because they believe it is their religion. This teaches us that everyone should follow one's religion. Good happens with Dharma (religion/religious), not with *adharma* (non-religious); do good deeds, not evil deeds."

India cannot survive without religion either as a land or as a nation. Babasaheb expressed his views on this subject very firmly, that the State must always be secular and must think of governance and other materialistic things; at the same time the State must also follow the rules of religion. In a speech in Mumbai on 14 April, 1951, he said, "Religion is shadowed now, but I am sure that everyone needs a religion too. One thing is certain from my view–society cannot live without religion and that religion must be Buddhism. If equality, love, fraternity are necessary for the salvation of the world, then they can be found only in Buddhism. I have concluded after studying all religions, that the whole world must embrace Buddhism."

Lord Gautama Buddha was born at Lumbini, in Nepal. He attained the title of Buddha (after enlightenment) in Gaya; his first Dhamma *chakra* was performed at Sarpattan near Varanasi and his *mahaparinirvana* took place at Kusinara. All these places fall in India and are very sacred from a religious point of view. All Indians along with a large number of followers of Gautama Buddha travel to these places. India is the holy land for the Buddhist brethren. That could be the reason Dr. Babasaheb never accepted the religion which was devoted to a foreign land. There are numerous Buddhist monuments on this land and all are considered holy. *Stupas* have been erected at various places and these places are extremely sacred.

Sculptural and architectural development was at its peak in this country after the *mahaparinirvana* of Gautama Buddha. Magnificent caves and architecture were built on the trade centres and routes. Of these, Ajanta-Ellora and the Kanheri caves at Borivili (Mumbai) are very famous. There are magnificent statues of Buddha erected at many places across the country and people visit them with full faith.

Similarly there are many places associated with Bodhisattva (great soul). The Modi government has revived and upgraded these memorials and made them more magnificent and this government has paid the highest respect to Babasaheb.

Babasaheb was born at Mhow, a place near the city of Indore. His early education took place in Satara and later in Mumbai. His house in the Hindu colony is known as *rajgruha*. He passed away in Delhi and his last rituals took place at Dadar, Chowpatty. The place is now known as a Chaitya Bhoomi. The ground in Nagpur on which he converted in 1956 is now known as Diksha Bhoomi. Millions of Buddhists visit Chaitya Bhoomi and Diksha Bhoomi every year.

Dr. Babasaheb was born on the soil of this country and his funeral also took place on the same soil. His *nirvana* has further enhanced the sanctity of this ancient sacred land. In a press conference held on 13 October, 1956, before conversion, Dr. Babasaheb said, "I promised Gandhiji that I would take the least harmful path (while going through conversion); therefore, by accepting Buddhism, I am doing a favour to the Hindu society because Buddhism is a part of Indian culture" (*Dr. Babasaheb Ambedkar-Conversion to Mahaparinirvana*, p. 272).

Dr. Ambedkar's role has to be observed carefully during the introduction of the Hindu Code Bill as a Law Minister. All religious scriptures and texts were taken into account while preparing this Bill. To whom it was supposed to apply? Dr. Ambedkar asked, "Are Hindus, Sikhs, Buddhists and Jains included in this Bill?" It meant he had studied all types of scriptures of all religions and then formulated this Bill. It shows his deep cultural sense as well.

Babasaheb's contribution to Indian nation building is worth remembering even today as it is no less relevant.

□

10

Aryan Invasion and Who are Shudras?

Europeans started travelling around the world after their dark age and tried to discover new, unexplored territories all around the globe. In the 15th and 16th centuries, they went to the Americas, across the African continent and far away, all the way up to New Zealand and Australia also. Most of these travels were made for exploration of nature and natural resources, trade and for occupying new lands. However, some of them were made to find new trade routes as well. Europeans set up their footholds in many of these lands; however, all these lands were previously inhabited by human beings. So they trumped up a new term for them–aborigines; and called themselves as inhabitants of the land so that no one could call them outsiders who had occupied this land. They created such lies for many parts of the world and not only that, they usurped these new lands.

They did the same in India as well; they named the tribes inhabiting the hills as Adivasi and introduced a false theory that these tribes were the aborigines of India. All were trumped up just to fulfil their vested interests. British rulers with the help of their so-called scholars popularised the equation that tribals (Adivasis) who are inhabiting the jungles are the aborigines of this land and non-tribals are all invaders. They further created the doctrine of Aryan invasions and deliberately raised controversies, such as Arya-Anarya, Arya-Dravida, natives and non-natives, etc. They profoundly popularised these controversial theories to break the social fabric of India so that they could rule peacefully over the newly occupied land.

The British created this new controversy of Aryan invasion to create differences in the minds of the people inhabiting the north and south of India. They plotted a theory that the Aryans came from outside, invaded the aborigines; fought with them and drove them into the jungle, where these tribals started living in their own communities and became Scheduled Tribes. Those who didn't flee to the jungles and were living in urban regions were exploited by Aryans. Their means of earning livelihood were distributed unevenly and they are now known as Scheduled Castes. The world is aware that Europeans massacred natives in the conquered territories and they also converted the rest. The world was witness to the horrors of European invaders and they tried to impose the same theory in terms of Indians, the only difference being that they replaced Europeans with Aryans to form this false theory for India.

This doctrine of Aryan-Dravidian was the mirror copy of what Europeans did on conquered territories and that is how the British perpetrated this scam. The fact is that nothing like this happened in India, but there is no evidence of it in history.

There are about 350 different tribes living in jungles in India since ancient times. Their method of worship, dialect-language is different, yet their cultural roots are the same as in Hindu religion and culture. The British tried to attack these very roots of united India by introducing the false principle of 'tribes' being 'indigenous' and impose the non-factual theory in the matter of tribals of India by doing intellectual exercises on matters related to indigenous people in the rest of the world. The definition of aborigines given by the United Nations and the rights granted to aborigines need to be re-examined when calling tribals as aborigines in India. The Belgian thinker, Koenraad Elst wrote in one of his books: "This community indigenous is not a matter to be decided. It is a matter to be determined by universal valid methods of history, anthropology–methods which can be applied by the non-indigenous as well as indigenous" *(Indigenous Indians: Agastya to Ambedkar,* p. 175).

The cultural cord of about 80 million tribals living in India is firmly attached to this country, but Christian missionaries are trying to break that cord through violence and temptations. Tribals and other Indians in the broadest sense are intertwined with the same culture, the same faith, the same tradition and the same history. Therefore, it will be completely artificial and irrational, if one classifies the two as Indigenous and non-indigenous.

Concepts like indigenous, tribals, etc. did not exist before the British came to India. It was only after their arrival that the Indians were introduced to these concepts; in fact the concept was forcibly imposed on us. The British wanted to strengthen their rule, so they declared the Aryans as invaders. Once a group is declared as an invader, then on the other side, people who have been attacked must also exist. That is how the doctrine of indigenous and non-Indigenous was derived and Arya-Dravid or aboriginal and non-aboriginal theories were floated. In fact, all Indians are of the same origin; there are no natives or invaders in India. So the standards used by the British for the natives of America or Africa cannot be applied to the society here.

This false doctrine regarding aborigines in India was first introduced by British scholars, British authorities as well as Christian missionaries who came here to preach through temptations and services. The British rulers studied about the various castes and tribes of India to strengthen their political base; they found that the weakest link in Hindu society was its caste system. They thought of attacking this weakest link and so first targeted the tribals of India. Initially, they established major centres for campaigns at Lahore and Benaras to propagate the theory that Aryans came here from outside and Dravidians are indigenous inhabitants of this land. T. H. Griffith and A.C. Wooler were assigned this responsibility in Benaras and Lahore respectively. English scholars and priests found that they wouldn't be able to succeed in their endeavours unless they weakened the roots of Vedic religion. And that's why they undertook the first task to distort Vedic literature. A person named Colonel Bowden donated a huge amount to Oxford University for the task of creating distorted meanings of Sanskrit texts.

Professor Max Muller held the highest position among the

European scholars of Sanskrit, who was appointed by Lord Macaulay. He revealed his real purpose of his translating the *Vedas* from Sanskrit to English in a letter to his wife. Muller wrote: "The edition of mine and the translation of the *Vedas* well hereafter tell to a great extent the fate of India. It is the root of their religion and to show them what the root is, I feel sure, is the only way to uproot all that has sprung from it during the last three thousand years" (*Life and Letters of Frederick Max Muller*, vol. 1, Chap. XV, p. 34).

That is to say, "This version of mine and the translation of the *Vedas* will have a far-reaching effect on the destiny of India. That is the origin of their religion and I will show them what this origin is. It's the only way to uproot everything that has arisen in the last three thousand years."

Proud of his success, Max Muller wrote in a letter to the Secretary of State for India on 16 December, 1868: "The ancient religion of India is doomed. Now if Christianity does not step in, whose fault will it be?" (Ibid., vol. I, Chap. XVI, p. 387).

Thus, on the one hand, Max Muller began to distort the Vedic literature in order to create hatred and suspicion in the minds of Indians about their religion, culture, civilisation and history, while on the other, Monier Williams outlined how to propagate Christianity. The Arya-Dravidian theory has arisen from such a perverse scheme, so that conflicts arise within India. This Aryan theory had come into existence long before Dr. Ambedkar was born.

This is how the scheming British developed a completely false theory of Aryan invasion in order to maintain their power. The British actually wanted to establish that the country had been invaded by Aryans and it does not belong to them; so we also came here as invaders just like others and occupied the territory here. The theory of Aryan invasion developed by the British was merely to justify their own invasion. Max Muller formulated this theory and anti-India historians as well as Christian missionaries working in the name of service in India, helped to spread the lie.

Nowhere is the term 'Adivasi' (tribals) used in the then Indian Constitution. There is no such mention of separate terms as tribals and Aryans in any literature of India. It proves that the British rulers and British missionaries created this racial controversy only to separate the tribal society from the mainstream Indian society and to convert them to Christianity.

Some (so-called) scholars are trying to mislead people that casteism in India is similar to the racism issue in the United States by citing the example of Blacks and Whites. Dr. Ambedkar did not agree with such a comparison and wrote in *Castes in India*: "The real situation in India is quite different than in the U.S. The people of India are one as a people and its proof is their cultural unity."

'Caste formation due to racism' is a favourite theory of Europeans. Western scholars have deliberately mixed races and castes to create illusions, but that is denied by Dr. Babasaheb Ambedkar: "People of every caste are of the same race, all are one culturally, despite thousands of castes." This is clearly stated by Babasaheb in his writings.

Dr. Ambedkar does not equate 'race' and 'caste'. After publication of his book, *Annihilation of Caste*, Babasaheb exchanged correspondence with Mahatma Gandhi and said, "'Race' and 'caste' are two different concepts. 'Race' is based on a person's merit and strength while caste is by person's birth. Two of them are as different and opposite as clay and butter." He also wrote in his book, *The Untouchables* that there was no caste in ancient India. Untouchability started just after AD 400.

The flattering Marxist and hypocritical secularists with English mindset, who had infiltrated the education system, inserted the theory of Aryan invasion in textbooks even after the Independence of the country in 1947, this lie continues. The Indian children have continued to learn these lies of Aryan invasion, cleverly developed by British, in the name of history in their schools and this repeated lie has now become the truth. But, a new research has proved that it was only fabricated by the British to maintain their power. It was fortunate for the country that Babasaheb refuted these lies of the British on the basis of his in-depth research. He has provided proof that the Aryan invasion theory is a white lie in his book, *Who are Shudras*? However, some of his opponents and foreign church-inspired organisations are not ready to accept these facts and are trying their level best to prove that Babasaheb was wrong. Writers, like Eleanor Zelliot have also written about his ideas in a distorted manner and that is a great injustice to Babasaheb. Let me clarify what Babasaheb had written in his book, *Who are Shudras?*

He said, "What evidence do we have that the Aryans came from outside and defeated natives by attacking them? There is no mention of any incident in the *Rigveda* to confirm that the Aryans invaded India." Mr. P.T. Srinivasan Iyengar wrote about this issue, "A careful analysis of the *mantras* suggests that wherever words like Arya, Das, Dasyu are used, they do not refer to the caste but to the branch. These words are mostly found in the *Rigveda Samhita*, where the word Arya is used 33 times in *mantras*, while the total number of words is 153,972. The very rare use of the word Arya is proof that the so-called Aryan race was not an invader and that if they had conquered the country and uprooted the local people, the winners would have repeatedly lauded their achievements." (*Sampurna Akshardeh*; book-13, pp. 88-122 in *Who are Shudras?*) As mentioned by Professor D.S. Trivedi: "The way seven sacred rivers mentioned in the *Rigveda* (10: 75-5) is very meaningful, the rivers have been addressed as my Ganges, my Jamuna and my Saraswati. No foreigner would make such an address to rivers of this land; only those with emotional attachments can make such statements." Further there is no such special story of a war between Dasyus and Aryans, where the Aryans are on one side and Dasyus on the other. Only at eight out of 33 places in the *Rigveda* are the Aryans mentioned as opponents of Das and in seven places this is mentioned in opposition to Dasyus. This shows that there may been some kinds of casual fights between them, but it does not mean a victory or defeat story. People who consider words like Das and Dasyu as reference to castes provide evidence like the words *mudharvak* and *anas* used in the *Rigveda* featuring the Dasyus. Das are called *shyamlang* (dark complexioned people) in *Rigveda*. The word *mudharvak* appears in the following verses in the *Rigveda* 1:174-2; 5: 32-8; 7:6-3 and 7: 18-3. *Mudharvak* means, 'one who speaks a crude language, a language like a hog but can this be considered as a measure of a different race or different caste? It is sheer madness to consider it to mean a different race. The word *Anans* is used in the *Rigveda* at 5:29-10. There are two meanings or definitions of the word *anas*. Professor Max Muller defined it as 'noseless' or 'flat-nosed', but Sayanacharya defined it as 'bad mouth' or *amrudubhashi* (hard-speaking). Those who derived the meaning 'flat-nosed' concluded that this was a different race than Aryans. Sayanacharya's interpretation of the word seems to be correct. The word *anas* seems to be a synonym of the word *mudharvak* and implies that there is no evidence to show that Dasyu was a lower caste' (*Sampurna Akshardeh,* Book-13, pp. 88-122; *Who are Shudras?*) Now, talking about Das, it is true that Das is called as *Krishna yoni* (of black origin) in *Rigveda* 6: 47-21, but it is used only once in the *Rigveda* and may have been used as a decorative word and the third thing is that we cannot say that the word refers to hatred. 'Das' cannot be considered as black race until these points are resolved. Some other verses from *Rigveda* should also be considered in this regard. Firstly, it is said in the *Rigveda* 6: 22-10: "O Vajra, you have made Das an Arya; you have turned wicked into good with your powers. Grant us the same power by which we can defeat our enemies. Secondly, in *Rigveda* 10: 49-3, Indra says that he has deprived the Dasyus of the title 'Arya'. Thirdly, *Rigveda* 1: 158-8 says, "O Indra, check who is Arya and who is Dasyu? Separate them." What does these verses mean? It proves that there was no racial distinction between Arya and Das-Dasyu on the basis of colour or complexion. It is also true that Das and Dasyu could become Arya and that is why Indra was given the task of distinguishing between Das and Dasyu. Any scholar who examines this issue carefully will not doubt that Western scholars had adopted a double standard in this matter. The first is that the theory of Western scholars is based on imagination and therefore has no basis for conclusion; secondly, the theory of Western scholars lacks scientific research and is not based on facts (*Sampurna Akshardeh*, Book-13, pp. 88-122; *Who are Shudras?*).

Why did Western scholars have to fabricate the story of Aryan invasion? In response, Babasaheb said, "The story of the Aryan invasion is a new discovery. Western scholars needed to discover this story because they had to prove the fact that today's 'Indo-German' people are of pure Aryan origin; their original homeland is expected to be somewhere in Europe. So the question before them was how did Aryabhasha (Indo-Aryan language) come to India? In order to find an answer to these questions, first the Aryans had to come from outside; second, the theory that the Aryans came from Europe had to be popularised because the prevailing European race is the best and is superior to the Asians. After accepting this fact, there was a need to find a basis to prove the superiority and this story proved to be helpful to them" (*Sampurna Akshardeh*, Book-13, pp. 88-122; *Who are Shudras?*).

Babasaheb categorically denied that "Aryans came to India from outside". He wrote: "It does not seem true that the Aryans came from outside and that the Das-Dasyus were natives of India. If we consider racism as the basis of the four-caste system, then it is to be noted that there are four castes and there is no explanation as to which breed was included in it; it is also not clear what the four colours were. Initially it was started with Arya and Dasyu, where Aryas were whites and Dasyus were blacks; that's all. Proponents of this theory of origin of Aryan race have just tried this or they may have lost their patience as well and that's why they have not even thought about the kind of complications that would result from this. Their goal was just to prove their theory and they wanted some evidence for that. They picked up only those from the *Vedas* which proved to be helpful to them. This false theory of origin of Aryan race is misleading; it should have come to an end a long time ago, yet it influences the masses rapidly" (*Sampurna Akshardeha,* Book-13, pp. 88-122; *Who are Shudras?*) This theory should have been opposed by Brahmin scholars, as they are Hindus but they have been projected as belonging to the European race, showing them to be superior and so the Brahmins supported it instead of opposing it.

"One of the strange reasons for this is that Brahmins believe in the principle of two nations. They themselves believed to be representatives of Aryans and the rest of the people as descendants of the Anarya (non-Aryan) race. This gave them the seal of excellence and boosted their ego because this theory helped them to establish their blood-clan relationship with the European race and thus their superiority. The theory says that the Aryans came from outside and they defeated the Anaryas (non-Aryans). This becomes one more reason to support because this theory is useful in maintaining their dominance over the non-Brahmins and in providing worthiness as well. Western scholars define *varna* (caste) as 'colour' and emphasise it; this was largely accepted by Brahmin scholars and may be one of the reasons that this theory did not come to an end. As long as this definition of *varna* prevails, the Aryan theory will also survive. On analysing the opinions of Western scholars, we can clearly conclude that *Arya* is not considered as a caste anywhere in the *Vedas*; that there is no instance or mention in the *Vedas* to prove that the Aryans invaded India and conquered the native Das and Dasyu; that there is no evidence in the *Vedas* to prove the separation of Arya, Das and Dasyu castes and the *Vedas* do not support the view that the Aryans were of a different colour than the Das and Dasyu" (*Sampurna Akshardeh*, Book-13, pp. 88-122; *Who are Shudras?*) I can recall some *mantras* (verses): (1) *Rigveda* (6: 33-3) 'O Indra! You killed both our opponents, Das and Aryans'; (2) *Rigveda* (6: 60-3) 'O Indra and Agni, guardians of religion and justice; oppress the Das and Dasyu who hurt us'; (3) *RigvVeda* (8: 24-27) 'O Indra! You have protected us from the demons and the Aryans living in the coastal areas of the Indus. Now you also disarm the Das'; (4) *Rigveda* (6: 81-1) 'Indra and Varuna killed Das and Aryans and protected the Sudras; (5) *Rigveda* (10: 38-3) 'O! Revered Indra, Das and Arya are from heretics, they are our enemies. Give us your blessings to suppress them. We will destroy them with your help'; (6) 'O Mameyu, give strength to your worshipers. We will destroy our enemy Aryans and Das with your help.' The facts contained in these *mantras* disprove the Western concept."

The only thing to say about Western theory is that it does not cover the facts in full and the conclusions drawn are hasty, based on preconceived notions of ancient Aryans and preconceived notions of similarity and uniformity in assumptions they believed it as truth. This doctrine has been established only on the basis of tale-tell facts" (*Sampurna Akshardeh*, Book-13, pp. 88-122; *Who are Shudras?*)

Based on his research, Dr. Ambedkar wrote: "Shudras had a place in the Suryavanshi (Sun-clan) caste in the Arya community. Shudras are originally Suryavanshi Aryans–Kshatriyas. Among the Aryans there were three–Brahmins, Kshatriyas and Vaishyas and there was no different caste called Shudras. They were an integral part of the Kshatriya caste. The fourth caste, the Shudras, originated from the Suryavanshi Kshatriyas."

Let's stop here and see what the representative of an NGO which has been propagating the theory of Aryan aggression say, "Why does Ambedkar need to write these? He affected our movement a lot by writing this..."

Many organisations in the country and around the world are still working to make the Arya-Anarya conspiracy run by Christian missionaries, Western scholars and Leftists a success. Its main objective is to discredit India, to break the country. In a nutshell, the attempt to break India has been the Arya-Anarya principle, which was rejected by Babasaheb years ago and saved India from collapse.

The research based on human skeletons found in Rakhigarhi, Haryana, some time ago, proved that there is no such thing as Arya. All the people living here were residents of India. The Arya-Dravidian theory is a fiction created by Western scholars and all were residents of this place and Shudras were Rajputs of Suryavanshi branch.

□

11

Women Power–Power of Nation

Women are the backbone of society; they are a power of perception; they are the real power to advance society and culture. The Gujarati poet Nhanalal has said, "If there is any creator in the world, it is the *janani* (mother) and *jagatajnani* (mother goddess)." A Hebrew proverb says, 'God could not reach everywhere, so *He* created mothers.' Indian scripture *Devipurana* says, "Mother has solemnity like the ocean, forbearance like the earth, potential to lay out fragrance like the air, coolness like the moon and magnanimity like the sky."

There was a time when women were considered weak, but times have changed. A great revolution took place in the social life of India and the so-called weak have now become strong. The poet Karsandas Manek said, "Those weak women who never held unsheathed knife, now became strong like Goddess Amba and Bhavani."

Babasaheb was an ardent advocate of women's power along with national power. He protected the dignity and honour of women by providing a legal shield to their liberty, equality and their rights. He studied the ancient scriptures in depth regarding the condition of women at that time. He depicted an overview of the status of women in the then India, based on different scriptures and texts composed at different times. He said in an article that women were enjoying a high status and proud position in ancient times but later their pride waned.

As Labour Minister in the Viceroy's Executive Committee from July 1942 to 1946, he enacted about 40 labour welfare laws. Even today, workers are enjoying the good fruits of those laws, which include less working hours–eight hours of work, privilege leave, provident fund, casual leave, accident compensation, safety of workers in gold/copper/coal mines, and ban on women workers in underground jobs, easy work for women, maternity and post-maternity leave (he introduced these in the Legislative Assembly on 28 July, 1928. Also women farm workers in rural areas were granted leave). Credit for implementing numerous laws, rules and schemes like cash for women workers in factories, free education for their children, free medical treatment, insurance schemes, etc. as well as welfare programmes goes to Dr. Babasaheb Ambedkar. He said, "Women are embellishments of the society and the paradigm of the rise and fall of any society can be determined from the position of women in that society."

He showed concern at the interests of the untouchables as well as the women while drafting the Constitution of India, showing that he was a guardian of all. As a 'framer of the Constitution' he proved that he was a proponent of liberty and equality by including fundamental rights in the Constitution.

The Constitution includes the right to equality under Fundamental Rights (Part-3: Articles 12 to 35). Babasaheb called this right to equality the 'soul of the Constitution' because it removed discrimination such, as different linguistics, sectarianism, sexism and casteism. Which is also a reflection of his intuition was his belief that this right would develop a sense of fraternity, thereby maintaining the unity and integrity of the country. This single right alone not only reflects his foresight, but also the sublime and strong nationalism in his heart. Through the right to equality, Babasaheb made a sincere effort to give freedom, social justice and legal equality to the untouchables as well as the entire women's society, thus ensuring that Indian women were independent citizens of the country. Women also now have freedom of speech and expression, right to education; they can roam all over the country without any inhibition, they can also hold rallies and even form organisations. Women will have all kinds of religious, cultural, educational and economic rights and the right to equal opportunity and equal pay for a job or position in public service, government or private organisation. They will also have the right to protection against exploitation. Babasaheb didn't stop here; he campaigned for the protection of the rights and interests of women workers. The government and the industrialists were forced to give women workers extra financial help and maternity leave with full pay.

Babasaheb wanted women to recognise their own power and strength and help solve social problems. Addressing women agitators during the Mahad *satyagraha* in 1927, he said: "You have courage and fortitude. As the men and women solve problems together in the family, so should men and women solve problems together in society as well! It will take a long time for men to shoulder this responsibility alone, but they will succeed sooner if women are also helpful in this responsibility."

Today, we have the slogans, *'Beti Bachao, Beti Padhao'* (save girl, educate girl) but Babasaheb talked about the upbringing and education of girl-child in 1927. He expected that at least women would educate their daughters along with their sons. He said, "You should also educate your daughters. Knowledge and education is not only for men, but also for women. If you want to improve your future generation, you must educate your daughters."

To provide even more rights and social security for the betterment of Indian women, Babasaheb included many revolutionary Articles in the Hindu Code Bill–the Hindu Samhita Bill, which was prepared by him after in-depth study of numerous Hindu scriptures, memoirs and social traditions of Hinduism. This Hindu Code Bill with 139 Articles and seven appendices divided into nine sections was introduced in Parliament on 11 April, 1949.

The Bill restricted the diversity of marriages, with restriction of single wife. Women were also given the right to divorce and to acquire property. The consent of the wife was made mandatory during child adoption. Many such innovative and revolutionary reforms were included in the Hindu Code Bill, which gave women many legal rights, including *(1) Civil marriage*: Any adult couple of man and woman can register at the government office and marry each other on mutual consent; such a marriage is permitted as 'legal marriage' under this Bill. This reform was likely to end up in breaking down barriers of casteism. *(2) Divorce:* This Bill provided protection and security to women in the case of divorce. *(3) Adoption:* The Inheritance Bill empowered women to play a decisive role in the case of adoption. *(4) Wealth or property rights:* With this reform, the wife became an equal stakeholder in all the property. This Bill provided adequate justice to women if there was any drawback in constitutional rights. These are just just a few highlights of a Bill; it included many sections to remove social inequality and traditional cruel beliefs and traditions. The introduction of this Hindu Code Bill caused a stir in the society.

Finally, it received an expected response–the Bill prepared by Babasaheb with great zeal, assiduity and conscientious work of day and night, when introduced in Parliament, was opposed vehemently and Babasaheb's golden dream of uniting society by way of liberty, equality and empowerment of Indian women did not come true. Opposition to the Hindu Code Bill frightened the government and the powers that did not want the Bill passed at that time. Babasaheb was very distressed. However, there was a silver lining in the dark sky, when the women parliamentarians stood firmly with Dr. Babasaheb, irrespective of party politics. Among them were women MPs like Sucheta Kripalani, Hansa Mehta, Begum Aziz Rasul, Renuka Ray, Dasanyi Velayudhna, Jayashree, Padmaja Naidu, Ammu Swaminathan and others. Babasaheb, a lifelong activist for women's empowerment and equality, did not compromise with his principles and finally resigned from his post as India's first Law Minister. However, the government then passed the Hindu Code Bill step by step, but Babasaheb's struggle for women to be empowered in every way would be remembered for centuries.

□

12

Education : Building Block of Character and Patriotism

Gyan (knowledge), *swabhimaan* (self-respect) and *sheel* (character) were three deities of importance for Dr. Ambedkar. In his speech on 28 October, 1954 at Purandare Stadium, Mumbai, he said, "I have three deities–the first among them is *gyan*. I worship knowledge; a man cannot have humanity and peace without knowledge. Everyone should gain knowledge. It is like an ocean. My second deity is *swabhimaan*, self-respect. I have never pleaded to anyone. My principle is that we should fill our stomach, but at the same time, serve people. Humans should be humble. My third deity is *sheel*, virtuous character. I have never cheated or betrayed my followers. I do not remember having committed any sin for my selfishness by trapping someone. I travelled abroad many times, but never smoked cigarettes nor consumed alcohol. I have no bad habits. I love books and clothes. I have a great quality of modesty and I am very proud to admit it. These three gods created me as what I am now. I have reached here today as the result of the power of these qualities."

He believed that the youth of the country was the future of the nation. While addressing college students on 28 October, 1951 at DAV College, Jalandhar, he said: "I like the teaching profession very much. I also love students. I have taught them and I feel immense pleasure in talking to them. The future of this country should rest on the shoulders of students. Students are an intellectual class of society and they can influence public opinion."

Compassion and modesty are necessary for the success of students. He said to the students at Milind College, Aurangabad: "Knowledge , wisdom, compassion, modesty and friendship– every college student should build their character on these five elements. Maintain your modesty and loyalty, even if you are alone on this path. Follow your conscience. If you need to choose between intellect and conscience; take the path which you think is right on the basis of conscience." "Wisdom means understanding, modesty means virtue, compassion means love and friendship for the entire human race means a sense of self-realisation for all and all should go hand in hand with education. Education is useful only if these become your four dimensions. A human being without mercy despite education shall be considered as a butcher."

Dr. Babasaheb Ambedkar envisioned that students should be ideal citizens of the nation. In a speech at Elphinstone College, Mumbai on 15 December, 1952, he said: "Today's students who are studying in a university do not pay any attention to its management. The university decides what should be studied and what students should pursue; however, students too should be vigilant about the issue–whether what we study is conducive to our intellectual development or not? The foundation of a student's future life is laid in the university; whether a student becomes an ideal citizen of the nation or a failure in life is determined by the education system. So students should keep an eye on every activity of the university, but today's student is careless in this regard."

"Ideological and moral values are never steady in human life as they keep changing from time to time; not only changing but also evolving. Indian students should embrace these new values of life and strive to put them into practice."

"The level of intellect of the past people cannot be compared. The sad thing is the intellectual and ideological level of modern students is declining. Students should be worried about this declining intellectual level. As such, the reason for this decline is also quite clear. Today's student is much more involved in football, cricket and politics, instead of that, a student should make a thorough study of past intellect, reflections and philosophy. Acquiring an education is very important. Our ancient schools of education–the *gurukulam*–used to impart education in solitude. *Gurukulams* were established far from the urban or rural civilisation; in the forest areas. The main reason behind it was to impart a new vision of education; a student would get the knowledge of true life values. But today's students are trapped in sports and politics and keeping away from clairvoyance."

"The teacher is imparting education just because it is his/her job; they are not doing it by heart; not because they are willing to teach. The teacher lacks the intuition; they are also lacking the longing for teaching and hard work required for that. Today the teaching profession has been distorted. Teachers have become lazy with the mindset of just finishing the course work. That's why professors have failed to impart thought-provoking knowledge to students. School fees have been raised sky-high. If the fees continue to rise in the same manner, then it will have an adverse effect on the lives of the students. Their future will be bleak. Knowledge is a great power. If students want to develop and save our country with the help of knowledge, they should pay special attention to the (management of) university."

Dr. Ambedkar addressed the youth conference in Mumbai on 11 September, 1938, and told the youth, "One can become mighty and wise only by working hard. No person is intelligent and mighty by birth. When I was in England in my student life, I completed my studies in just two years and three months, which normally takes eight years to complete. But, that was not possible without hard work, I had to study 21 hours a day out of 24 hours."

"Today I am over 40 years of age, yet I study for 18 hours, sitting in a chair every day. Kudos can be achieved only through hard work. Nothing is going to happen by merely attaining the title. "*Sheel* is essential along with knowledge. There is no importance of learning in the absence of modesty. Reason is similar to *vidya-shastra* (weapon of education). If someone has a weapon of education and is modest, then he will protect others with that weapon."

"In the absence of *sheel*, anyone can kill or get killed with the weapon of learning. But its importance is based on its use. An illiterate person cannot cheat others because he does not know how to harass others, but an educated person can deceive others with his skills. At once, he can make the truth feel like a lie and a lie like a truth and no one will doubt him."

"Education, society and nation will be spoiled by the group of educated people in the absence of modesty. Therefore, modesty is more important than education; it is necessary for every human being. You must pay attention to this."

In his speech at Dhobi Talao Night School in Mumbai, during the elocution competition on 15 January, 1948, Babasaheb said, "There is a saying that whose hands hold the cords to raise, he does salvation of the world. Similarly, nothing is going to happen without education."

Dr. Ambedkar was one of the brilliant students ever born on Indian soil. He was devoted to education and wanted to use it as an instrument for resurgence and transformation of Indian society. He perhaps inherited his educational consciousness from his father Ramji Sakpal, who served the Indian army in the educational core. Ramji Sakpal paid proper attention to the education of young Bhimaro and even took loans to pay his fees and buy books. Later, the Maharaja of Vadodara, Shri Sayajirao Gaekwad granted him a scholarship and gave financial support for his higher education. On meeting the Maharaja, when asked about his goal after higher studies abroad, Babasaheb very humbly yet boldly stated that he wanted to study sociology, economics and public finance and would like to work for the emancipation of Indian society with the help of his knowledge. Such a candid statement from an adolescent Bhimrao impressed the Maharaja very much and indeed Bhimrao dedicated himself to the cause of social transformation and bringing equality and freedom in the society after completing his education. He was a source of inspiration for all those modern students who were fleeing to America and Europe to acquire materialist prosperity.

Having completed his graduation in the year 1913, from Mumbai University, he went to Columbia University for his MA and PhD degrees. During that period, he presented his papers in different seminars and conferences and later got the opportunity to study at the London School of Economics and other internationally renowned institutions. He was awarded degrees in MSc., DSc., LLD, Bar at Law etc and D. Lit. by Columbia University in 1952. His dissertation and thesis were published in the form of various books that became very popular worldwide. These books contained his socio-economic and political views.

His studies continued even after returning to India–he studied the condition of society and wrote his views and recommendations to rectify the ills plaguing the Indian society. He died at the age of 67 after completing his book on *Buddha Dharma.* The 15,000-page book was published in 22 parts after his death.

His first contribution in the field of academia on returning from England was to serve at Sydenham College of Mumbai as a lecturer in Economics. He worked there for two years before joining a private institute as a professor in Mercantile Law. He then joined the Government Law College as a professor in the year 1928, where he became principal in 1935. He was popular as a sincere and disciplined professor and administrator during his tenure here. His teaching was very effective and powerful due to his in-depth knowledge of the subject and gift of oration. His communication skills, special command over the English language and extensive subject knowledge were reflected in his lectures.

Along with the normal course of academia, Dr. Ambedkar also imparted practical skills and social wisdom to his students. He presented his recommendations about social problems through his articles in periodicals like *Mooknayak, Bahishkrit Bharat,* Janata, etc. He also participated in social reformation movements through organisations like the Bahishkrit Hitkarini Sabha, Samaj Samta Sangh, etc. besides propagating his ideas and views in many councils and conventions of Dalits and untouchable community through powerful speeches. His speeches became very popular when he participated in the Mahad Council and Chowder Lake *satyagraha*, in the year 1927. He was the founder of the Dalit Liberation Movement and even made inspiring speeches through the All India Radio–Mumbai and Delhi, BBC, London and Voice of America. "Many of his ideas expressed in different forums highlighted various social and political issues." His contribution in restructuring the Indian society was purposeful, his message universal and charismatic and his contribution as a public educator will always be remembered.

Dr. Ambedkar founded the People's Education Society and

established colleges to provide higher education to the Dalit community in Mumbai and Aurangabad. These colleges were not only the centres of knowledge but also of liberation for the students of untouchable communities. He ran his institutions with emphasis on transparency, truthfulness and far-sightedness. His vision of an ideal social and educational institution was such, where public money would never be misused and where the accounts would be available to whosoever wanted to check.

Dr. Ambedkar insisted on proper arrangements in hostels, libraries, and laboratories for students. However, while making appointments of teachers in his institutions, he never considered anyone's caste, but always emphasised on qualification and merit. He wanted his students to acquire the best possible knowledge through the best possible teachers.

In his address to the college professors, Dr. Ambedkar advised that they should be so engrossed in their teaching that they would have no time to think of the family. They should not only be scholars in their subjects but also be capable of making learning recreational and joyful. He also told the teachers that every generation is an independent nation needed to make their own rules in life. No previous generations had the authority to impose their rules on future generations. This, he considered to be the spirit of true democracy.

Dr. Ambedkar used to say that school is a sacred institution where students not only gained knowledge but also built their character. Therefore, the school had to practice discipline and transparency in its affairs. If there were financial irregularities in school, it would have an adverse impact on the life of the new generation. In an article in *Bahishkrit Bharat,* he wrote: "The mind of a student must be diverted to social interests because schools are factories for making good citizens. The quality of the product of these factories will depend on the quality of the foreman."

He also suggested that even the political parties could have a network of good educational institutions and supported the system of co-education because the real test of discipline and self-restraint was possible only in such a system.

Babasaheb taught students about the value of self-confidence, discipline, humanity and truthfulness. He said knowledge was futile without these qualities. Even though he wanted his students to be socially conscious, he never wanted them to join politics because he felt they would only cause greater harm to them. He said that students should focus not only on obtaining a degree, but also in acquiring knowledge, wisdom and good conduct. He said that modern students were lacking in analytical ability, logical discussion and deeper understanding. He told the students of Siddhartha Degree College to develop a vision, thinking ability and problem-solving skills and the ability to use their mental power in solving the problems faced by the country. He wanted the students to intervene if they found the politicians at fault. Being a good teacher himself, he believed that education was an on-going process and that the teacher was its foundation, it was necessary for the teachers to have curiosity and aptitude for learning. His formula for attaining knowledge was to read, to think and to contemplate. He applied his educational philosophy in his own life, and taught those principles to others as well. According to Ambedkar, teachers had to play a great role in nation building.

Dr. Ambedkar expressed his views on education through his periodicals and speeches given on different occasions in different fora and to communities. He spoke about his educational policy at the higher educational institutions, Mumbai Vidyapeeth, Mumbai Assembly, Governor Council, Constitution Assembly and Parliament. He wanted the educational system to be autonomous and independent and that "no individual or political institutions should have direct interference in education." He stressed upon the value of primary education and literacy. In his view, education served as food in life and so it was the responsibility of the government to ensure that everyone was educated in due time. He presented figures on the basis of available statistics claiming that 82.5 per cent people of Hindu society were illiterate and 98 per cent belonged to the backward class. He believed that the main cause for educational backwardness lay in social and economic backwardness and that is why he recommended special facilities for the backward and deprived communities. He did not approve of giving scholarship but called for establishment of good training centres, hostels, *balwadis* and *sanskar kendras* to help create a conducive atmosphere for students from the deprived communities. The policy of reservation incorporated in the Indian Constitution had its seeds in the social and educational philosophy of Dr. Ambedkar. That is why Dr. Ambedkar considered education as the foundation of all cultures and civilisations.

Dr. Ambedkar said that the ideal human character was formed through learning, wisdom, compassion, humility and friendship. Pure learning or knowledge could have no value without these supplementary qualities and the society could never benefit from this. He emphasised not only on the acquisition of information and skills but also on developing high values and strengthening the character.

Mahatma Buddha said that knowledge is radiance and Babasaheb also accepted this definition. He was of the opinion that this radiance should inspire social, economic and political revolution. 'Education must have social orientation as it must guide us to the path of salvation from exploitation. Education is the great instrument for the upliftment of downtrodden. Education opens the doors of their self-respect and self-dependence.' He said that for raising the standard of life of the downtrodden, not only democracy, but our society must be based upon equality, values and character. This was possible only through education.

Dr. Ambedkar was very studious, studying in the libraries of foreign universities for 18 hours at a time and subsisting by eating some slices of bread and a cup of milk. He purchased thousands of books and studied them minutely. In most of the books his jottings in the margin are ample proof of his sincere studies. He even denied, when Pandit Madan Mohan Malviya wanted these books for the BHU library, saying that giving away his books was like giving away his life and soul.

Ambedkar taught people to educate, organise and agitate. He thought that education and society were inseparable because education was the basis of social and cultural development. There could be no other medium for creating a society based on equality. Without equality there was no chance of gaining freedom.

□

13

Industrial Growth of India and Benefits to Labour

Dr. Babasaheb Ambedkar knew the value of labourer's sweat, whether he was engaged in agriculture or in industry. He was conscious of their suffering and problems. That is why he agitated against the *khoti* system and worked for the welfare of the landless, farm labourers, farmers and industrial labourers.

His involvement in the Indian labour movement went through various stages. During the period 1920-30, the Indian labour movement was dominated by communists, who were using the labourers for their own benefits. There were several strikes in 1924, 1925, 1928 and 1929, with as many as 75,000 workers from 43 different (mostly textile) mills participating in 1929. Another public strike was announced in April 1934 as he considered it was motivated by vested interests. He vehemently opposed the strike in his weeklies *Bahishkrit Bharat* and *Janata*, advising the untouchable workers to desist from participating in the strike. Eventually, the Dalit workers suffered a huge financial loss after the strike. That is why Dr. Ambedkar called the communists as enemies of the workers; in return, the communists also started calling him an enemy of the workers.

In 1934, Dr. Ambedkar became president of the Mumbai Municipal Corporation Employees Union. When the British government decided to grant territorial autonomy under the 1935 Act, Dr. Ambedkar founded a political party in 1936 and called it the Independent Labour Party. The Opposition then staged its first successful strike against the government in 1938. Dr. Ambedkar and the Independent Labor Party played an important role in the strike and was appointed the labour leader at the national level.

He was labour representative in the Viceroy's Executive Council in July 1942 but the committee was disbanded in 1946. He worked very hard in order to give a new direction to the attitude of the British government towards the interests of the workers and their issues.

Labour Leader–Dr. Ambedkar

Dr. Ambedkar vehemently opposed the strike in the mid-1920s though he was instrumental in making the 1938 public strike a success. This was indeed contradictory and surprised many. However, an analysis of the Indian labour movement clears the role of Dr. Ambedkar. The fact was that he was working only in the interest of the workers but this was beyond the comprehension of his opponents, the communists.

He supported the right of the workers to strike, which he considered a very important weapon for them, but it was not meant to be used for political purposes. The initial strikes were carried out by communists for political motives because of which Dr. Ambedkar opposed the strike in 1929. He argued in his weekly, *Exiled India* (31 May, 1929) that "previous strikes have worsened the economic situation of the workers. The grip of creditors and moneylenders on them has become stronger. It is not in their interest to strike again." He introduced a Bill in the Mumbai Legislative Assembly to curb the unscrupulous dealings of the lenders.

Similarly, he advocated strongly in the Mumbai Legislative Assembly granting of maternity leave to women workers. He, while speaking on the Bill at MLC on 28 July, 1928, explained that maternity leave to working women was in the interest of the nation. He said, "An important component of this Bill is the mother who works during pregnancy and then takes care of the child after giving birth. I think it is in the interest of the nation to give mothers rest during and after childbirth; the government should bear the burden."

This was in consonance with his decision to support the strike against the 1938 Industrial Disputes Bill. According to the Bill, the right to strike was to be taken away from the workers and there was a provision to declare the strike illegal. Dr. Ambedkar said the strike may be a civil error but it cannot be considered a crime. "Forcing someone to work against his will is like enslaving a person," he said. According to him, the word "strike means 'the right to work on one's own terms'. If a government elected by the people considers freedom to be a divine right, then strike must also be considered a divine right."

According to the same ideology, he, along with other parties, including the Communist Union, opposed the Industrial Bill. He created history by making the strike a success. But the communists considered him as their enemy and were spreading various lies about him.

If we look at the events chronologically, Dr. Ambedkar's formal entry into the labour movement came in 1934 when he became the president of the corporation's Employees' Union. He emerged as a full-fledged labour leader in 1936 when he founded the Independent Labour Party. The manifesto of this party was unusual and unique though later, it became a historical document. In a way his manifesto became a source of inspiration for a number of programmes to alleviate poverty in India over time, including the 20-point economic programmes.

Dr. Ambedkar said in this manifesto, "The main cause of poverty is unlimited population growth in villages and fragmentation of land," and so he "stressed on the need for technical knowledge to increase efficiency and production capacity. It also upholds the principle of public ownership wherever necessary."

The manifesto also included a legal requirement to control recruitment, promotion and dismissal of industrial workers. He mentioned setting maximum working hours and enacting legislation for the provision of paid leave as well as affordable and clean accommodation. It also included building houses at the village level and health-related schemes and modernisation of villages.

As the chairman of the Independent Labour Party, he said at the opening of the Central Province and Varad branches, as to how concerned he was about the interests of the workers. He said, (*Janata* magazine, 30 July, 1938): "Today, the Congress is dominated by moneylenders and tycoons. At a time when these moneylenders will never allow the Congress to speak for the interests of the farm and other labourers, the only duty of the farm labourers and the working class is that they should achieve power through their own organisations."

He also said that the Independent Labour Party was not just for one caste or religion, but had been "established to protect the social, economic and political rights of all the working people of India. There is no discrimination between the untouchables, the Brahmins and the non-Brahmins, the Hindus and the Muslims. Anyone can be involved."

Communists were not happy with the Independent Labour Party and felt that this would divide, instead of uniting the workers. They also feared a decrease in their dominance over the workers because of Dr. Ambedkar. Communists believed that the interests of any section of the working class were the same, so there was no need for an independent labour party. Their argument was that the labour movement should continue under one banner. Communists were provoking workers against Ambedkar, but the untouchable class of labourers had faith in Dr. Ambedkar's views.

Railway Employees Convention held on 12 and 13 February, 1938 in Manmad town of Nashik, discussed in detail the reasons for the establishment of the Independent Labor Party. Dr. Ambedkar said, that the communist leaders fought for the rights of the workers, but was indifferent to the human rights of the untouchable workers. "Untouchables are not given the opportunity to work in departments of textile mills where they can get more economic benefits. Communists have never spoken out against such injustices. The only reason for this may be that the communists fear that they would lose the support of the upper-class workers if they raise their voices for the human rights of the untouchables."

Speaking in front of 20 thousand workers in Manmad, Dr. Babasaheb said: "As a teenager, I used to deliver tiffins to my family. So I know the problems of the workers and their issues.' He also said: 'Until now we used to gather as untouchables, but today we have gathered here as labourers. It is said that I am the enemy of the workers (communists made such propaganda against Dr. Ambedkar). In fact, Brahminism and capitalism are the enemies of the workers. Brahminism means lack of liberty, equality and fraternity."

In this conference, he elaborated on the racial aspect of the economic question of labour and discussed in detail the two enemies of untouchable labourers–"Brahminism and capitalism. Our critics do not understand the way we have to face Brahminism. When I say that Brahminism is to be confronted, it should not be misunderstood. I have not used the word Brahmin in the sense of power, rights and interests of the Brahmin caste. Opposition to Brahminism means opposition to the elements that oppose liberty, equality and fraternity. If someone thinks in this sense, one can understand that even if the Brahmins have originated this, it is no longer limited to them; it has spread everywhere and it controls the behaviour of all classes."

He further insisted that the opportunities and facilities available to untouchables and non-untouchable workers should be compared. He proved that untouchables had less opportunity to get employment and promotion. He cited the example of workers who had lost their jobs in (textile) mills and railways because they were untouchables. 'If communists, who are committed to the unity of workers around the world, cannot solve the problems of the untouchables in their movement, how can they get the support of untouchable workers? The communists do not have any answer to this question.'

Making a fierce critique of communism, he said, "Communism and the labour movement are two different things. The state of the labour movement in India is extremely pitiable. The labour movement has become ineffective due to fearful, selfish and directionless leadership. Its condition has become like a stinking puddle of mud. This is because communists did not use their prime power properly."

Considering the interest of all the workers during the public strike against the Industrial Disputes Bill-1938, he constituted a union with communists, despite sharp differences with them. According to him, it was required to fight against thc extremely furious and blood-thirsty Bill, even though one had to sacrifice everything. However, he was able to keep the Independent Labour Party free from the influence of the communists even after forming a union with them.

The Independent Labour Party organised several movements on its own. Their main purpose was to solve various problems of the employees of the Mumbai Municipal Corporation. It did a commendable job for the rights of the *bidi*-industry workers in the region called Berar in the Central Provinces at that time.

Labour Member: Dr. Ambedkar

Dr. Ambedkar's activism gave a new turn to the Indian labour movement in 1942. On July 2 of the same year, he was appointed as a member of the Labour Welfare Department in the Executive Council of the Governor General. "This is the ideal post for the person who has dedicated his life to the rights of workers and the emancipation of the untouchables," wrote the *Sunday Standard* newspaper.

Speaking after the appointment, he said, "Even if I have got the post, I will not stop fighting to protect the interests of the workers."During his tenure as a minister, he intensified his work for the welfare of the workers and chalked out many schemes for the labourers. He enacted several welfare laws and schemes for maternity benefits for women labourers, protection of their children, equal pay for working women and for their health.

He wanted the labour unions to get government recognition for which he introduced a legislative Bill. The Bill was introduced in the Assembly in 1946. He took many such initiatives and laid the foundation of the labour policy.

As Labour Minister in the Viceroy's Executive Committee from July 1942 to 1946, he enacted about 40 labour welfare laws from which the labourers benefited. It included reduced working hours (eight hours of work), while providing privilege leave, provident fund, casual leave, accident compensation, safety of workers in gold, copper and coal mines as well as ban on female workers on working underground, light work for women during pre-and post-maternity for women. (He even introduced in the Legislative Assembly on 28 July, 1928 that women in rural areas should be granted leave). He was credited with implementing a number of laws, rules and schemes as well as welfare programmes for the children of female workers in the factory, including free education, medical treatment, insurance scheme, etc.

His performance as a labour member can be evaluated in two ways. Made a perceptive demand for women labourers in the Central Legislative Assembly (*Central Legislative Assembly Debates*, vol.-1, 8 February, 1944, p. 131). He said, "Women workers should be paid equal to men. I think the principle that men and women should get equal pay for equal work without any sex barrier has been accepted; which has not happened in any industry till date."

He discussed numerous important issues concerning the labour movement in his speeches as a labour representative and emphasised the need for uniform labour law as well as the need to maintain order in industry at the Joint Labour Conference in New Delhi (7 August, 1942). He said, "The order of industry depends on two things–first, hands-on arrangements for speedy resolution of industrial disputes; second, to bring down the standards of ethics of those involved in the industry and to eliminate conflicting situations."

In the meeting of the Mumbai Pradesh Committee of the Indian Labour Union on 10 May, 1943, he clarified that the Indian labour movement had been weakened by internal divisions. On the same day, in a speech before the Maharashtra Chamber of Commerce, he said, "Why don't Britain and the United States, which spend Rs 14 crore every day on war for the destruction of human civilisation, spend even half as much on alleviating poverty and human suffering in peace-time? This is difficult to understand."

Similarly, in his inaugural address at the Seventh Indian Labour Convention in November 1945, he appealed to the workers to ask the rich taxpayers, "If you have no problem paying the extra taxes for the war situation, then what is the problem in raising payment to improve the condition of workers? If the money spent on the war had been used for public welfare work, many illiterate people would have become literate and many patients would have been able to recover and enjoy a healthy life."

He was an advocate of workers' liberty, equality and fraternity and said on Akashvani (Radio Mumbai) on 1 January, 1943, "The

Central Government has imposed certain conditions on the employers for the welfare and benefit of the workers. It gives workers rights to safety, care and equality; second, the labourer is not satisfied only with the suitable conditions of work; they want liberty. Workers want equality and fraternity. From their point of view, fraternity means humanity."

Unlike communists, Babasaheb did not want workers to keep fighting; he wanted coordination, cooperation, harmony and positivity instead. He believed that welfare could be ensured only in a positive way and as a Labour Minister, said Labour Convention held on 6 September, 1943 in New Delhi: "In order to make proper arrangements to solve industrial problems for the welfare of the workers, it is necessary for the three of them, i.e. the government, the industrialists and the workers to come together and formulate policies and rules by exchanging views and ideas. All three need to have mutual trust and a sense of responsibility to get together. They should also respect each others' opinions, understand each others' point of view and show willingness to work together in a spirit of exchange and cooperation. The Ministry of Labour has come up with a plan to exchange views, understand each other and build a relationship of trust and respect. We plan for workers to receive a fair wage, to fix their working hours and resolve other issues. I predict that this system will be beneficial to the country if it is adopted on a permanent basis as a part of the country's economic structure."

This Labour Convention included eight agendas of labour interest. It mainly covered unemployment, social security and minimum wage, rules for fixing dearness allowance, establishment of three-tier unions in the provinces, representation of workers in legislative and other organisations as well as ideal rules for provident funds.

Inaugurating the Conference of Regional Labour Secretaries in Mumbai in December 1945, Dr. Ambedkar mentioned three points necessary to avoid industrial dissatisfaction: (1) settlement system for resolving industrial disputes, (2) amendment in the Trade Disputes Act, and (3) Minimum Wages Act. In the same speech, he discussed far-sighted measures to maintain industrial order. It is impossible in the future to maintain industrial order on the basis of power alone; even if the law is formulated for it, it will not be credible. Such industrial order can only be achieved on the basis of social justice and by maintaining it forever. This required coordination among all three parties. First, the labourer had to understand his work as the ultimate duty–remain dutiful towards work and not become just a labourer. Employers should pay fair compensation or wages, avoid exploiting workers, provide a healthy working environment, and think for the welfare of workers. The government and society should pay attention to the fact that a healthy industrial relationship was not only the responsibility of the employer or the labourer, but the responsibility of the society as a whole. This vision was as unique and integral as it was original and far-sighted.

At another level too, Dr. Ambedkar was vigilant about special reforms for labour welfare. At the third meeting of the Standing Labour Committee on 7 May, 1943, Dr. Ambedkar pointed out the need to set up 'Employment Exchange Centres' to regularise employment opportunities. While presiding over the tripartite labour convention held in September 1943, he explained the definition of food, clothing, housing, education, cultural needs and the need for a health plan for workers.

Influenced by his remarks, a resolution was passed at the convention to set up a committee to consider issues related to wages and income, as well as to set up a committee to gather necessary information on the social security of workers. He introduced a Bill in April 1944 for paid leave for those working in the factory, which worked round-the-clock. He was appointed chairman of the Standing Labour Committee in August 1945 when industrial rules and responsibilities of industrialists were taken into consideration.

Babasaheb wanted industrialisation of India so as to move faster in the race for development. But the development had to be in line with social justice. He said, "India's industrial progress is our goal, but at the same time we have to make sure that India's development is in line with social justice."

Babasaheb thought about agriculture, farmers, farming conditions, employment, industrialisation from the economic point of view and everything was centred around labour. He enacted a number of laws and schemes to address the concerns of the industrial and agricultural workers.

Contributing to the Interests of Labourers

Babasaheb's association with the labour movement was very long. As a child he even planned to run away from his home in Satara and work in a (textile) mill as a labourer. He woke up in the middle of the night, opened his aunt's wallet, but found nothing in it. He was disheartened and relinquished the idea of going to Mumbai. From his childhood determination to be a labourer, he spent his life fighting for workers' rights and for upliftment of the untouchables. He became known as a leader for untouchables and a labour leader. He was even honoured to be the first untouchable labour-member of the Supreme Working Committee of India.

In this capacity, he played an important role in laying the foundation of the industrial policy of independent India. On the basis of the foundations he laid, India's industrial policy, the basis of the interests of the workers and the development of modern India received a new direction. However, what he did as a Labour Minister, unfortunately, has not been properly evaluated and has been forgotten deliberately after 1947.

□

14

Population Control and Common Civil Rights: In the Interest of Nation

The nation was the top priority for Babasaheb and wanted it to prosper. He spoke out against Islamic fundamentalism, China's territorial ambitions, the betrayal by some people in the country, Article 370, the common civil code and the anti-constitution and anti-national Marxists.

If there was one monstrous problem which may engulf the country, it is the population explosion. Babasaheb expressed concern over the problem of population growth and believed that it would increase poverty by thwarting all the good plans of the government. His important speech in the Mumbai Assembly (1938) to control population growth is still relevant today and is worth considering in the interests of the nation.

Babasaheb was scheduled to deliver a speech on population control in the Mumbai Provincial Legislative Council in November 1938, but for some reason he could not reach on time. At the request of Ambedkar, the written discourse (*Mumbai Legislative Assembly Debates*, vol. 2) was read by P.J. Roham. Here are the 17 key points from the discourse:

1. This Assembly recommends to government that in view of the urgent need of limiting the family units, Government should carry on an intensive propaganda in

favour of birth-control among the masses of this province and should provide adequate facilities for the practice of birth-control. The educated class has, by this time, fully realised the necessity of birth-control and fortunately the leaders in our country also are unanimous on this point. Pandit Jawaharlal Nehru, Sir Ravindranath Tagore and Mrs. Sarojini Naidu know very well the importance and urgency of the movement for birth-control and are in favour of contraceptives. Babu Subhash Chandra Bose, the president of the Indian National Congress, said in his presidential speech: "If the population goes up by leaps and bounds, as it has done in the recent past, our plans are likely to fall through."

2. Even Mahatma Gandhi had written long ago as follows: "I must not conceal from the reader the sorrow I feel when I hear of births in this land." Very few have an adequate idea of the immense loss incurred by children born of persons who are handicapped, either physically, mentally or financially. The parents as well as the society suffer. The prevention of the births of such children would considerably reduce the death rate among mothers who succumb in childbirth and its concomitant diseases. So the need is for lower infantile mortality, improved public health by removing the many diseases due to want of even the prime necessities of life felt by many persons, check the offences perpetrated by persons suffering from intense poverty and bring about an all-round uplift of society by affording full scope to its spiritual advancement.
3. The present struggle of life renders timely marriage impossible for many and thus exposes them to various diseases and habits. Many women become invalid for life and some even lose their lives through the birth of children in their diseased condition or in too great numbers or in too rapid succession. Attempts at abortion, resorted to for the prevention of unwanted progeny, extract a heavy toll of female lives. Unwanted children are often neglected by their mothers and hence they become nothing but a burden on society which is further deteriorated by the

addition of defective progeny from diseased persons. Birth-control is the only sovereign specific that can do away with all these calamities. Whenever a woman is disinclined to bear a child for any reason whatsoever, she must be in a position to prevent conception and to bring forth progeny should be entirely dependent on the choice of women. Society would in no way profit by the addition of unwanted progeny. Only those children who are welcomed by their parents, can be of social benefit and hence, every woman must be enabled to resort to prevention of conception quite easily.

4. Poverty is the root cause of immorality. The following passage from the essay read by Prof. Dr. Tondler before the Congress at Vienna in 1933 would show the evil consequences of insufficiency of living accommodation. The professor said, "On the average, every family gets one room in Germany, two-and-a-half rooms in France and three rooms in England. Seventy-five thousand families had no tenements of their own in Berlin in 1925. The result is that children sleep with the adults not only in the same room but also in the same bed. Many children lose their lives by overcrowding in insanitary dwellings... The boys learn to commit thefts and the girls become prostitutes. The same condition prevails in Vienna. In 1919, out of the tenements let out, 10 per cent had only one small room; 37 per cent had one big room and 23 per cent had one small room and one big room. Out of the children between the ages of 14 and 18 who maintained themselves, 20 per cent had no separate beds of their own. Towns and villages fare even worse." In our country, the same condition prevails in cities like Bombay. A few exceptions apart, it is observed that virtue is palsied where poverty prevails. Further, on it will be shown how it is well-nigh impossible to uproot poverty without the aid of birth-control.
5. When we have thus realised that birth-control is the sine qua-non for every progress, we must consider the means to attain that end. To be satisfied with only that much of

sexual enjoyment that is necessary for getting the desired number of children and to banish sexual thoughts from one's mind when progeny is not required, is one of the ways. The use of modern contraceptives is the other way. As for the first way, it must be remembered that while continence in the unmarried state may be possible, it is nothing but displaying ignorance about human nature to expect that young and healthy married couples, living together and fond of each other, can observe continence for years together. The cases of strong-willed persons, whose minds are not affected in the presence of objects of enjoyment, apart, there is no doubt that ordinary human beings are bound to fall prey to the influence of enticements. Is it not strange, therefore, that this fact, which is as clear as daylight, is denied by some.

6. Self-control has been proved to be absolutely useless for birth-control from the experience of several countries and ages. Even the advocates of continence cannot claim that ordinary persons will be able to eschew sexual intercourse altogether throughout their lives. The laying aside of continence even for a single day every year may lead to an annual conception. Even, if we assume that self-control enables certain persons to bring about birth-control, we cannot draw the conclusion that others will be able to follow them. It is necessary to remember that just as appetite for food differs in the case of different persons, so sexual appetite also varies from person to person.
7. Strict observance of certain rules laid down in Hindu scriptures necessitates the neglect of the ideal of family-limitation. For instance, verse 8, Chap. 54, of *Vishnu Smriti* enjoins sexual intercourse on certain specified days.

   As a doctor has wisely remarked, if men had to bear the pangs which women have to undergo during child-birth, none of them would ever consent to bear more than a single child in his life.
8. It is wrong to hold that because the ideal of large families is before society up to this time, nobody wishes to limit

his family. Human beings, who earnestly desire to be saddled with large families, are rare. Ordinary persons do want to limit their families and do not even flinch to take recourse to diabolical methods, such as abortion, infanticide, etc. Such attempts are witnessed everywhere. From an account published by *The People's Tribune* in 1934, it was found that in 1933, over 24,000 dead bodies of little infants were picked up in the streets of Shanghai alone and the same state prevails throughout most of China...It is, therefore, established that there is no way without recourse to modern contraceptives. To deny the necessity of these remedies is to show one's preference for abortions, infanticides, etc.

9. Some people think that they would be losers if the numbers in their particular race, religion, or region are lessened. They are afraid that their adversaries would thereby be enabled to gain ground over them. In the first place, it is necessary to remember in this connection that the rate of increase of a population does not necessarily dwindle down as soon as family limitation is resorted to. That rate is dependent, not merely on the birth-rate, but chiefly on the survival-rate. The experience of several scientists from different places has proved that the higher the birth-rate, the higher is the death-rate also and no sooner the birth goes down, the death-rate also declines. The result is that not only is the survival-rate not adversely affected but very often it even rises. Dr. Maria Stopes has found from the experience gained in The Mothers' Clinic that the greater the number of conceptions the higher is the rate of maternal and infantile mortality...Due to excessive child-mortality, the rate of growth of the population of countries like India is not equal to that of countries like England though the birth-rates in countries of the former type are higher than those in the latter type. The birth-rate of England is nearly half that of India. Yet we find that the population in England increased by nearly 23 per cent between 1901 and 1931, while the population in India rose by only 17 per cent in the same period. This

will show that even for a rapid growth of numbers, the better way is to adopt the practice of birth-control and thus cut down on infantile mortality.

10. It must also be remembered that for modern wars, comparatively few persons are necessary. An army, well-equipped with modern materials for warfare, can rout an army much greater in number than itself, if the latter one is not so well-equipped. In the former world war, countries of low birth-rates vanquished those with high birth-rates.

    In the world, we can witness many societies that are small in numbers but distinguished in respect of wealth, culture, etc. In our country, the Parsee community is an illustration of this point. To hanker after quantity is, therefore, not a very profitable ideal.

11. The example of Western nations shows us that modern contraception is utilised by persons of all races, religions and strata. For instance, it is found that the notion that the Roman Catholics are against birth-control is unfounded. France is a Roman Catholic country and still it is notorious that the birth-rate in that country is quite low. The following countries had the lowest birth-rates in 1932:

Country	Birth-rate
Germany	15.1
Sweden	14.5
Austria	15.2
England & Wales	15.3
Norway	16.3
Australia	16.7
New Zealand	17.1
U S A	17.3
France	17.3

Among the three lowest countries is Austria, which is entirely Catholic, and Germany, which is one-third Catholic.

The following figures, the birth-rates of important cities, illustrate the very point. They are all for 1927 or 1928:

City	Birth-rate
London	16.1
Cologne	16.0
Geneva	14.6
Turin (Italy)	14.5
Prague (Austria)	13.2
Munich	12.5
Vienna	10.6

With the exception of London, all the above towns are solidly Roman Catholic, yet they all have a lower birth-rate than London. Three of them are in Mussolini's Italy. It is thus seen that the fear that other communities will neglect birth-control and will thus become stronger in numbers, is altogether a baseless one.

12. The result of the movement will thus be dysgenic instead of eugenic–is also groundless. The experience gained in Western countries establishes the fact that the lower classes do take advantage of contraceptives as soon as they are made cognisant of them, the need being greater in their cases. The masses in our country, though illiterate, are intelligent enough to know in what their own interest lies and hence there is no doubt that they will fully utilise this invention as soon as they are made aware of its existence. Vasectomy would be found to be useful in the case of such persons and hence government and municipalities must provide facilities in this respect in their hospitals, etc....The opponents of this movement try to show its futility by pointing out the examples of France, Germany and Italy but they forget that we cannot follow these countries unless it is proved that their attempts at the increase of their populations are justified. In the first place, it must be kept in mind that the birth-rates of these nations are much lower than the birth-rate of our country. Our birth-rate is 35 whereas in 1936, the birth-

rates of Italy, France and Germany were 22.2, 15 and 19 respectively. In 1900, the birth-rate in Germany was 35.6 but in 1933, it came down to 14.7. Italy and France also have their birth-rates much lower since that time. In England, the birth-rate was 33.9 in 1851-55 but in 1931, it lowered to 15.3. Our birth-rate has been practically stationary for the last 50 years and hence it would be unwise for us to imitate the efforts of other countries towards raising that rate.

13. Some think that as soon as child-marriages are given up and late marriages are introduced, the increase in population will be checked. But this belief also is an unfounded one. In the first place, years must elapse before the ages at which girls are married would be sufficiently higher in our country. The years of greatest fertility in the case of girls are those between 18 and 22. In Western countries, women marry after this period. That is, they marry when their time of greatest fertility is over. When we notice the difficulties in the enforcement of the Sarada Act, fixing the minimum age of marriage of a girl at 14, we can easily see that it is almost useless to hope that in the near future women in our country will postpone their marriages up to 22 and population will be checked thereby. Mr. P.K. Wattal has drawn the following conclusions from the fertility-enquiry conducted specially in connection with the 1931 Census.

(1) That girls married at ages below 20 give birth to a smaller number of children than girls married at ages above 20.

(2) That the survival-rate of children born to mothers married at ages below 20 is much less than that of children born to mothers married at age above 20.

These conclusions show us that even when late marriages would come into being, there is no chance of the population being appreciably checked thereby. More children would live up to mature ages and hence there is a chance of an increase and not a decrease in the rate of growth of our population.

14. The view is held that economic independence of women will lessen the growth of population but it also does not hold water. Economic independence has no power to free a person from the clutches of Eros. Few women can observe perfect continence throughout their lives and hence this remedy would be found to be fruitless. Even now, women of the lower classes are actually helping their families with their own earnings but that fact does not seem to help family-limitation to any extent.

    Some people hold the view that though birth-control may be necessary on medical and hygienic grounds, it is still not required for solving economic difficulties. They maintain that our country has got much scope for economic and agricultural development and efforts in these directions would raise the standard of life of our people appreciably. On close examination, however, this view also is found to be quite untenable. Want of sufficient capital and rich customers would prevent any material development of our industries. Similarly, insufficiency of fertile lands, rainfall and manure stand in the way of any substantial increase in our agricultural production.

15. Through the excessive growth of population, our country suffers from deficiency of forests and pasture-lands. In Canada, 34.3 per cent of cultivable land is reserved for pasturage. This proportion is 21.5 in France, 18.3 in Italy, 14.3 in Germany but in our country, it is only 1.6. These figures will show to what extent our cattle are forced. Our agriculture, therefore, is suffering from insufficiency of useful cattle and organic manures like cow-dung, and hence it is very difficult to effect many appreciable improvements in it. Some persons point out the large produce per acre of rice in Japan and China and hold out the hope that there is scope for materially increasing our produce of that crop. Besides this, notice also must be taken of the facts that Japan is blessed with plenty of timely and all-the-year round rainfall and abundance of manure due to her extensive forests and also with a climate ideally suited to her rice crops; a combination of

advantages is rarely witnessed anywhere else.

16. Although it may be admitted that self-rule may effect some betterment of the lot of our masses, no lasting and appreciable improvement in the economic condition of our people can be hoped for unless the growth of our population is deliberately checked. As has been already explained, with every opportunity afforded for its expansion, the population begins to grow rapidly and thus nullifies all the advantages secured through great efforts. The fact that mere self-rule is powerless to effect an all-round improvement in the condition of a people is demonstrated to the hilt by the examples of many independent nations. Although, through various reasons, including a low birth-rate, the economic condition of the inhabitants of countries like England and America is superior to that obtained in this country–poverty prevents many of our countrymen from obtaining a nourishing food–still it is far from satisfactory. Even there, many find it difficult to maintain a standard of life necessary for perfect health. In the Bombay Presidency, the amount of milk available per head per day is only one and a quarter 'tolas'. According to authorities on nutrition, every individual must get on average at least one pint of milk per day.
17. The main object of the movement for birth-control is to bring about a state of things wherein every country will have its birth-rate suitably reduced, so that it would thus be able to maintain its population decently with the aid of its own produce. Some are under the impression that modern scientific discoveries have solved the problems of food for mankind and that it is only mal-distribution that is at the root of the present economic difficulties. Fair distribution of property would, in their opinion, bring about plenty everywhere. There is no doubt that in many places, injustice prevails in the division of property and every impartial public worker must take all steps to secure justice for wronged persons in this respect. It is, however, necessary to remember that mere equal distribution will

never be able to bring about a permanent and material amelioration of the condition of the masses unless the growth of population is controlled by means of family-limitation.

These were the extremely important 17 points of Dr. Babasaheb Ambedkar's concise discourse and which are still relevant today. The only thing we must clearly understand from Dr. Ambedkar's speech is that the population explosion has thwarted all the schemes of the government, families cannot be happy and poverty is on the rise.

Population Control in the Interest of Society and Family

Babasaheb also believed that population control was not only in the interest of the nation, but also in the interest of the society and the family. He cited his own example in his public speeches to explain to the youth why population control is necessary. He knew that students were the future builders of the nation and that is why he advised students to keep their (future) family small. "Most of you will be unmarried," he commenced his speech at the Untouchable Student Convention in Mumbai (*Janata* magazine, 17 December, 1938). "Some may have been married, but what will you do after you get married? Marriage carries responsibility with it. Let me give you an example of my father instead of yours. I am his 14th *gem* out of a total of 14 children of my parents. My condition was extremely pathetic when I was studying at Elphinstone College. There were no shoes to wear; I had a simple cotton shirt and my father's torn coat over it for my classes at college. You may find a picture of Mr. Muller at Elphinstone College whenever you get a chance to visit; he donated me shirts during the last two years. I think my days would have passed better, if my father had only four kids instead of 14!"

"What are your future plans for your career? I think most of you will become clerks. You will get a maximum salary of Rs. 50 or 60 and what will happen to your children if you have 14 of them? Will you be able to bear their responsibility or just hand it over to society? You need to think about it. I know you are not going to get renunciation, but it's good if some of you get it" (*students laugh*).

"Please, don't laugh; this is not a laughing matter, it's very important. I had five children, four of them passed away. If they all survived, their education, food, accommodation would all be a burden on me and a problem for me. I now have the responsibility of only one boy. It would be much better if you carry even 10 per cent of that responsibility for your children. It will be good for society as well. How will you raise and give good education if you also have five or six children? I don't think there will be any upliftment in such a situation; there will be only decline. It is therefore considered a disgrace for mankind if men and women live like animals."

One thing becomes clear out of his both above-mentioned discourses that Dr. Ambedkar wanted population control in the national interest, social interest and family interest–at all three fronts.

One can see how important it is to curb population growth even today in all three aspects. No matter how perfect any government plan is, it becomes incapable of fulfilling the aspirations of the people just because of uncontrolled population. Population growth is also a major obstacle in combating poverty; not only that, it can be a threat also in terms of national security. Implementing ideas of Dr. Ambedkar is not only necessary but it is inevitable to secure the future of India, to make India poverty free and maintain the well-being of the society and the family. The horrific population explosion must be curbed to make India as per Babasaheb Ambedkar's dream.

The way Dr. Ambedkar associated population control with national interest could be seen from his desire for a Uniform Civil Code in the country. He did his best to enforce the Uniform Civil Code in the Constituent Assembly, but he had to endure opposition from the Muslim delegates. Muslim representative insisted that they could resolve their issues in accordance with Shariah law. Dr. Ambedkar said, "I personally do not understand how a religion can be given such a vast and important jurisdiction that one's whole life will be governed only by it and the legislature has no right to interfere in it! So what is the use of our freedom? We must use our freedom to improve the social fabric of all forms of inequality and discrimination, which is full of all kinds of inequality and discrimination. All this is a violation of our fundamental rights."

But the then Prime Minister Jawaharlal Nehru was not in favour of enforcing the Uniform Civil Code. He, like many other issues, did not support Dr. Ambedkar.

Dr. Ambedkar had made strong arguments in favour of a Uniform Civil Code. It would have come into force at the time of drafting the Constitution if he had been given a complete free hand at that time.

Opponents of the Uniform Civil Code during a debate in the Constituent Assembly, were Hussein Imam, B. Poker, Mehboob Ali Beg, Mohammad Ismail, Naziruddin Ahmed. They said that the issue of marriage and inheritance should be decided according to the Quran and Shariah. Now the question is, why do all Muslim leaders want different rules for themselves in matters like marriage and inheritance? In both cases, there is a great deal of discrimination and oppression against women in the name of Personal Law. If anyone raises a voice on the issue of atrocities on Muslim women, the Muslim party repeatedly cries of interference in their religious issues. They used to make the same argument regarding the Personal Law. Babasaheb gave them a scathing reply, on 23 November, 1948 in favour of a Uniform Civil Code, which is still on record today. He said: In India, most of the issues that fall under the Uniform Civil Code have already come up. I would like to challenge those members who say that Muslim Personal Law is unchangeable in this country and there is a uniformity about it in the whole country. They seem to have deliberately forgotten that the North-West Provinces did not come under Sharia Law until 1935. They used to follow Hindu Law in matters, like inheritance. The story doesn't end. The Murumakkathayam Law applies not only to Hindus but also to Muslims of North Malabar and the law was not patriarchal, but Marumakkathayam was a matriarchal one. And Muslims followed it; so it is baseless to say that Islamic law is immutable, because they have been following for centuries. We have had enough discussion on the Uniform Civil Code; there is no point in discussing it any more.´However, just like the Population Control Act, Dr. Ambedkar's wish for a Uniform Civil Code remained unfulfilled. As Article 370, which was included in the Constitution against the wishes of Babasaheb and has been removed by the Modi government, it is now in the national interest to fulfil his wish by applying the Population Control Act and Uniform Civil Code.

This country suffers from personal laws based on religion. The Supreme Court has also directed the government to apply the Uniform Civil Code on several occasions. The idea is already there in the Constitution, but it could not be implemented due to appeasement and political ideology of prestige of Muslims. The Congress divided the country into Hindu-Muslim in the name of hypocritical secularism. There is also pure politics behind the protests against the CAA.

In fact, the makers of the Constitution have made it clear in Article 44 that India should work towards enforcing the Uniform Civil Code for all its citizens. In 1954, the Supreme Court held that religious freedom granted under Articles 25 and 26 did not mean that it was above the law. The Supreme Court repeatedly pointed out the need for Uniform Civil Code during the Shah Bano case and during the case of Saira Bano. Uniform Civil Code grants the same civil rights to everyone; it has nothing to do with religious freedom. Whether Hindu or Muslim, they are free to practice their religion and religious rituals without hindrance even after the application of Uniform Civil Code.

In Dr. Ambedkar's words, "Overpopulation thwarts all plans of the country and Uniform Civil Code gives equal justice to all. Hence, Population Control Law and Uniform Civil Code, both are in the interest of the nation."

□

15

Indian Constitution : Foundation Stone for Nationality

The Constitution of India, the most important document for the country, was conceptualised, drafted and finally framed by the most eminent personality for that task Dr. Babasaheb Ambedkar. He was initially invited to the Drafting Committee as a representative of one class of people and was then unanimously elected as Chairman of the Committee. A draft for the discussion on the Constitution was prepared by B.N. Rao and each clause was discussed in detail on its basis. Babasaheb framed the Indian Constitution by penning down this discussion, although the process was not that simple. There were many innovative ideas and researches were presented and some serious allegations were also made on various Articles of the Constitution. However, everything was addressed and answered properly by framers of the Constitution and in particular, by Babasaheb. He faced many challenges and difficulties in drafting this Constitution; it was not possible to comprehend his contribution to nation building without knowing the difficulties and challenges.

Granville Austin described in the preface of his famous book on the Indian Constitution–*The Indian Constitution: Cornerstone of a Nation*: "The importance of the social revolution is highlighted when national unity and stability are the only goals and that is the prerequisite for social upliftment. It is clear in many places in our Constitution that national unity has been the central issue in the making of constitutional and federal as well as linguistic Articles. The result of the need to maintain internal unity is that the Constitution has a federal structure and has a special effect when it includes some clauses for emergency. Other objectives, such as protection of minority interests, efficient governance, building up governance and national security, which are directly or indirectly included in the Constitution and they have also influenced the Constitution largely, because the Constitution was the only means to achieve these objectives and it was in a way neglected by the Members of Parliament."

We were liberated on 15 August, 1947 and achieved political freedom. Before this date, the country was occupied by Muslim invaders for 762 years and remained under British rule for about 200 years. This means that the people of this country were not running their own State for nearly 1,000 years. Many aspects have to be considered in running one's own State, like: What does the State mean? What is the meaning of State power? How is it ruled? How is it managed? What should be the relationship between the people and the rulers? Which system will achieve political stability? What are the principles of making the State a public welfare State? Where is the source of power? We have forgotten words like self-government, self-rule, freedom due to the slavery of hundreds of years. The people of our country had become accustomed to being 'slaves' of foreigners. Saying 'yes sir' and '*Ji Huzoor*' were entwined in their thinking. India and her people were suffering from this mentality when India got Independence. It was the responsibility of the Constituent Assembly to establish a system of independent governance.

The Constituent Assembly discussed each clause and points in this regard and it was the responsibility of Dr. Babasaheb Ambedkar to verbalise all such discussions that took place in the Constituent Assembly.

Babasaheb dreamed and envisioned a united and strong nation which is full of the feeling of brotherhood. But, he knew that we were not one nation at that time in 1947. There had to be a strong national spirit among all the people of the nation for a nation to be built as a 'nation'. There should be a feeling that we all are one; we all are brothers. Indian society is a bouquet of people of different castes and different faiths; in simple words, there were communities in India. Community means a group of people living in a particular class and the task was to reach to the word 'people' from the word 'community'. Here 'people', if we define as per political science, means all the people living in any one region of the world and they are aware of their common interest. That is why the preamble of our Constitution uses words like "we-the people of India..." instead of "we-the nationals of India..." Our Constitution shows us the path from 'people' to the 'nation' and the biggest contribution in making this path was made by Babasaheb.

As an ardent believer of democracy, his faith and devotion to democracy was unique, and this can be seen in the Constitution. There are many definitions of democracy made by prominent personalities; among them the most popular and most quoted was given by Abraham Lincoln. Babasaheb delivered one of the best speeches on the subject of 'Conditions for the Success of Democracy' at the District Library in Pune on 22 December, 1952. He said, 'What is the meaning of democracy? Democracy is defined by many personalities in their own words. A constitutional expert, Walter Bejuat defines democracy as 'governing the state through internal debate', Abraham Lincoln defined democracy as 'a government of the people, for the people and by the people' in a famous speech at Gettysburg. My own definition is different. I believe that the only true 'democracy is to bring about a bloodless radical change in the political and social life of the people.' Running a democracy means those who have a duty to run democracy and those who have such a right should establish social and economic equality in the society by taking care that it is completely bloodless! Only then I will call them true servants of democracy. This may be an assumption, and some people think–is there any possibility of coming true? Yes, there is a possibility, but it requires an understanding of how democracy can succeed; and there are many different ways to understand it. But there are no such principles, rules, by-laws to run a democratic government; no philosopher has mentioned it. We need to look at the history for that."

Babasaheb showed some ways to make democracy successful and they were:

- "There should not be any distinction in society, like someone is premier and the other one is trivial, to make democracy successful. The whole society should be on the same level. If there is division in the society, the power of the society is divided and the society becomes pithless.
- The second thing which makes democracy immortal is a strong Opposition. Democracy stands on pillars of the ruling party and the Opposition party.
- The third vital element which makes democracy immortal is equal treatment for all before the rule of law and the State.
- The fourth vital element is strict adherence to parliamentary policy values and discretion. The mental readiness to adhere to constitutional policy values is invisibly enshrined in the Constitution."

He was very insistent on morality in the Constitution. He gave two examples in his speech. In his own words, "George Washington was the first President of the United States. He was so popular among the people that people would have elected him for ten terms, if he would have run for it. But he was not ready to run for re-election. When the people insisted, he said, 'We have made our Constitution. For what? The main objective of our Constitution is to uproot the tradition of dynasty rule we had until now and to hand over the power to a suitable and best person of the people's choice. It is true that you will elect me a second time but it will tarnish our Constitution,' although he had to accept people's strong insistence and became the President for the second time. But he flatly refused to run for a third term."

He then gave another example, "The eighth king, King Edward wanted to marry an American woman who was not of royal blood. This news caused a stir in England. The marriage was vehemently opposed by the Conservative Party. The then Prime Minister did not want the king to marry the woman out of dynastic bloodline and remain on the throne. But Churchill had no objection to the matter. The Labour Party wanted to take political advantage of the situation and remove the Conservative Party from power. Professor Harold Laski wrote several articles on the Labour Party's intentions and warned the Labour Party that if the king disobeyed the Conservative Party's advice and the Labour Party supported it, it would be tantamount to endorsing the king's arbitrariness. The king will have the right to break the tradition of England without following the advice of the Prime Minister. Even if the Labour Party comes to power after this happens, it will have to suffer the consequences. However, King Edward later abdicated his throne on the advice of Professor Harold Laski."

Although the subject of his speech was democracy, Babasaheb focused on the specific issue of one nationality in this speech. He also described in detail what kind of society it should be in which the democracy would be adopted. He said, "The environment that is conducive to moral values is essential for the society to adopt democracy so that evil activities do not enter politics. Unfortunately, such an environment is not present in Indian society. It is difficult for our democracy to survive in Indian society."

Such an environment could be created, but should also be nurtured for the welfare of society. The power of discretionary thinking in the common public is required to nurture this environment. Justice and injustice, sin and virtue have good or bad effects on the power of society. There was a law in England that if a Jew died, all his wealth and property would be deposited to the State treasury instead of his/her heir. This law continued for many years, because Christians were not affected so they did not mind whether the law continued or was removed; at the same time the king's treasury grew richer, so the king didn't want to remove the law. So, when the Jews started a movement against it, they had to endure persecution of both–the Christians and the king. Later, many intellectuals came forward to amend the law and became a good example of social conscience for the society. When injustice ever happens to people of any religion, creed or sect, everyone should support those who help to diminish it. It is the duty of every human being, even if it is not affecting them."

Among the many speeches of Babasaheb in the Constituent Assembly, three are very important–on his patriotism, national outlook, challenges and problems facing our nation and his guidelines to solve them. The first meeting of the Constituent Assembly was held on 9 December, 1946 as per its fixed schedule under the chairmanship of Sachchidanand Sinha. On 13

December, Pandit Jawaharlal Nehru presented the objectives of the Constitution and an eight-point proposal in the Constituent Assembly. India's independence, sovereignty and republic were declared in this presentation. His proposal gave lesser powers to the Centre and was likely to weaken the Central Government. His proposals included: the provincial constituents will be autonomous, they will have special rights, they will have the right to make laws, enforce them and to administer certain matters; there will be a federation over constituent provinces. Babasaheb opposed the proposal strongly, "I do not approve the idea of forming such a one-sided faction," he said. "I would like to have a stronger Central Government."

Babasaheb addressed the Constituent Assembly on 17 December, 1946: "I have no doubt about the bright future of this country; the social, political and economic development of this great country is sure to happen in years to come, if not today. I am aware that today we are divided socially, economically and politically. We are in fact a group of different camps fighting against each other and I would go even further and say that I also lead one such camp. But despite this being true, I am confident that at the right time and the right circumstances, this vast country will achieve unification. No power in the world can interfere with its unity. In spite of the fact that there are so many sects and castes in this country, I have no doubt that somehow we will all become one. Today the Muslim League is striving for the Partition of India but a united India is in our interest. I have no hesitation in saying that one day they will also understand this."

In a sense, Babasaheb introduced the concept of a united India in the Constituent Assembly. Praising this historic discourse, the daily newspapers carried the title: 'Dr. Ambedkar: Proponent of United India'. He was worried about the future of the country as can be seen when he said, "Everyone's ultimate goal is the same; no one can doubt it. What will happen in the future is not our issue; our issue is how we can take such a decision in our country with different castes and sects so that we can become one people, one nation. Our problem is–how to start. My advice is to try to end the rift between the Congress and the Muslim League once again. This is such a great and important subject that it cannot be decided on the basis of the prestige of any one party. When it comes to making decisions about the future of the nation, there should be no place for the prestige of people, leaders or parties. The future of the country should be given importance."

"I am saddened that there are still some people in our country who believe that political problems can be solved through war. They think that they are going to fight the war against the enemy. I do not mind if such a war takes place at the border, but can such a war to be confined to the British only? I want to make it clear to this house that if there is a war and if it will be on this issue, the war will not be against the British; it will be only against Muslims. Whether the war is against the Muslims or against the joint opposition of both the Muslims and the British, it is not possible in any other way than the fear I have."

"The use of force is fleeting. This allows the enemy to accept a momentary defeat, but it often requires defeating the enemy again and again; and a nation that needs to fight over and over again cannot rule."

"The result of force is not always fear and the army does not always mean victory. If you do not succeed, then you won't have any solution, because if you fail, then the compromise is the only solution left. Sometimes love buys power and strength, but the losers of war cannot beg for love and charity."

"If anyone is thinking that the issue of Hindu-Muslim will be solved forever, in other words, to fight with Muslims and force them to accept the Constitution unconditionally, then believe me, it will be an indefinite war against them–winning once will not be a final victory. Now, I will not take much time and will remember Burke once again on concluding my speech. Burke had said that it is easy to provide power but difficult to provide wisdom.' If this assembly has erred in believing that it has got all the powers, then it has to prove by its conduct that it should use such *suo motu* powers wisely. No one should be left in the lurch that this is the only way we can work together with all sections of the country; there is no other way for the unity of the country." This speech in the Constituent Assembly predated the Partition of India when Muslim League insisted on it. Muslims who wanted Partition, went to Pakistan in 1947; now, we have to bring the remaining Muslims into the Indian mainstream and into fold of nationalism.

Babasaheb had toiled to draft the Constitution of India. It was tabled in the Constituent Assembly for final approval and was discussed all over the country. Many questions were raised on certain issues of the Constitution and errors were also pointed out. It was also criticised by some who said that there was nothing new in the Constitution or it did not reflect the Indian political views or that it was just a copy of the Government of India's 1935 Act. Some also made allegations that it was a copy of the Constitutions of other countries. However, Babasaheb responded to all these allegations, questions and errors in his speech on 4 November, 1948. His original speech covered extensive details, but this speech does not mention much contemporary politics. It was based on some theoretical principles for the Constitution.

Babasaheb presented the written draft in which the first three or four paragraphs gave technical details, like reports which came from the drafting committee of various subjects. He did not advocate the demand for a Constitution; his point of view was neutral and introduced features of the Constitution as a legal expert. Overall, it was an ideological speech on the fundamental qualities of the Constitution.

The most remarkable feature of his speech was his vision. His approach was non-partisan while drafting the Constitution. Although, he had been known as a leader of the Scheduled Caste community before he was appointed Chairman of the Constitution Committee,but his speech showed that he was a leader of the nation who cared only about the nation.

Indian Constitution combined parliamentary democracy and a presidential system like the American system. Seeing the situation prevailing in the country, he could gauge that the British had decided to divide the country when they gave the freedom to princely states to decide their future by staying with India or by merging with Pakistan. This clearly meant that British wanted to balkanise India, but Sardar Vallabhbhai Patel united all the princely states and merged them into India, thus creating one united country. At the same time Babasaheb created a Constitution that bound them together as one unit.

It was very difficult to decide which system of governance

would be appropriate for a huge country like India. India has had a long history as an ancient nation and is one culturally, but its national spirit had been weakened for numerous reasons. There was a complete vacuum of a strong central authority. It was therefore required to establish a strong central power in independent India and at the same time the system had to be democratic. There are two types of democratic governance–one is presidential democracy as seen in the United States and other is parliamentary democracy as found in England. Presidential democracy provides immense power to the President, who is not responsible to the Parliament; even his cabinet is not accountable to Parliament. No-confidence motion cannot be brought against the President by Parliament and no one can remove the president from power for four years, once he comes to power.

There are several advantages to this system. This system keeps the regime stable and the President can take his own decisions at his own responsibility. It does not need the approval of Parliament to support the decisions. He can make any dutiful person of the society a minister. A person can only be President twice and there is no provision for a third term in their Constitution. All follow this rule and the President also adheres to the constitutional policy. He does not behave like a dictator and his role is to take the country along.

Such a system is not conducive to India. At that time, many demanded introduction of a presidential system in India like the United States, but Babasaheb, with foresight, rejected the American system of government. Indian people did not have the political maturity in 1947 like the American voters who considered a candidate's views while voting, his role on various issues, the nature of voting on various Bills in Parliament and his speech in public meetings. While the Indian voter's first consideration is the candidate's caste, then comes his family, his wealth and social status. The candidate's conduct and character come last for the Indian voter. In such a situation, if there is a presidential system in India, then any person who with an impressive personality could be elected as a President. It may not be surprising for a famous actor or a cricketer were to become President, but would he possess the ability to run the country responsibly.

Coming to the parliamentary system, here the members are responsible for answering to the Parliament. The Prime Minister has to answer in Parliament. He can remain in office as long as the Parliament has confidence in him. We have witnessed an example in the case of Atal Bihari Vajapyee's government in recent history, when his government collapsed as it was short of just one vote in the Parliament. That is why neither the Prime Minister nor his Cabinet can make decisions as they deem fit. Babasaheb said in this regard, "The Executive Council in America is non-parliamentary, so the American Congress cannot dismiss it. But in the parliamentary system, the government has to resign if there is no majority in the House. The non-parliamentary cabinet is not connected with Parliament. Therefore it has less responsibility towards the judiciary system as well. On the other hand, parliamentary cabinets run on the majority of parliamentarians, so they have a larger responsibility to Parliament."

India is a country full of diversity; at the same time, cultural unity is necessary in diversity. Casteism and untouchability are equally prevalent throughout the country. The attainment of supreme (spiritual) happiness is the goal of life and this happiness is not based on materialism. In India, there is a positive unity in some matters and a negative unity in others, which makes it very difficult to build political unity in the country. It was really a difficult task to eradicate diversity and casteism to create a secular society while protecting the diversity of the country. Babasaheb was able to accomplish this most difficult task because 'interest of the nation' was the topmost priority for him. Some excerpts from his speeches indicate his unique ability.

Babasaheb was a staunch supporter of a strong Central Government. The various states of India are also independent but the unity and integrity of the country is primarily in the hands of the Central Government. There are also several states in America. Each state has an independent Constitution and each has its own laws which often contradict one state to another. The law that exists in one state becomes illegal in another state. Americans have a system of dual citizenship-state and Union. Because, the United States is a union of different states, India is also a union of different states. Comparing the two, Babasaheb said, "The

Indian Constitution has a dual state system, but citizenship is one. Citizenship in the whole of India is same. A citizen of any state is considered as a citizen of India, and that is called 'Indian'; his/her basic rights remain the same. This system of the Indian Constitution differentiates us from the US Constitution."

- The Indian Constitution gives freedom to the states to develop in their own way, but no state is allowed to become independent by separating from India. The Indian Union is inseparable. Clarifying this important matter, Babasaheb said, "It is true that there is diversity in the states; it is also worthwhile to preserve its diversity. But it must uphold the vision of India." He further added, "Some basic uniformities are built to keep the unity intact. The draft Constitution shows three solutions for this:
- A single judiciary system.
- Uniformity of the basic law, uniformity of the legal system.
- Same Civil Service Commission for appointments to important posts."

Sense of nationalism is of utmost importance and it can be achieved when everyone, every citizen is involved in building the country. Participation creates nationalism; it imparts a sense of togetherness. Participation in administration is required to create attachment with the country, to create sense like, my country, my democracy, my country's brothers and sisters. That is why Babasaheb included several Articles in the Constitution for administrative matters. Adherence to constitutional ethics means honest adherence to every rule set out in the Constitution. Babasaheb said, "Constitutional morality is not a natural feeling; it needs to be cultivated. We need to understand that it has not been created in the people even today. In such a situation, it is not appropriate to trust the judiciary to build an administrative system. That is the purpose to include them in the Constitution."

Administrative system means the system that runs the government. Various clauses have been included in the Constitution in view of the cooperation of all in the system governing the administration. Babasaheb did not assign the task of determining it to any legislature or any other autonomous body.

The Indian Constitution contains guidelines called the

'Directive Principles of Policy'. There were no such Articles in the Constitution of any other country in the world at that time, except in the Irish Constitution. The peculiarity of these guiding elements is that they are not binding on the ruler. This means that one cannot go to court if these elements are not enforced. Fundamental rights are different; rulers are bound to enforce fundamental rights, failing which justice can be sought through the judicial system.

Inclusion of these guiding elements was an original and far-sighted idea of Babasaheb. Polls take place every five years (sometimes it is mid-term) and a new government comes to power. No matter which party that government belongs to, they have to act in accordance with the country's Constitution. Not only that, they have to follow the guiding elements. Babasaheb said, "The decision of who will form the government is entirely up to the people, but whoever comes to power will not be free to act arbitrarily. Ruling government represents the whole nation and has to rule accordingly. They shall have to remain loyal to the Constitution of the country. And guiding elements must be respected while exercising authority. They can't ignore it. They may not have to answer in the court, if they violate these elements, but they will certainly have to answer to voters when they will go to the people for the next election." In other words, Babasaheb placed a huge and important responsibility on the people, who had to be vigilant and ensure that the regime kept in mind the welfare of the people. In a way, the key to the welfare of the country lies in the hands of the citizens.

Babasaheb introduced the final draft of the Indian Constitution before the Constituent Assembly on 25 November, 1949. He delivered his third important speech on nationality. Babasaheb said, "Both the members of the Constituent Assembly and my colleagues in the drafting committee have showered greetings on me. It is so overwhelming that I cannot find the words to express my gratitude to them. I did not come to the Constituent Assembly with any greater aspirations than just the protection of rights of the Scheduled Castes. I had no idea that I would be requested for more responsibility. So I was very surprised when the Constituent Assembly selected me to the drafting committee. I was shocked when the drafting committee elected me as its Chairman. Although the drafting committee had bigger, better and more capable members than me, like my friend Sir Alladi Krishnaswamy Iyer, I owe the Constituent Assembly and the drafting committee for putting so much faith and trust in me and choosing me as their tool and giving me the opportunity to serve the country."

"The credit given to me is not really mine. In part, it goes to the constitutional adviser to the Constituent Assembly, Sir B.N. Rao, who prepared a rough draft for consideration of the drafting committee. Part of the credit should go to the members of the drafting committee. As I said, they sat for 141 days and without their expertise in formulating a new theory and their ability to tolerate and accommodate different points of view, the task of drafting a Constitution would not have been so successful. Much of the credit for the success goes to Mr. H.N. Mukherjee. Hardly anyone can match his ability to put the most complex proposals in the simplest and clearest legal form. He has been an achievement of the Constituent Assembly. It would have taken many more years to finalise the Constitution without his help."

"I do not want to dwell on the pros and cons of the Constitution because I think that, no matter how good the Constitution is, it can be bad if the people who work on it are bad. No matter how bad the Constitution is, if the people who work on it are good, it will be good. The functioning of the Constitution does not depend entirely on the kind of Constitution. The Constitution can only provide components, such as the legislature, the executive committee, and the judiciary. These are the factors on which the functioning of the components of the State depends. The people and their aspirations and the political parties will realise their tools to run their politics. Who can predict how the people of India and their parties will behave? Will they support the constitutional conditions for achieving their objectives or will they choose revolutionary ways to achieve them? If they adopt revolutionary methods, no matter how good the Constitution is, it does not need a prophet to predict that it will fail. Therefore, it is useless to give a verdict on the Constitution without mentioning the people and their parties who are going to take part in it.

"Criticism of the Constitution is often from two parties– Communist Party and Socialist Party. Why do they criticise the

Constitution? Is it because it's a really bad format? I dare say 'NO'. The Communist Party wants a Constitution based on the principle of 'proletarian dictatorship'. They criticise our Constitution because it is based on parliamentary democracy."

Regarding the ideas expressed in the Constitution, Babasaheb said: "The principles enshrined in the Constitution are the ideas of the present generation or if you consider this an exaggeration, I would say that they are the ideas of the members of the Constituent Assembly. Why to blame the drafting committee for including them in the Constitution? I say, why blame the members of the Constituent Assembly too?"

In support of his point, Dr. Babasaheb quoted American constitutional scholar, Jefferson:

"Jefferson, the great American politician who played a major role in shaping the US Constitution, has expressed some very important views. The framers of the Constitution cannot ignore it. At one point he said: '*The question whether one generation of men has a right to bind another, seems never to have been started either on this or our side of the water... (but) between society and society, or generation and generation, there is no municipal obligation, no umpire but the law of nature. We seem not to have perceived that, by the law of nature, one generation is to another as one independent nation to another...On similar ground, it may be proved that no society can make a perpetual Constitution, or even a perpetual law. The earth belongs always to the living generation...*'

"Let's elaborate in simpler language. Consider each generation as an independent nation that is able to impose its views on the majority, but that privilege is only up to us. It cannot be imposed on the next generation. How can one nation have a special right over another nation? The practices established for the national interest can neither be touched nor changed by institutions even to address their purpose, because the unsolicited rights of those engaged in conducting them in the faith of people may be a benevolent provision against the king's abuses, but that fiddles against the nation. Nevertheless, our lawyers and clergymen often hold to this principle. Suppose the previous generation had the right to impose their laws if they held the earth more freely than we do, and in the same way we can make laws and impose them on next generations, which they have no right to change. In short, the earth belongs to the dead, not to the living."

Babasaheb said in the context of change in Constitution in future that if the country needs it, "The provision for amending the Constitution has to be looked into. The Constituent Assembly is not stopped after checking possibilities of denial to people of the right to amend the Constitution like Canada or to amend the Constitution subject to extremely stringent conditions, like the United States and Australia; but it has made it extremely easy to amend the Constitution. In the circumstances in which this country exists, I challenge any critic of the Constitution to prove that if any Constituent Assembly anywhere in the world has provided such a simple procedure for amending the Constitution. Those who are dissatisfied with the Constitution have to get only a two-thirds majority and if they do not get a two-thirds majority in their favour in a Parliament elected by adult voters, then the general public cannot be considered a partner in their dissatisfaction with the Constitution."

Babasaheb's statement clarifies that the Constitution is neither a document that cannot be changed nor a traditional religious scripture; hence the future generation has every right to do the necessary amendment, if the need is felt.

Expressing concern that the country should remain united, independent and not become dependent again, Babasaheb said, "From 26 January, 1950, India will be a democracy, (*applause*) but what about its freedom? Will it retain its freedom or lose it again? This is the first thought that comes to my mind. It is not that India has never been an independent country. Not only has India lost its independence once before, but the fact that it has lost its independence due to the betrayal and disloyalty of some of its own people makes me very upset. When Muhammad bin Qasim invaded Sindh, Raja Dahir's General refused to fight on the king's side but took bribe from Muhammad bin Qasim's agents. Jaichand invited Muhammad Ghori to invade India and to fight against Prithviraj. While Shivaji was fighting for the liberation of the Hindus, other Maratha chiefs and Rajput kings were fighting on the side of the Mughal emperor. When the British were trying to destroy the Sikh rulers, their chief General Gulab Singh remained silent and did not help save the Sikh state. The Sikhs remained silent in 1857 when the freedom struggle broke out against the British in most parts of India. Will this history repeat itself? This thought makes me anxious. In addition to our old social enemies in the form of castes and sects, the fact that there are political parties in the country with different and opposing ideologies makes this concern even more serious. Will Indians put the country above their sect or will they consider their sect above the country? I don't know that but it is so certain that if the parties put the sect above the country, our independence will be in danger again and if we lose it this time, it will be lost forever. The country should be strongly protected against any such possible incident. We must be determined to defend our freedom to the last drop of our blood."

Babasaheb expressed concern for the country as well as for democracy, "The first thought that comes to my mind is that India will become a democracy on 26 January, 1950 in the sense that from that day on, the government will be of the people, by the people and for the people. The next that thought comes is–What will happen to the democratic constitution? Will India be able to keep it or lose it again? This makes me as anxious as ever."

"It is not that India does not know what democracy is. There was a time when India was full of republics and also a monarchy, but it was either selective or limited; it was never absolute. It is not that India did not know Parliament or parliamentary procedure; it appears from the study of Buddhist monk associations that there were Parliaments. Buddhists Sangh–unions–were nothing but Parliaments. The Sangh knew and followed all the rules and procedures of the parliamentary system known to the modern age."

"India lost such a democratic system; will it lose it a second time? I don't know that, but in a country like India, where democracy has not been around for a long time and is considered as a brand new thing, it is almost impossible for this newborn democracy to maintain its form without establishing democratic dictatorship in the country. In the situation of any kind of collapse, the second possibility is more likely to become a reality."

"What should we do if we really want to maintain democracy? In my discretion, the first thing we must do is to hold fast to constitutional practices in order to achieve our social and economic goals. This means that we should abandon the ways of *savinay* (modesty) violations, non-cooperation and *satyagraha*. Unconstitutional methods are justified when there is no way left for the constitutional system to achieve the economic and social goal! But there can be no justification for such unconstitutional methods when constitutional methods are open. Any other methods are nothing but creation of chaos and the sooner they are abandoned, the better for us."

"The second thing we should do is follow the warning given by John Stuart Mill to all of us who are interested in maintaining democracy. That is: 'Do not put your freedom at the feet of the great man, nor trust in him with so much power as to overturn his own practices.' There is nothing wrong with being grateful to great men who have served the country throughout their life, but gratitude has its limits. According to Irish patriot Daniel O'Connell, 'No man can be grateful at the cost of his honour, no woman can be grateful at the cost of her chastity and no country can be grateful at the cost of her freedom.' This warning is more necessary in the case of India than in the case of any other country. *Bhakti* (worship) or *veerapuja* (worshipping of heroes), which we call *bhakti marg*, is unique in the part that plays in the politics of India. Devotion in religion could be the path to the liberation of the soul, but devotion and worshipping heroes in politics is the sure path to fall and possibly a dictatorship."

"The third thing we should do is not be content with just political democracy. We must also make our political democracy a social democracy. Political democracy cannot function without the foundation of social democracy. What is social democracy? It means a way of life that accepts the principles of liberty, equality and fraternity as the principles of life. These principles of liberty, equality and fraternity should not be treated as separate entities in the trinity. They form a unity of the trinity in the sense that to separate one from the other is to defeat the very purpose of democracy. Liberty cannot be separated from equality; equality cannot be separated from liberty; at the same time liberty and equality cannot be separated from fraternity. Liberty without equality will produce superiority of a few over many. Liberty without equality will destroy individual initiative, as well as liberty and equality cannot be natural ways of things without fraternity. We must begin by acknowledging the fact that Indian society lacks two things. One of them is equality. On the social front, we have a society based on the principle of gradual inequality in India, that is, progress for some and decline for others. At the forefront of economic life, we have a society in which many live in abject poverty while some have abundant wealth. We are going to enter a paradoxical life on 26 January, 1950. We will have equality in politics and we will have inequality in social and economic life. We are going to accept the principle of one person and one vote, one value in politics. But, we will deny the principle of one person, one value in our social and economic life, because of our social and economic structure. How long will we continue to deny equality in our social and economic life? How long will we continue to live such a contradictory life? If we continue to deny it for a long time, we will only be able to do so by endangering our political democracy. We must overcome this contradiction as soon as possible. Otherwise, those who have to deal with inequality will blow up the structure of political democracy which this assembly has diligently prepared."

"Another thing we lack is the acceptance of the principle of fraternity. What is fraternity? It means a spirit of brethren within all Indians. It is the principle that gives unity and fraternity to social life. This is difficult to achieve."

Dr. Babasaheb's points of view were directed at how a country, divided into thousands of castes, be called a nation? At the same time, he wanted the abolition of castes to be called a country; a one nation; he considered castes to be deadly to the country. Babasaheb added, "In my opinion, we are afraid of being known as one nation. How can a people divided into thousands of castes become a nation? Only when we will realise that we are still not a nation in the social and psychological sense and we need to become one, we will seriously consider the fundamental resources to achieve the goal, and this goal is not so easy to achieve. Casteism is not a problem in the United States, but there are numerous castes in India, and that is anti-national in the first place because that creates inequality in social life and this inequality produces jealousy and hatred among castes. We must overcome all difficulties if we really want to be a nation; then the fraternity will become a reality. Equality and liberty without fraternity is no more than daubing (a superficial covering)."

"These are my thoughts on the task at hand. It may not be pleasing to someone, but there is no denying that the few have for long monopolised the political power in this country, and many are not only beasts of burden, but became violent beasts. This monopoly has deprived them of the opportunity to get better chances and not only that, but the very essence of life has been destroyed by these monopoly rulers. Attempts have been made to rule over these oppressed classes. Now, this oppressed class is longing to rule themselves. This longing for self-realisation in the oppressed classes should not be allowed to lead to class struggle or class rage. Indeed that day will be a day of calamity, as the house divided against itself cannot last long as Abraham Lincon said. So the sooner the opportunity is given to realise their aspirations, the better for those 'few', the better for the country, the better for maintaining its independence and the better for its democratic structure. Creating equality and fraternity in society in all aspects is the only way to achieve this, and that is why I put so much emphasis on it."

"Freedom is undoubtedly a matter of pleasure, but we must not forget that there are heavy responsibilities attached to it. Now, after Independence, we do not have an excuse to blame the British if something goes wrong; we cannot blame except us. And there is a great danger of something going wrong. Time is changing rapidly; there is always new thinking in the air and that affects our own people also. They are tired of government by the people. They need a government 'for the people' and they do not care whether it is a government of the people or by the people. If we really want to uphold the Constitution where we have tried to enshrine this principle of government of the people, for the people and by the people, then we must neither be slow nor be weak in our efforts to identify and eliminate the evil elements that stand in our way to entice people to choose the government for the people instead of the government by the people. This is the only way to serve the country. I don't know any other best way for it."

The above excerpt from Babasaheb's historic concluding discourse in the final meeting of the Constituent Assembly is everlasting; it contains the roadmap of how a nation can become great and reminds us of his contribution to the nation.

Babasaheb initially opposed the creation of a province on the basis of language because he feared that if the demon of linguistics infiltrated the already multi-caste society of India, the society would be further divided and the country would become weaker and that was not acceptable to him under any circumstances. Later, he wrote a dissertation, *Thoughts on Linguistics*, in which he wrote in support of the reconstruction of states on the basis of 'one state, one language': "The State is formed on the basis of intimacy with each other. Intimacy meant the spirit of oneness; the sense of inner closeness with one another. If that feeling is strongly present in people, then it seems that they are closely connected with each other and those who are outside are not ours. This feeling is called 'consciousness of kind'. On the one hand, such a feeling binds them closely together and gives them the power to rise above economic and other conflicts as well as social discrimination, but on the other hand, it creates a distance with outsiders (who do not speak their own language). The basic requirement of democracy is that the mutual intimacy between the people is stable."

He explained in this research that there was a need for one language to build the national spirit. He believed that this language had to be Hindi. He was very good in English, but his strong patriotism led him to favour Hindi as the lingua franca of the country. "There is no point that any regional language be the national language," he said. "The one national language of the country should be Hindi; however, the nation shall run by English until this situation (of accepting Hindi language) is created. Indians have to accept it. There will be a crisis in language-based states, if they do not accept it. Language nurtures culture and binds people. Since Indians are desirous to unite and to develop a common culture, their primary duty is to make and accept Hindi as the national language. Language-based states are an integral part of India. In such a situation, those who do not approve of the concept of Hindi as the national language, do not have any right to call themselves Indians. Such citizens may be 100 per cent

Maharashtrian or Tamilian or Gujarati, but cannot be Indian in its true sense; yes, s/he will be geographically an Indian."

"God seems to have laid a curse on India and Indians They shall always remain divided and they shall always be slaves," he said. By quoting this, Babasaheb challenged all the Indians to disprove the curse of God of creating small states on the basis of the same language and that such states should be given the freedom to solve their problems. He laid a special insistence on people developing themselves in a democratic way.

India is an ancient nation, but it is not an ancient State-nation according to our history. Our long history says that we were one nation with many states. There were many small kingdoms in existence in India during the period of the Mahabharata war or in the era of Gautam Buddha. A state called India came to existence in 1947. The part which was under British rule became independent at that time. Babasaheb wished that the same could become a truly modern nation-state. Therefore, it is suitable to say that the concept of 'nation-state India' took birth in 1947. Babasaheb expressed his view on India becoming a nation of many states. India has cultural unity with diversity, but there was no social unity and consequently no political unity. That was the situation we had in 1947.

It was necessary to eradicate casteism in order to build social cohesion. The religious rules established against the backdrop of untouchability had to end. Article 17 of the Indian Constitution criminalises the practice of untouchability. Similarly, the Fundamental Rights clause guarantees no discrimination, equal opportunity for all, protection of all freedoms and equal treatment of all. Our society has traditionally adhered to social heterogeneity. As a citizen of the nation, Babasaheb gave every citizen an independent identity and the nation's guarantee of protection of his rights was established. The basic premise behind this was that a citizen should abide by the law of the land and the freedom to control all these transactions could not be given to any religious leader. Babasaheb made a uniform law for all Hindus. His wish was to make common laws for all citizens, but that was not possible at that time. A uniform civil law strengthens nationalism.

Babasaheb has given citizenship to all Indians while

developing the concept of India. The judiciary is the same. Everyone has the same civil rights. Theoretically, he has abolished the monopoly of those who rule by tradition and dynasty. Although it is not reflected in practice, there is no legal impediment to its elimination. As a result, the monopoly will end as people become socially and politically literate.

Babasaheb has a profound knowledge of the nature of Indians and the Indian psyche does not accept fundamentalism. Granville Austin has beautifully commented on this in his book, on p. 396. He said, "The most notable characteristic in every field of Indian activity... is the constant attempt to reconcile conflicting views or actions, to discover a workable compromise, to avoid seeing the human situation in terms of all black or all white...As India's philosopher Vice President (now President) Sarvapalli Radhakrishnan has put it: 'Why look at things in terms of this or that? Why not try to have both this and that'?"

Today, after 70 years, every citizen of India has easily got two types of identity. His first identity is of his state and then his second identity is as an Indian. Whenever there is a rift between the two identities, the feeling of 'I am Indian first' comes to the surface. Natural calamities and disasters are clear examples of display of such feelings. The feeling that 'disaster has befallen my country' inspires them to help their fellowmen. The feeling of patriotism is felt throughout all the citizens of the country when a soldier is martyred on the country's border. Similarly, everyone react with the same anguish to *jehadi* terrorist attack anywhere in India. This is an emotional element of the concept of nationalism and we are moving strongly towards this concept. The *mantra* 'first an Indian, then an Indian and finally an Indian' was given by Babasaheb and we are moving ahead towards the same in this 21st century. Undoubtedly, the credit to achieve the 'one nation' concept of India should be given to Babasaheb.

□

16

Dr. Babasaheb and RSS—Friends or Foes

Despite being two different entities and contrary to the general view that Babasaheb Ambedkar was opposed to the Rashtriya Swayamsevak Sangh (when he had publicly burnt a copy of the *Manusmriti* which favours the Brahmins), their goals, dreams and aspirations were almost similar, especially on the following 22 points:

1. Nation first and supreme priority.
2. This is an ancient 'Hindu' nation.
3. Formation of a casteless Hindu society.
4. A society based on equality, harmony and brotherhood.
5. Cultural integration of India.
6. Nation's downfall because of sectarianism and treachery.
7. Untouchability is a sin, a perversion.
8. Strong belief in democracy–humanity.
9. Service and upliftment of the exploited and victims of the caste system.
10. Views of Hinduism are best but not put into practice.
11. Theory of Aryan invasion is false and perpetrated by the British to serve personal gains.
12. '*Roti*' and '*beti padhao*' (meal and women's education) of prime importance.
13. Anything in scriptures that nurtures casteism is unacceptable.

14. Sanskrit should be the language of the nation.
15. The 'saffron flag' should be the national flag of the Independent India.
16. Religion is not just a ritual or a method of worship; it's the path leading of human welfare.
17. Importance of character, Morality and Personality development.
18. *Chaturvarna* system is unacceptable.
19. It is a national task to unite Hindus'.
20. Babasaheb established the Samaj Samata Sangh in order to propagate social equality, the RSS founded the Samajik Samrasata Manch for fulfilling the same objective.
21. Casteism stratification creates divisions in Hindu society, adversely affecting the spirit of nationalism.
22. Let India become the best.

A study of Dr. Ambedkar's life philosophy, work and views indicate that his goal, aspirations and objectives were similar to those of the RSS (Rashtriya Swayamsevak Sangh). He was conscious of the work and philosophy of the RSS, kept in constant touch with the RSS *swayamsevaks* (volunteers) and held frequent discussions with them. He held clear views about the Sangh and had realised that only the RSS who fulfil his dream of a single *varna* (hierarchical caste system) system instead of the *chaturvarna,* that Sangh's activities were in the interest of the nation and the Hindu community as a whole, and that only the RSS could destroy the social evil for establishing a harmonious Hindu society. However, he was sceptical about the scope and speed of the Sangh's growth and therefore advised the latter to expand further. He also knew that there was a wide gap between some other pro-Hindu organisations and the Sangh to understand which, it is necessary to analyse Dr. Babasaheb Ambedkar and the Sangh's contributions..

The Hindu Mahasabha was another major Hindu organisation which was working to unite the Hindu society at the time, but unfortunately Babasaheb Ambedakar's views about them were farm from complimentary. He knew that the leaders of the Hindu Mahasabha favoured unity among all the Hindus but, without destroying the caste system and caste differences. Only a few exceptional leaders like Bhai Paramanand, Lala Lajpat Rai, Veer Savarkar were appreciative of Babasaheb's work. However, Babasaheb was aware that these leaders had no hold over the minds of the high-caste Hindus and their religious leaders. Babasaheb was also sceptical about the sincerity of the leaders of the Hindu Mahasabha.

Crystal clear Ideas about Hindutva and Hindu Organisation

Babasaheb was absolutely conscious about the importance of unity among the Hindus and made it clear that despite his and his followers' conversion from Hinduism to Buddhism, he would work towards uniting the Hindus of the nation. Dr. Keshav Baliram Hedgewar was the great personality who prioritised unity among the Hindus. He didn't resort to any propaganda but adopted grass-root methods for uniting the Hindu society. He created a small replica of a caste-free and class-free egalitarian society in the form of establishing the RSS. He used to proclaim that social harmony cannot be built from a system that has not been adopted by anyone till date, on the basis of psychology; only hope for bringing about social equality was through social harmony.

In a speech in Delhi on 25 November, 1947, he said, "It is our fault that we do not have brotherhood in our conduct. We Indians are brothers to each other. If there is one element that infuses unity in social life, it is brotherhood. Bringing this brotherhood into practice in our daily lives is a difficult but necessary task. There are many different castes in India and that is destroying the idea of a nation. The first reason is that castes produce isolation in social life. The second reason is that it produces mutual hatred, contempt and jealousy. If we want to stand united as a nation, we have to remove all these obstacles from our path because brotherhood can only arise where a nation exists. How can there be equality and freedom without brotherhood?" In the resolution prepared for the meeting, he said, "The aim is to build equality and unity within the untouchables and the touchables; even if they don't know about it, but there is an idea of social harmony. In the same way, social equality is ingrained in the minds of those who fully insist on social harmony. The difference is just to emphasise.

What social egalitarians know as social convergence also requires social harmony."

Dr. Ambedkar and Dr. Hedgewar took different paths because their starting points were different. Dr. Hedgewar's view was based on emotions to build a mindset of social harmony in the whole society.

'Look at the condition of our large nation and what was the condition of a small nation like Japan. Today the same Japan has progressed and made its place among the major nations of the world. The artificial casteism that exists in Hindustan today also existed there, but the people of the higher 'Samurai' caste gave up their racial seniority and made their ignorant and miserable brethren knowledgeable and happy. Acquiring love in this way, they created a new national spirit of ownership in them, which became a reason for the advancement of their motherland.'

—(*Mooknayak* magazine, Issue 15, 28 August, 1920)

Dr. Babasaheb Ambedkar's inclination towards the Rashtriya Swayamsevak Sangh was well known. He knew that only the Sangh could realise his dream of creating a casteless society. He never criticised the Sangh over the issue of casteism or on the issues of the Dalits except once in the Rajya Sabha, where he mentioned the name of RSS instead of Jana Sangh, and that too in reference to communalism. (Although it is quite possible that the sagacious great man like Babasaheb Ambedkar, knowing the working style of the Sangh and the Jana Sangh, may not have said 'RSS' instead of 'Jana Sangh'; it must be the copywriter of this volume who must have deliberately inserted the word 'RSS' instead of 'Jana Sangh'.) At this very time, he also criticised the Akali Dal, but never believed that the Sangh subscribed to casteism.

It is well-known that only RSS can build an egalitarian and fraternal society. Babasaheb also had the same viewpoint and that is why he attended the Sangh camp and stayed overnight at one of the Sangh officials' place in Badlapur, Maharashtra. The very fact that he visited the Sangh camp was described by a follower of Dr. Babasaheb and who was the leader of the Scheduled Caste Federation and a Member of Parliament during the second Lok Sabha session (1957-1962). His name was Dr. Balasaheb Salunke, who was the only elected MP from Scheduled Caste Federation. In his diary, Balasaheb had written on the page 25 of his book that on Babasaheb's visit to Poona on 19 August, 1939, a meeting took place between Dr. Babasaheb and Dr. Hedgewar, the founder of the RSS at Bhausaheb Gadkari's bungalow. Thereafter, Bhausaheb Abhyankar, Balasaheb Salunke and others paid a visit to the Swayamsevak camp organised at Bhave School, where Babasaheb gave a talk on 'military discipline and organisation'.

Dr. Babasaheb Ambedkar also had great respect for Dr. Hedgewar, on whose death, he published an obituary paying tribute in his *Janata* magazine in June 1940. He wrote: "Dr. K.B. Hedgewar, the founder of the Rashtriya Swayamsevak Sangh met with a tragic death due to high blood pressure on the date 21.06.1940. He was fifty-one when he died. He has set up more than seven hundred *shakhas* of the Rashtriya Swayamsevak Sangh and has about one-and-a-half lakh registered Swayamsevaks. His demise is a loss of a great and zealous Hindu leader of Nagpur." (*Janata*, 28 June, 1940).

Dr. Ambedkar was steeped in patriotism and he also knew that the Sangh was an organisation dedicated to patriotism. That is why he said in his book, *Annihilation of Caste* that 'working for a Hindu organisation is a national task'. He dreamt of single *varna* society which could come true only by uniting all the Hindus, where the spirit of brotherhood flowed flawlessly, 'but, that requires action; not only words'.

"We should become the ideal soldiers of the country a part of our duty. Our glory should resonate not only in India, but in the world. A sense of virtue and equality should be within us."

—(speech at the Samata Sainik Dal Conference held in Mumbai on 8 February, 1939)

The ideal of harmonious social life set by Dr. Hedgewar by founding the RSS was based on Hindu unity. The united Hindu society meant unity in Hindu society on the basis of equal faith and equal values of life by destroying social inequality in Hindu society. That is why Dr. Ambedkar said that 'uniting a Hindu is a national task'. Secondly, Dr. Ambedkar, while presenting the aim behind organising the Mahad *satyagraha*, was: 'elimination of untouchability which is a national task.' Thus, in the light of Dr. Ambedkar's ideology, the Sangh is engaged in uniting the Hindus.

Progress through Harmony

Unity and heterogeneity are two opposites. A system based on casteism creates social inequality and this is not suitable for creating a united Hindu organisation. One whose mind is engrossed in the distorted mentality of casteism, he can never unite the Hindus. Patriotism means unity in the whole society. The goal of the RSS is to take the nation towards prosperity by building a united, egalitarian and harmonious social power, where social discrimination or inequality in the society are simply out of question. The splendour and security of the nation is possible only where exists a harmonious society.

Babasaheb Ambedkar also believed that if one part of the society was weak then it would be detrimental for the entire Hindu society and the nation as well; only a harmonious society could make the Hindu society stronger. He therefore wrote in the very first issue of his magazine *Mooknayak*: "Development cannot take place if one caste is oppressed; other castes would also ave to experience that damage. Society as a whole is like a boat in the middle of the sea. If a passenger travelling in a boat makes a hole in the boat with the intention to harm other passengers due to his suicidal nature, sooner or later he also must drown with all his fellow passengers. Similarly, harming one caste is akin to harming the society." The RSS placed the goal of a harmonious Hindu society in front of all the Hindus. Dr. Hedgewar, through the Rashtriya Swayamsevak Sangh, eradicated the distorted mentality from the minds of millions of Hindus through an innovative concept of *shakha*. To work for the Sangh does not require revealing one's caste identity; just being a Hindu is enough. Dr. Hedgewar was able to perform such a miracle through the Sangh *shakhas* because he never uttered a word of criticism against casteism, the *varna* system, etc. He was not concerned with such systems; he gave only one identity to every Hindu and that was the word 'Hindu' without identification of one's caste. He awakened the identity as a Hindu among the Swayamsevaks and as a result, Hindu brotherhood was established. The kind of *bandhutva*, brotherhood, that Babasaheb Ambedkar wanted in Hindu society, the Sangh, through its *shakhas*, created the same feeling of brotherhood among the Swayamsevaks of the RSS. Swayamsevaks used to hail Mother India by saying

'*Bharat Mata ki Jai*' in unison at the Sangh *shakhas*. This meant that by removing our internal vices and protecting our national pride, we can make India all-encompassing, prosperous and harmonious, elevating it to the highest peak. The only resolution of the Sangh was: '*Param vaibhav netumetat swarashtram*'–to unite Hindus to take our great nation to the ultimate glory.

"The principle of linguistic region formation is correct. But it is my sincere opinion that implementing it will be detrimental to the country. If there is one thing that is lacking in this country, it is the national spirit. There are several reasons why nationalism could not be established in this country. One of the main causes is the many languages of the country. And the origin of nationalism is impossible until this cause is destroyed. The creation of territories on the basis of language is a blow to the spirit of unity. It is imperative to make efforts to have a single language of the entire nation instead of creating a region according to language. I firmly believe that this is in the interest of the nation."

—(18 January, 1929, *Bahishkrit Bharat* editorial)

The work stated by the two doctors, Dr. Babasaheb Ambedkar and Dr. Keshav Baliram Hedgewar proved effective in diagnosing the 'social diseases'. Both of them suggested the right prognosis and treatment for the disease by making correct diagnosis. The goal of their life's work was same – the resurgence of Hindu society through unity, which was on the brink of collapse. Importantly, both were born at the two extreme ends of a distorted view of casteism. Dr. Hedgewar was born into a Vedapathi Purohit family while Dr. Ambedkar was born into an untouchable family. Both began their lives in extreme poverty, deprivation and hardship. Dr. Ambedkar was humiliated by the social stigma of poverty as well as untouchability. The two doctors however, agreed on one thing and that was the upliftment of Indian society which was not possible as long as the British remained in power. At the first round table conference of 1930, Dr. Ambedkar told the British in no uncertain terms: "The untouchables of India also want the government elected by the people and for the people instead of the present British government. Dalits will not be liberated from injustice as long as there is a British government in power. Has the

British government done anything to eradicate untouchability? Has it given us the right to draw water from a public well? Can we visit the temples today? Does the British government recruit us into the police? Do they recruit us in the Army? Injustice with us is still there; its wounds are not healed. Even after a hundred and fifty years of British rule, it (British rule) has made no effort to remove (the injustices)." He declared: "We want a government where the person in power is dedicated to the best interests of the country; one who can accurately estimate where obedience ends and the resistance begins and who does not hesitate at all to change such socio-economic rules. Given the demands of social justice and time, such rules have to be changed."

No Hatred; simply National Interest

"If my mind was full of hatred and revenge, I would have wreaked havoc in this country in just five years," Babasaheb replied to those who used to say, "Dr. Babasaheb's movement is based on hatred". Since he thought only of national interest, he was not capable of creating social chaos in the country. Instead, he presented his ideas as well as his programmes to remove social vices prevailing in the Hindu society and make Hindu society united and harmonious. A writer, Dhananjay Keer, has said in his book, *Dr. Babasaheb Ambedkar*, that every movement of Babasaheb was intended for the revival of the Hindu society. He further writes: "That is why the wise citizens believed that the life of Babasaheb is an important link in the revival and the transformation of Hindu society and they described Ambedkar as a great reformist Hindu leader." He has written even more clearly in his treatise, by describing the chronology of reforms of Hindu society till date: "The *Upanishads* made the first revival, and thereafter Mahatma Buddha did the second revival of Hindu society. Third revival was done by the saints like Ramanuj, Chakradhar, Kabir, Ramanada, Nanak, Chaitanya and Gyandev. While, Raja Rammohan Roy, Mahatma Phule, Swami Dayanand, Justice Ranade, etc. revived the Hindu society for the fourth time and the fifth revival began with Dr. Ambedkar's movement."

Dhananjay Keer further writes: "The movement of Babasaheb Ambedkar marked the beginning of the fifth revival and reorganisation of the Hindu society. The revolt by Dr. Ambedkar against Hinduism and Hindu society was shocking like an earthquake. The form of this revolt was different from the form expressed by the revolutionaries right from the time of Lord Buddha to Savarkar. Babasaheb was the first such revolutionary leader during the past 2,500 years to be born in a downtrodden society. Not only did he revolt against the heterogeneous social structure of Hindu society and Hinduism, but he also started a revolution, unprecedented in the history of Hinduism. The motive behind this revolution was very high and great. Dr. Babasaheb's aim was to purify Hinduism, restructure it and bring about a revolution to prevent the degradation of Hindu society and Hinduism and loss of lives."

Dr. Babasaheb Ambedkar had constantly rebuked the society for this and warned against the practice but he never broke the rules.

Summary of Annihilation of Caste

He was scheduled to address the Jat-pat Todak Mandal (Association to Eradicate Caste System) in Lahore in 1936, but the organisers asked him to give the speech in writing prior to its delivery. The organisers found the speech very harsh and ultimately decided to cancel the programme. Dr. Babasaheb's discourse was then published in the form of his book, *Annihilation of Caste,* in which he gave some answers to pertinent questions raised by Mahatma Gandhi regarding this discourse in the 11 July, 1936 issue of *Harijan*. Saying that Mahatma Gandhi did not even touch on the questions posed by Dr. Babasaheb in his discourse, Babasaheb wrote: "The main point which I have tried to achieve in my speech is as follows:

- Caste has destroyed Hindus.
- Reorganisation of Hindu society on the basis of *chaturvarna* is impossible.
- Reorganising Hindu society on the basis of *chaturvarna* is detrimental as it degrades the oppressed people by denying them their right to knowledge and makes them weaker by depriving them of their right to bear arms.
- Hindu society should be restructured on the basis of theology in which equality, freedom and brotherhood are harmonised.

- In order to achieve this goal, the support of religion to casteism and the *varna* system must end.
- As soon as the belief that the scriptures are the voice of God is removed, the religious abode of caste and race would also cease."

Warning against the Mistakes of the Conservatives

An incident took place before the second Round Table Conference when some orthodox Hindus from Bengal sent a cable to a Muslim representative named Ghaznavi, who was attending the conference and requested him to support them (the orthodox Hindus) against the entry of Dalits into the temple and place their grievances before the council.

Dr. Ambedkar warned that the fact that orthodox Hindus had to approach Muslims for the protection of their religion posed a serious warning to the Hindu reformists. He did not approve of any arrangement that left the Dalit class at the mercy of some orthodox Hindus. Given the mentality of the common Hindu masses in those days, he did not believe that the Dalit class would ever get justice. That the incident occurred at the time of the second Round Table Conference indicates the direction in which his mind was working. He found that his speeches were being used by the British in support of the anti-Hindu demands of the Muslims. He quietly handed over a petition to Ramsay McDonald, then the chairman of the Round Table Conference and also to the Prime Minister of the United Kingdom. In this petition, he defended the Hindu interests against the Muslims.

However, critics did not hesitate to call Dr. Ambedkar an enemy of the Hindus, a destroyer of Hinduism, etc. He was condemned all over the country for standing against Gandhiji in the second Round Table Conference and demanding privileges for the Dalit class. Speaking at a rally in Pune a few days later, he said: "I am the most hated person in India today. I am defamed as a traitor, Hindu enemy, destroyer of Hindutva and enemy of the nation. However, I am confident that this storm will subside and future historians and the coming Hindu generations will congratulate me for my service to the nation when the work I have done will be fairly evaluated at the Round Table Conference."

Dr. Ambedkar was called anti-Brahmin, but when some non-Brahmin leaders in Maharashtra proposed non-participation of the Brahmins in the Mahad *satyagraha*, Dr. Ambedkar replied, "It is wrong to believe that all Brahmins are enemies of untouchables. My opposition is against Brahmanism, i.e. Brahmins who are engrossed in the mentality of higher and lower caste. It is because of this mentality, some human beings are considered untouchable and some people are given privileges which creates inequality. In my mind, a non-Brahmin with the mentality of higher and lower castes deserves to be despised and a Brahmin not only free from such feelings, but who does not lust for privileged rights, should be revered."

Dr. Ambedkar had staged peaceful *satyagraha* against the use of Mahad's Chavdar Lake only by upper-caste Hindus, when all others, like Muslims and Christians and even animals like dogs and cats, could use that water except for the untouchables who were alleged to render the water impure through their touch. The protests were also attended by thousands of people who had firsthand experience of World War I. A single outrageous command from the leader could have prompted a bloodbath at the Chavdar Lake, but the participants exhibited great discipline by obeying their leader. He certainly demanded rights of untouchables from the British government, but at the same time he also demanded freedom for India from the clutches of the British even in a louder voice. He was given a ministerial post in the cabinet of Independent India, though never harboured any fascination for such posts or positions and he soon forsook his Cabinet position. He, along with his three lakh followers, eventually converted from Hindu religion to Buddhism, but avoided every harm to the spirit of the nation. He said, while addressing a large function at the Deekshabhoomi in Nagpur, "I once told Gandhiji that I do not agree with you on the issue of untouchability, but I will choose the path that will be least harmful to the country in due course. Today, by embracing Buddhism, I am doing the greatest service to the country. Buddhism is an integral part of Indian culture. I have always taken care that the tradition and history of this land is not harmed by this conversion."

The Role of the Congress

It was Gandhiji who declared that the country's goal was to eradicate untouchability, but the Congress made it part of its programme. Dr. Babasaheb did not trust him over this issue. He made it clear to Gandhiji in a face-to-face meeting, "I don't believe that the Congress is honest about this. If they were really honest about it, then they would have made untouchability also a condition to become a member of Congress, just like the use of *khadi*. The one who does not have untouchables as servants at their homes, who doesn't take care of an untouchable student and doesn't take a meal with the untouchable at least once a week shall not become a member of the Congress. If such a condition had been placed, it would not have been possible to witness the ridiculous scenario where the president of the district Congress Committee opposes the entry of Dalits into temples."

Prevention of Untouchability: Route and Programme

A letter written by Dr. Ambedkar to Thakkar Bapa, who dedicated his life to the welfare of the Adivasis (tribals) has been included in Babasaheb's biography, suggests some ways and programmes to eradicate untouchability and so did Dr. Hedgewar. Surprisingly, many similarities are found in the programmes suggested by both these great men. The letter of Dr. Babasaheb was very long, so some excerpts are given below:

Dr. Babasaheb wrote: "There are two perspectives for the upliftment of the untouchables. The future of a Dalit society member person depends on his conduct. With this principle in mind, Dalit reformers have to work to build personal virtues amongst Dalits." Subsequently Babasaheb further wrote: "Activists of this ideology should start programmes to eliminate alcoholism, health prevention and co-operation issues as well as to establish schools and libraries." He emphasised eradication of untouchability: "The situation or constraint in which a person has to live his life is the situation responsible for the person's future. It is possible that the social environment around the person can be extremely hostile and difficult; that the environment will influence his/her future. The second point to work for the Dalit upliftment has been formulated on the basis of this principle." And then he adds, "The method shown in the first point is useful for personal development; it is effective for the society as a whole. It is necessary to change the situation around us for the development of the whole society and the second point is required for that change."

He was well aware that the mere acquisition of some constitutional rights would not solve the problem of untouchability. He wrote, in a letter to Thakkar Bapa, "Only law will not keep untouchables and upper-caste Hindus together. And that is also not possible through joint constituencies instead of separate constituencies. The only thing that will keep the two of them together is a conduct full of love. The liberation of Dalit society is possible only when the upper-caste Hindus will feel or when they experience that we have to change our behaviour (towards Dalits). I just want to revolutionise the mindset of the Hindus (as a whole)."

Babasaheb also stressed on celebration of all festivals together, "Even though Hindu festivals are similar, they do not create the sense of organisation as they are celebrated differently, based on different castes. When a person is made a partner in group activities, he/she feels that the success or failure of the group is his/her own success or failure and only then the internal relations between the people are strengthened and all this leads to a united society. Casteism prevents the celebration of such good programmes and for this reason, Hindus could not unite in the form of a society which has a united life and has its own identity."

Considering the reasons for the weakness, dependence and lack of self-confidence of the Hindu society, Dr. Hedgewar also came to the conclusion that in order to create harmony and intimacy in the Hindu society which was divided into many castes, creeds, languages, etc., various programmes were needed where one could participate equally without any discrimination. He founded a simple organisation system on the basis of *sangachchhadhvam, samvadadwam, sanvo manansi jayatam* as mentioned in the *Vedas*. He used to say, "We should treat every Hindu brother, whether he is of high or low caste, with equal intimacy. It is a great sin to despise any Hindu brother. At least the Sangh Swaymasevaks must not have this kind of narrow-mindedness within them. Our dealings with every Hindu who loves India should be like a brother. If our behaviour is ideal, then all Hindus will not be unattractive to us."

It is because of Hedgewar's introspective vision that from the very beginning of the Sangh activities, there has been no place for vulnerabilities, such as high and low and touchable and untouchable. That is why both Mahatma Gandhi and Babasaheb Ambedkar could not help but be impressed by the lack of untouchability in the Rashtriya Swayamsevak Sangh. Both these great men were fortunate enough to be present in the Sangh camps and witness the wonderful spectacle of love, equality and harmony. But, the Sangh never wanted this lack of untouchability to be confined only to the Sangh branches and Sangh camps. The Sangh wanted this problem to be removed from the entire society.

Purification of Goal and Setting the Target

Today, Some elements are trying hard to disintegrate and create rift in the society for their selfish and malign motives in the name of Dr. B.R. Ambedkar. They even do not hesitate to receive inspiration and resources from foreign countries and work as their pawns. In this context, Dr. Ambedkar's warning in the Constituent Assembly on 5 February, 1950 is worth considering. He said, "Over the centuries, slavery has resulted in some of the distortions that have arisen among us. We will not tolerate any foreign element trying to usurp our property by using it as a weapon. We will disappoint them for their aspirations. This is a matter of our home, so we will solve it by ourselves. It is not our desire just to get benefits or to get out of a state of social degradation. We will not be pawns in the hands of foreigners. We must be wary of the Jaichands (traitors) that emerge amidst us. We must properly recognise the interests of the nation and society we are a part of."

The Goal of both Dignitaries was One

The revolution that Dr. Babasaheb Ambedkar wanted to bring in the psyche of the Hindu society was the same as that in Dr. Hedgewar's mind. Dr. Hedgewar, like Dr. Ambedkar, desired to create a harmonious and united Hindu society which was free from the feeling of high/low rank, untouchability, etc. Keeping this as a sole goal, i.e. unite the entire Hindu society, Dr. Keshav Baliram Hedgewar started that the Rashtriya Swayamsevak Sangh did not work only for one class just to eradicate untouchability; but the tradition of untouchability to be eliminated naturally and that the new feeling of unity must become a practice. His dream was to create a Hindu society that would end wrong customs and discrimination of high/low prevalent in Hindu society. He wanted to bring the scattered castes of the Hindu community under a broader umbrella of united Hindu society. To unite Hindus meant eradication of the perversions of caste and race from their minds and to make them think that they were components of a united Hindu society. His aspiration was to unite Hindu society with the sentiment of 'I am a Hindu' instead of taking pride in individual castes. He always gave a positive message to the Sangh volunteers, "We all are brothers; we want to establish unified life in this country; we need to be powerful." Social conflict or negative thoughts can never create harmony. Great men like him, who wanted to unite the society, would never support social conflicts and with these ideas at the centre, the Sangh, in its nine-decade old history, has never launched a single campaign which shall create social conflict.

This does not mean that the R.S.S. did not want to change the mindset of the Hindu community, which considered untouchability a part of religion and so kept the untouchables suppressed. The Sangh has a unique vision to unite the entire Hindu society and shun all social vices. The Sangh never thought of the Hindus as belonging to a single caste or class or that the Hindus belonged to any one region. Dr. Hedgewar considered the entire Hindu community, from Kashmir to Kanyakumari and from Kutch to Kamrup as one social group.

Sangh's Unique Vision for Unification

The social problems of Hindu society can be found all over the country. The stigma of untouchability is also nationwide. So, a nationwide organisation is needed to solve the nationwide problem and for this, such dedicated volunteers have to be created who consider the Hindu unity as their life-goal before serving from every corner of the country. These volunteers should awaken the spirit of brotherhood in Hindu society and form a nationwide organisation. Dr. Hedgewar began his work of the RSS with this central theme in his mind. He sent extremely dutiful, dedicated young volunteers across the country to work for the Hindu organisation.

Madhavrao Mule went to Punjab, Balasaheb Deoaras went to Bengal, Bhaurao Deoaras took charge of Uttar Pradesh, while Dadarao Parmarth took over Tamil Nadu. Shivram Pant Joglekar also actively joined the Sangh. These are just a few leading names. Hundreds of such young enthusiasts left their homes to work for the Sangh with dedication. Dr. Hedgewar urged many students to go to other regions for their education in order to spread the Sangh's message in that region. The base of his work was that it was not possible to deal with nationwide problems without building a nationwide organisation.

Who is really Responsible for the Evils Prevalent in Hindu Society?

Hinduism is always blamed for the vices present in Hindu society, but that is also true. When we observe superficially the many customs and traditions observed as a part of the religion, untouchability too is considered as a part of religion. Thus, social reforms and Hindu unity are not possible without a true understanding of Hindutva.

The belief that things written in the scriptures thousands of years ago must be followed religiously is utterly ridiculous. It is in the best interest of the society to give up many things that are not relevant to the times. Superstitions, outdated customs, etc. are obstacles to the unification and progress of the society. Great men, like Maharshi Dayanand Saraswati, Swami Vivekananda, Sri Aurobindo, Mahatma Jyotiba Phule, Mahatma Gandhi, Swatantryaveer Savarkar, Dr. Babasaheb Ambedkar, etc. made every effort to reform the religion. Swami Dayanand Saraswati made a logical attack on false traditions by saying that Vedanta was our religion; Swami Vivekananda preached the Advaita philosophy; Veer Savarkar insisted on looking at religion on the basis of merit and intellect, while Dr. Babasaheb's insisted on curbing discrimination on the basis of religion. He converted to Buddhism because the process of reformation was very slow and every change, big or small, takes time.

Religion is of paramount importance in the prevailing beliefs in Hindu society. If we study carefully, it seems that Dr. Hedgewar's path was different from other reformers but one thing that was common was that a reformist should be in deep love with his/her own religion. It is impossible to make improvements without this deep love for one's religion. And at the same time, if one who has an attitude of denial or desire to sabotage the religion, it can never bring reforms. Hindu society can be transformed by attacking abhorrent, perverted norms or by abandoning Hinduism and creating a new creed within it; it is also possible to bring transformation by simply accepting the word 'Hindu' or by abandoning relationships with Hindu theology. Which of these remedies was the appropiate way according to Dr. Hedgewar?

Here Dr. Hedgewar's vision must be examined on the basis of his work in the RSS. He had immense love and devotion for Hinduism and Hindu culture. He had said, "The goal of the Sangh is to protect our religion, society and culture. Some may think that hatred towards another religion is to protect one's own religion, but I don't understand how hating another religion can protect one's religion. There is no question of sectarianism or caste discrimination in the working of the Sangh. The Sangh thinks in unison with the entire Hindu community." Speaking about Hinduism, he said, "We Hindus are religious, we are proud of it, but we do not know the difference between protection of religion and observance of religion. Those who want to revive religion should have the power to resist the attack on religion...This country is known as 'Hindustan'. Hindutva is the life-blood of this nation; so the only wish of the Sangh is that the responsibility for the protection of this culture should be borne entirely by the Hindus."

Dr. Hedgewar's attitude becomes abundantly clear from his remarks on Hinduism and Hindu culture and the goal of the Sangh, but the question that arises is as to which part of religion is to be protected? There are two distinct parts of religion – one is the eternal philosophy of religion and the other is the actual practice of religion. If we consider the situation at the time when Dr. Hedgewar started the Sangh, it will be noticed that there were many vices in the practice of Hinduism. Did he advocate practice of such outdated religious practices? The very clear answer to this is, 'NO'.

Everyone in the Sangh is Identified as a Hindu

Dr. Hedgewar was not fond of outdated norms and practices of Hindu society. He himself broke many such norms through his own dealings. He neither believed in untouchability nor practiced caste discrimination. Sangh was open to every caste in Hinduism; there were no caste barriers on the Sangh; its *shakhas* and meeting were open to all Hindus. Doctor used to go to every Swayamsevak's home and have meals with them. He also invited many of them to his home for a meal. There was no such thing as discrimination in his life. Sangh camps were true examples of Hindu unity because people from every walk and every caste of Hindu society lived together and took their meals together. A new Swayamsevak once got annoyed when he saw such practices in a camp at Sangli. He complained to Dr. Hedgewar, "Doctor, what have you started?" Dr. Hedgewar replied, "Why? What am I doing?" The Swayamsevak said, "What kind of mess are you making here?" But Dr. Hedgewar's concept was different.

Dr. Hedgewar never deliberately planned a mass meal to break the wall of caste discrimination, but the mass meal was as natural as a family meal in the RSS. He created a natural arrangement for such natural meals to continue in future too. He did not stop just by saying, "Untouchability is bad; it should be eliminated"; instead he gave the highest importance to the conduct of the person. He said, "We are all Hindus, so we are bound to get it into practice (elimination of untouchability). There is a philosophical aspect of such practice. That is, a unified idea about the whole Hindu society. This is our Mother India; we are all her sons, so naturally we are brothers (and sisters) to each other." He laid the foundation of the Hindu organisation with this idea. (I remember when working for *Organiser* weekly, RSS was not called a Hindu organisation because many Muslim men and women visited the office with their problems. RSS is neither a political party but a social organisation of volunteers. I think that calling it a Hindu organisation would be wrong particularly in the light of what Mohan Bhagwat recently said to set the Muslim minds at rest.)

Historical Heroes cannot be Divinities

Dr. Hedgewar was also against establishing and worshipping of any human being as a god. Some events in his life in this regard are worth mentioning. Once he visited the princely state of Aundh, where he was well acquainted with the Rajasaheb, the ruler of Aundh. Rajasaheb took him to a painting exhibition, where a picture of Jijabai, Shivaji Maharaj's mother was painted to show that Lord Shiva had taken birth in the form of Shivaji Maharaj to Jijabai. He was upset at this portrayal and remarked, "It is true that Shivaji Maharaj was a great hero, but there is no point in making him divine. By doing this, we find an easy way to become inactive."

He also got upset when he noticed a picture of Lokmanya Tilak in divine form with four hands holding divine articles like the conch, the *chakra*, a hammer and a lotus. He was saddened to see that they had placed Lokmanya Tilak as god instead of adopting his virtues. By placing any great man in the place of God, one tries to place the responsibility of one's protection and salvation on him. Hindu society has been severely damaged by such an attitude.

There was a third similar occurrence when Dr. Hedgewar asked a gentleman who was reciting the *Ramayana* daily, "If you read the *Ramayana* every day, will you be imitating its virtues too?" The said gentleman got livid at Dr. Hedgewar and replied angrily, "Rama was God; how can we imitate his qualities? One should read the *Ramayana* for its merit." By citing such examples Dr. Hedgewar used to guide the Swayamsevaks, "The belief in moulding great personalities into the image of God is indeed very strange! Whenever a great person appears, place him in the shrine. Worship him with sincerity, but do not imitate his virtues! Hindus have learned this wonderful art of avoiding responsibility!" Dr. Hedgewar believed that the practice of religion should change over time. He never criticised the theology, scriptures, or the religious practices of the people to bring about a change; his approach was positive. He wanted to strengthen the self-reliance of Hindu society.

He was very annoyed with the critics of Hindu society. Once a young doctor from Amravati came to a regular meeting of Dr. Hedgewar's. During the discussion, the young man remarked, "Our Hindu society is the worst and most degenerate society in the world. Why are you organising it?" Hedgewar became furious and shouted, "People like you, who do nothing for a degenerate society but above that, attack it shamelessly, are the most disgraceful in this society." Such occasions did arise, but thereafter for several days he used to repent for his anger at them.

It is not possible to arouse the society from its lethargy by insulting it. Repeated negative statements, like 'we are weak, depraved, worthless people'; 'that our religious practices are wild', do not motivate us to defend religion. Appropriate positive stories only can evoke regeneration of the society.

Even today, self-esteem-provoking songs, like '*Ame putro amrut na...*' (we are sons of nectar) and '*Manushya tu bada mahan hai...*' (human, you are great) are sung in the Sangh program,es. It is actually the belief in many human beings and society that such songs create a positive atmosphere and produce positive vibes. We, in India, have an eternal way of reforming religion. Perversion in religion had occurred even earlier, but, there has been a great tradition of reforming the religion from the times of Buddha, Shankaracharya, Madhavacharya, Vallabhacharya, Maharshi Dayanand, Tukaram to Swami Vivekananda.

Dr. Hedgewar convinced his Swayamsevaks effectively by saying, "Today's epoch-making religion is the social religion; it is the national religion to free ordinary Hindus trapped in the shackles of religious orthodoxy, both individually and in the family.' He inculcated the feeling that 'serving the community is the service of God' in the minds of the Swayamsevaks. These Swayamsevaks rightly consider that 'the land of India is my abode' which stretches from Kashmir to Kanyakumari and from Kutch to Kamrup. They are emotionally connected with the Hindu society and with all their countrymen as a whole. So they don't need any command to run for help when Morbi is flooded or if a storm arises in Andhra Pradesh, or an earthquake occurs in Killari or Gujarat or if a plane crashes at Charkhi Dadri. Such calamities are taken as vagaries of weather or as malfunctioning of machines. This is the result of the feeling of social service that Dr. Hedgewar had awakened within them through the Sangh.

It is not possible to change people's religious practices by traumatising their thoughts and beliefs. This was a method adopted by Martin Luther King, but it is not possible to reform religion in India because people's religious life is closely connected with their social and national lives. Any reformation in religion is possible only by explaining the appropriate meaning of religion according to today's age and for that, Dr. Hedgewar envisaged a nationwide social organisation where the Sangh Swayamsevaks could be self-motivated, self-aware and self-governing. Results are bound to come in every sphere of life if such a nationwide organisation of patriotic volunteers is constituted. The broader meaning of Dr. Hedgewar's statement that 'the only solution for all the problems of Hindu society is the Hindu organisation' comes to force in different ways–that he did not start the Sangh for the reformation of religion, but as a natural consequence of the Sangh's role in it.

"The country is divided into about 4,000 castes. There are also casteism, provincialism, religious discrimination and hundreds of other conflicting issues, which keep the country unorganised. It is difficult to imagine that India will ever be united as long as there are such separatist forces."

—(Samata Sainik Dal meeting, presidential speech, Damodar Hall, Parel, Mumbai, 8 November, 1936)

What could be the Form of Reformation of a Religion?

It was a historical moment when the Vishwa Hindu Parishad (Global Hindu Committee) was constituted in 1964 at the Sandipani Ashram in Powai, Mumbai through sustained efforts of Guruji or Guru Golwalkar, the second Sarsanghchalak (president) of Rashtriya Swayamsevak Sangh. It was the first time in the history of 1,000 years that all religious leaders and reverend personalities of Hinduism had come together on one platform. They came from all walks of life and sects of Hinduism including Master Tara Singh, saint Tukdoji Maharaj, Swami Chinmayanand, Muni Sushilkumar, etc. at the establishment of Vishwa Hindu Parishad. It had been constituted as a great challenge to define religion in an age-appropriate manner. The first convention of the Vishwa Hindu Parishad was held in 1966 at Prayag. This was a revolutionary event in the history of Hindu society when religious leaders of every hue and colour came to one platform. Suryanarayana Rao, the All India officer of RSS, wrote a beautiful article describing the historical role of Guruji on the issue of untouchability and conversion. Here is an important part of this article which will help us to understand how Dr. Hedgewar's idea of religious reformation came alive through the efforts of

Guruji. "Dr. Keshav Baliram Hedgewar founded the Rashtriya Swayamsevak Sangh to free the Hindu society from all kinds of vices. He advised Swayamsevaks to identify all compatriots as 'Hindus', to leave aside the discriminations like different methods of worship, language, class etc. The Sangh believes in no caste and the Swayamsevaks do not believe in untouchability, but the Hindus outside the Sangh are victims of the norms that had prevailed for centuries. Although adhering to untouchability is a crime in the eyes of law after Independence, this bad tradition has not ended. Christians and Muslims have taken full advantage of this situation."

Guruji had done a very deep study of untouchability and conversion. He found that Hindus in general were religious and followed untouchability with religious spirit. Now, what was required was to involve religious leaders to reverse the process, i.e. to eliminate untouchability. It was Guruji's analysis that it required the involvement of leaders, who led the Hindu way of life and religion. The Vishwa Hindu Parishad was established in 1964 with this central idea and inspiration from Guruji. Such a platform was needed to bring the different forms of worship of the Hindu society and the heads of different castes to one platform and to think in terms of the whole Hindu society being 'one family'.

Conversion and Repatriation

The first national convention of the Vishwa Hindu Parishad was held at Triveni Sangam in 1966 at Prayag. About 50 thousand representatives from all sections of Hindu society and from all parts of the country, *dharmacharyas*, *jagadgurus*, *mahamandaleshwars*, etc. participated in it. Considering that this was the best occasion to think about the issues confronting the country, Guruji wanted the issue of conversion to be taken up by drawing up a plan to bring back those who had left Hinduism and converted to Christianity or Islam. Many speeches were delivered on this subject and a resolution was also passed. All religious barriers were to be removed if a decision was taken to bring back those who had converted from Hinduism to other religions. All the delegates strongly supported the resolution, but Jagadguru Shankaracharya of the Govardhanpeeth at Puri vehemently opposed the resolution. He said, "According to our scriptures, once a person goes to another religion, he becomes corrupt and therefore he is subject to exclusion. No one can go against the scriptures."

Guruji himself held a meeting with Shankaracharya and discussed the issue with him in detail. He explained to Shankaracharya what could be the deadly consequences for the Hindu society and the country if there was such a feeling for the Hindus who had gone to other religions and added, "Partition of the country, Kashmir problem, declining population of Hindu society, shrinking Hindu land, rise in anti-national activities – one prime reason behind all these incidences is conversion from Hinduism. The enemies of our country and culture are using the people who have left Hinduism as a weapon." Jagadguru realised the seriousness of the issue and thought that since he had strongly opposed the resolution, how could he retract from it now? Guruji explained to him and finally it was decided to present the seriousness of this issue to the representatives by Jagadguru himself.

So, the convention became curious when Jagadguru got up to deliver his speech the next day. He said that people were being exploited due to ignorance and poverty and taking to conversion. He clarified, "It is like stealing someone's money. The truth is that it does not belong to the thief; it belongs to someone else. Similarly, those Christians and Muslims who have been converted by exploitation are a component of Hindu society. They have been stolen away because of their ignorance; all these converted people are originally native Hindus. Just as there is no crime in getting back the stolen money, similarly there is no problem in getting our Hindu brothers back to Hindu society. Those who return to their home-religion should be happily welcomed."

This speech of Shankaracharyaji was greeted with loud applause. Everyone was happy. The resolution on the referendum was passed unanimously. Jagadguru Madhavacharya Panjavar Swami of Udupi declared: "*Na Hindu: patito bhavet*" – Hindus can never be corrupted.

It was decided that those returning to the fold of Hinduism should be welcomed by the religious leaders and blessed. Thus, the biggest obstacle to bringing back Hindus to their original religion was removed by the saints of Hinduism. This became possible only due to the untiring efforts of Shri Guruji.

"It is natural for Muslims in India to have a penchant for Muslim culture. This tendency is so strong that their goal is to spread Muslim culture and form a union of Muslim nations to bring non-Muslim (infidel) nations under their dominion. Because of such ideas, I feel that it is a mistake to think that a Muslim whose feet are in India but eyes are fixed on Turkey or Afghanistan, those who have no pride for their own country and no sense of belonging to their close compatriots will defend Hindustan against invasions by foreigner Muslims."

—(18 January, 1929, *Bahishkrit Bharat*, editorial)

The convention of the Karnataka branch of the Vishwa Hindu Parishad was held in Udupi, in December 1969 and received an overwhelming response. About 1,500 delegates came from 1,200 locations. Presidents of 40 different sects, namely Shaivite, Vaishnavite, Lingayat, Jain, Buddhist and Sikh were present at the convention.

Guruji felt that this was an opportunity to announce publicly that the practice of untouchability prevalent in Hindu society shall not be acceptable. He called on all religious leaders before the convention began and urged them to guide Hindu community in this regard. Thereafter, Jagadguru Mahamandleshwar Acharya and Muniji issued a statement with their signatures: "Following the goal of Vishwa Hindu Parishad to unite the Hindu society, impenetrable unity should be created in the entire Hindu society. Vices like untouchability create rifts in the society. That is why all Hindus in the world should have a spirit of unity, harmony and equality."

The same topic was first taken up for discussion after the opening session. The session was chaired by a retired IAS officer and member of the Public Service Commission of Karnataka state, Shri R. Bharanaiya. He was born into a so-called untouchable caste. After the sermons, he presented the resolution to the council: "Considering the guidance given by the Dharmagurus (religious gurus) and *acharyas* (clergies), this council calls upon all Hindus to renounce the spirits of discrimination like high/

low, untouchability, etc. Hindus should be treated religiously and socially with the same spirit of Hindu brotherhood, without any distinction of caste, creed, birth, etc..."

As soon as the resolution was introduced, the delegates welcomed it with loud applause. The clergy, seated on the podium, heartily blessed the resolution. It was a golden moment in the pages of history. "We are all going through a great historical moment," declared Panjawar Swamiji of Hindavah Sodaraha Survey. "All the Hindus are brothers and sisters. Religion or theology has nothing to do with all the perverted norms prevalent in Hindu society today." Mr. Bharnaiya was supposed to be present at the conference for only one day, but looking at the enthusiastic atmosphere, he changed his programme and was present at the conference full time.

Shri Guruji gave his speech on the last day of the convention to appeal, "Now our religious leaders have ordered us to renounce untouchability, so it is our prime duty to carry this order into our lives. We must all consider those who follow our religion and culture as our 'brothers'. Do not look at a person's caste and creed. We shall ignore the divisive issues in the society and focus only on strengthening the unity of the Hindu society; this way we can create everlasting unity and harmony. That is what has been my experience at Rashtriya Swayamsevak Sangh. Adherence to such rules does not create the slightest segregation or antagonism in the Sangh in matters of caste, creed, language, etc."

At the time of closing of convention, one by one, all the speakers and religious leaders came down from the stage, but Mr. Bharanaiya was so overcome with emotions that he forgot everything else, and remained seated on the podium. Someone had to remind him that the programme was over. As soon as he came down, he hugged Guruji tightly with his eyes wet. There was silence all around for a few moments. He then said to Guruji, "It's all because of you and as you have taken this responsibility for us. This is really a mammoth task you have taken up. It's a big deal for us." Guruji replied very politely, "Who am I? The whole society is with you. This is the task taken by the society into its own hands."

The conclusion of this convention was marked by two statements made by Hindu religious leaders-'Hindus cannot be degenerated' and 'All Hindus are brothers'. Guruji had performed this supernatural task which Dr. Babasaheb Ambedkar expected from Hindu religious leaders. Dr. Ambedkar was not successful while Shri Guruji had performed it successfully. So, the next question would be as to how was this possible?

The principal reason behind this was the strength of the RSS. Guruji held a powerful seat when he insisted on religious reforms before the religious leaders. His personality and his spiritual abode was very high. At that time, he held the highest position in the nationwide largest social organisation. The power of this organisation had a positive influence over the religious leaders.

Like the so-called untouchables, acceptance of the forest dwellers and the nomadic castes (tribals) was a natural consequence of devotion to Hindutva. Explaining the role of the Sangh in this regard, Guruji said, "Many activists blame the whole situation on others. Some blame political perversion in this regard' others have blamed the aggressive activities of Christians, Muslims and people of other faiths. Our Swayamsevaks should be free from such thoughts and continue to work for our society and religion with a pure spirit. A helping hand should be extended to those who need help. They will have to work hard to overcome the crisis for those who are in crisis. There should not be people to people discrimination while performing this act of service. We have to serve all."

"Some people think that our movement is just to remove the stigma of untouchability and to become upper caste people. It is not only the untouchables who have been harmed by atrocities, it has also harmed the upper castes, and the nation has suffered the most. If the untouchables come out of this stigma and contribute to nation building, then it contributes to the development of the country.

Thus the movement for the abolition of untouchability is truly a movement for nation building."

—(presidential speech, Berar Province Untouchable Council, Amravati, 13 November, 1927, *Bahishkrit Bharat*, 25 November, 1927)

Are the untouchables backward in terms of quality? Revered Guruji said, "Some people say that the intellectual and mental quality of this so-called untouchable caste is so inferior that they will not be able to match other societies even after a long period of time. This is their worst insult and that's the opposite of reality too. Right to perform rituals in Hindu society was given to only Brahmins. This is a discrimination based on birth; anyone born into (any caste of) Hindu society should have the right to perform the rituals and to worship God ceremoniously."

Many great personalities have strongly presented their views, opposing this. Following the Sangh practice, Dr. Hedgewar never touched this subject directly in his life. But, he created the cadre of Sangh Swayamsevaks who came forward and gave the right to perform rituals to all the people of Hindu society, instilling the feeling of 'I am Hindu' in every Hindu. The temple priests in Kerala and Tamil Nadu were non-Brahmins. Training was imparted to those who wished to become priests. The controversy over a temple priest in Kerala reached the High Court. The court gave an important verdict recognising the right of non-Brahmin priests to worship.

Sangh Swayamsevaks performed another important task in reformation of religion on 3 October, 1993 at Nagpur. It was the occasion of a meeting of Ram Janmabhoomi Trust Forum. Many dignitaries, saints, *mahants*, *acharyas* and other leaders of Vishwa Hindu Parishad from all over the nation had gathered at Nagpur to attend the meeting. They all visited the *Diksha Bhoomi*, where Dr. Ambedkar had taken *diksha*, initiation into Buddhism. Revered Shankaracharya Vasudevanand Saraswati garlanded the statue of Dr. Ambedkar and the Madhavacharya of Udupi, Shri Vishvesh Tirth Maharaj announced, "There should be no sign of untouchability in this country of Dr. Babasaheb. We have gathered at Ambedkar's *Diksha Bhoomi* (initiation ground). We, all devotees of Ram, will take Bhim-*prerana* (Bhim inspiration) and Bhim-*shakti* (Bhim strength) with us and guide the whole society."

Balasaheb Deoras, the then Sarsanghchalak (president) of the Sangh, while praising the work of the religious leaders, said, "Saints and *sadhus* from all over the country have come up with a great ideal of unity in Nagpur out of respect for the founder of the Sangh, Dr. Keshav Baliram Hedgewar and saviour of untouchables–

Dr. Babasaheb Ambedkar. It is of utmost importance that monks and saints have shown intimacy towards the work of Sangh, but the incident that all of them went to the *Diksha Bhoomi* and remembered the late Dr. Ambedkar is even more important and historically far-reaching. Both Dr. Hedgewar and Dr. Ambedkar had the same goal. Inspired by both; the ideal that one should renounce untouchability and live in harmony, has been put into practice by saints and Hindus on this occasion."

It was a revolutionary event in the history of Hindu society to pay homage to Dr. Ambedkar when revered Shankaracharya offered a garland to his statue. Such a big change was possible only with the inspiration of Dr. Hedgewar, who seemed to have used the *mantra* of two words–Hindu *sangathan*. Dr. Hedgewar was a worshipper of the goddess of power and had stated the goal of the Sangh in one sentence: "We want to make our Hindu society so powerful that no power in the world can even dare to look down on us."

Selfishness responsible for a Weak Hindu Society

Hindus, in India, were powerful in terms of population and numbers but they were weak as a society, at the time when Dr. Hedgewar founded the Sangh. Rather, he was required to found the Sangh because of this weakness of Hindus as a society. Surprisingly, the numbers didn't impart strength to the Hindu society because they were divided into numerous castes and sects. And almost all were convinced that the reasons for a weak Hindu society were caste discrimination, stubborn religious norms, etc. though Dr. Hedgewar's analysis was different.

He had said, "Hindus have always been careless about social issues and as a result, we have been weaker from within. We have a mindset of 'what do I lose even if society is reduced to dust?' and this instinct has gone all the way up into our veins and bones. We keep thinking about ourselves only as self and not as a society. We don't get up until our selfishness is hurt. This is indifference towards the society and unfortunately it has sunk deep into our minds and weakened us. The bitter fruit of our mental weakness is being suffered by our society today. This mental weakness is most deadly and is the biggest weakness of our society. We do have the potential; but unfortunately we have forgotten about it. If we become organised by recalling our potential, our power will become unlimited. The very root of our decline is our mental weakness."

How did Dr. Babasaheb Ambedkar express the same?

Dr. Babasaheb Ambedkar too had analysed this issue and tried to find the actual reason for the weakness of Hindu society. He wrote in his magazine, *Mooknayak* (issue 13, 31 July, 1920): "If you want the upliftment of our nation and wish that we should be respected among the major nations of the world, efforts should be made for this and there should be internal unity in any nation, any society."

He was hopeful that casteism would vanish one day, even hundred years before today. He said in the 31 July, 1920 in issue of *Mooknayak*: "No matter how much you water the tree of *varnashrama*, it is bound to collapse." And in the issue of the 14 August, 1920, he explained how a man can reach any height through his own deeds. "When the *varna* system came into existence in the era of *Puranas*, rules were not so strict then. A person could change his *varna* and shift from one *varna* to another through his own deeds. Sages, like Vishwamitra, Valmiki, Vashishtha, Tank, etc. are proof of this. In course of time, selfish, hypocritical, heresy people erected a whole barbed wire fence between different *varnas* and extended the distance further between different castes with the result leading to the emergence of a whole lot of castes. As these castes came into existence. Some patriarchs, in order to maintain their dominance, resorted to the *Puranas* and the *Smritis* to create these higher/lower distinctions by adding some fictitious and imaginary commands."

Dr. Ambedkar further wrote in an editorial (21 December, 1928) in *Bahishkrit Bharat*: "Sociologists say that caste discrimination has weakened Hindu society. Social works are being considered as an outcast activity because of the belief that one has to have 'birth in the same caste, death in the same caste, food in the same caste, marriage in the same caste.' The more a man stays away from people, the more his caste is considered pure. Caste discrimination in social cohesion is like a pair of scissors. Caste discrimination does not allow the spirit of unity and makes the lives of Hindus unbearable. People of different castes have become indifferent towards each other. In all their public dealings, it has become customary to think of the advantages for one's own caste to the detriment of other castes. This policy, no matter how unjust, is followed and as a result, an atmosphere of distrust has been created among the Hindu castes."

Dr. Ambedkar further wrote in the same editorial: "Hatred among castes cannot be vanished as long as there is a caste discrimination in existence. That has increased the fight between different castes, instead of leading to alliance between the castes. Even the social reforms are at a halt due to caste discrimination. People are not ready to understand that the tradition of caste is wrong and this has gone to the extent that those who act against this false tradition are socially ostracised. The development of Hindu society has been stalled because of caste discrimination, thereby weakened the society. It is a general belief that untouchables cannot produce the right and dutiful people, but the upper caste people seem to forget that higher efforts are not possible without high ambition and great work cannot be done without higher efforts. When you set all the boundaries for untouchables on the name of social restraints, those who have been left behind by the way of untouchability for thousands of years are not left with the mental powers to cross their own boundaries. And these boundaries have deprived them of the seed of ambition as well."

Let us have a look at some quotes of Babasaheb in this regard:

- "Morality of Hindus has been destroyed due to their loyalty towards their own caste. Such casteism has ended social loyalty and social generosity. A personal world of Hindu is limited to his/her own caste only. The centre of their fidelity and loyalty is only their caste. Their field of virtue is limited to their caste only. They lack empathy or generosity towards the deserving person" (*Annihilation of Caste*, written by Dr. Babasaheb Ambedkar).
- "Every Hindu has a tendency to follow the leader of only his own caste. That is to say, Hindus only appreciate the virtues of their own 'caste brother'; it is not in the nature of Hindu person to appreciate the virtues of a person

other than his/her own caste. The whole conduct of the Hindus is as narrow and corrupt as that of the savage tribes. 'Good or bad, amiable or a scoundrel, but if he is of my caste, I will take his side!' This is a very strong tendency among the Hindus. This has also forced them to ignore persons from other castes without observing their virtues. Isn't it a treason that someone's loyalty is limited only to the caste, even though being a citizen of a nation?" (*Annihilation of Caste,* written by Dr. Babasaheb Ambedkar).

- "The way to end casteism is to start with inter-caste mass-meal, but I think this idea is also incomplete and lacking because inter-caste mass-meal is already prevalent in some castes, but in reality even that has not succeeded in eradicating casteism or its spirit. So in my opinion, the panacea to avoid caste discrimination is inter-caste marriages. Intimacy cannot be created as long as blood relations are not formed and the feeling of segregation created by casteism will not end" (*Annihilation of Caste* written by Dr. Babasaheb Ambedkar).

B.R. Ambedkar wanted to establish a harmonious Hindu society that was based on equality. The letter he wrote to Thakkar Bapa on 14 November, 1932 is very long and every word of that letter is as valuable today as it was then. The last two lines of the letter are particularly important: "We need sincere, hardworking and faithful workers who are useful in eradication of untouchability. A spirit of love and self-sacrifice is essential for the success of such a task. The untouchables and the upper castes will not come together just by the constraints of the law; only love can keep them together."

Hindus Survived by Accepting Slavery

An editorial by Dr. Babasaheb Ambedkar's in his magazine *Bahishkrit Bharat* (21 December, 1928) is worth mentioning here. He agreed in that editorial that India was and is a Hindu nation, but, this Hindu nation did not accept changes over time. He further wrote: "It is a well-known fact that the Hindu nation (i.e. India) is one among the ancient civilisations. It is also known that the way civilisations of Egypt, Assyria, Rome and Greece were destroyed, the Hindu nation is still alive with its ancient culture. But, if Hindu nation is considered as a strong nation only on that basis, then it is akin to boasting. Surviving by defeating the enemy and surviving by being enslaved are two different things. Hindu society survived for hundreds of years as slaves. There was a time when conquerors would grab the property of a defeated king by killing his people. But, then they stopped killing and started enslaving them for farm work, etc. The Hindu nation does not dominate other nations because it requires flexibility and social justice for that. The reason for the Hindu nation's such infamous tradition is its inverse social structure. The structure of Hindu nation is made according to the religion, so religious theology is responsible for its condition. The world is reformed in terms of social structures while Hindu society has not adopted age-appropriate changes. It still has child marriage, meal bans and (inter-caste) marriage bans."

Dr. Babasaheb tried to eliminate untouchability and casteism and build a strong and single-caste Hindu society. Perhaps he wished for the welfare of Hindu society to the extent that he should be called its great reformer. He made plans for it but failed and in 1935, he announced his conversion.

Wait of 20 Years after the Announcement

He did not convert for 20 long years even after announcing it and he converted to Buddhism, which too had emerged from the cultural stream of India. It was like shifting from one room to another in the same house. He did not adopt the foreign-based non-national religions, like Islam or Christianity and this shows his love for the nation and Hindu interest in his heart.

It was futile to expect support for the Hindu organisation from him after the proclamation of conversion in 1935. In fact, such an expectation was inconsistent with his declaration of conversion. Yet the importance of Hindu organisation from the point of view of Hindu society is fundamental as well as indispensable and it is not based on the declaration of conversion. In the context of the Hindu organisation, the declaration of conversion meant that Babasaheb would no longer support the Hindu organisation, but, had someone else formed a Hindu organisation for Babasaheb, would he have opposed it? As far as direct conversion was concerned, it was impossible for Babasaheb to oppose the untouchable class as he was a part of the Hindu society in which he was interested. After announcing his conversion, he wanted the Hindus to unite and advised them to increase their inner strength by removing vices of Hinduism and Hindu society and empower the society for defence.

Therefore, after the proclamation of his conversion, in his discourse, *Annihilation of Caste* written in 1936, he praised the work of the Hindu organisation by calling it as an excellent work. He felt that the Hindus also needed to organise themselves for defence against Muslims. He, like today's hypocritical secularists, never considered such a statement to be bigoted. He gave a stern warning to the Hindu community that 'a day will come when it will be impossible for Hindus to save their society or caste, and that day is not far away.' Even after the announcement of conversion, Babasaheb further spoke about the organisation of Hindus thus: "In the end, all the responsibility is yours. I have already decided to convert. I am separating from your religion but I will keep an eye on all your activities and will continue to help as needed."

"What evidence do we have that the Aryans came from outside and defeated natives by attracting them? There is no mention of any incident in the Rig Veda, which confirms that the Aryans invaded India. Mr. P.T. Srinivasan Iyengar writes on the issue that, a careful analysis of the mantras, it seems that where words like Arya, Das, Dasya are used, they do not refer to caste but to branch. These words are mostly found in the Yajurveda Samhita. where the word Arya is used only 33 times in mantras, while the total number of words of which is 1,53,972. The very rare use of the word Aryan is proof that the so-called Aryan race was not an invader and that if they had conquered the country and uprooted the natives, the winners would have repeatedly lamented their achievement."

—(Dr. Babasaheb Ambedkar in his book,
Who are Sudras?)

The work of the Hindu organisation is more important than *swarajya*. Speaking from the bottom of his heart in the book, *Annihilation of Caste*, Babasaheb Bhimrao Ambedkar said: 'Hindu organization is a national task. It is even more important than *swarajya* (self-government). What is the use of *swarajya* if we cannot save it? It is more important to protect the Hindus of *swarajya* than to protect *swarajya*. If the Hindus do not have power, then *swarajya* will turn into slavery in no time.'

It should be noted that Babasaheb had turned down many tempting offers from Islamic clerics and Christian missionaries to join them after announcing his conversion. Rather, he gave the right advice to unite the Hindus, to become internally strong by removing vices in Hinduism and society, to create a powerful Hindu organisation and to empower the society for defence. He was disappointed not to see the possibility of cooperation from Hindutva devotees as well as Hindu Mahasabha leaders in his task of elimination of untouchability and building an integrated Hindu society.

Dr. Ambedkar, an advocate of a united India, had a strong hatred for the caste system within Hindu society (religion), but no animosity at all. If there was animosity and a sense of revenge, he would have converted to Islam or Christianity instead. He flatly denied Islam by kicking off temptations and knocked out Christians as well. Denying such conversions, he said in no uncertain terms, "I do not approve of my people becoming denationalised."

After much study and analysis, he finally converted to Buddhism, a religion close to Hinduism as well as a religion of Indian culture. This great obligation of Dr. Babasaheb to the nation is very little understood. From 1924 to 1956, during his public career, he never considered to appoint a Muslim to any important post, not even as a member of his socio-political organisations, though many upper caste Hindus held important positions. Moreover, not a single one of his organisations or magazines was named after any caste or indicated a caste! According to the information given by Dhananjay Keer about the informal meeting of the joint committee that went to London for the Round Table Conference: "Being in a desperate situation, I demanded an independent constituency," Dr. Ambedkar remarked. "I am deeply disappointed by the inhuman treatment of untouchable Hindus. If Hindus try to make their social system uniform, the untouchables will wholeheartedly help in that task."

At that time, the RSS was only ten-years old and had no influence on Hindu society. It was just the beginning, though Dr. Ambedkar knew enough about it and believed that the Sangh was the only organisation that could fulfill his hopes and expectations. He maintained contacts with the RSS till the end of his life. He went to Pune in 1935 to inspect the first Sangh Shiksha class in Maharashtra. At that time, when he went to Dapoli for his professional (advocacy) work, he went to the Sangh *shakha* and openly talked to the Swayamsevaks.

No 'Untouchables' Found!

In 1939, Babasaheb attended the Sangh Shiksha Varg (Sangh training programme) in Pune in the evening. That afternoon, he met Dr. Hedgewar at Gadkari's bungalow and visited the Sangh class at Bhave School in the evening. There were about 525 fully-uniformed Swayamsevaks at the place of training. He asked Dr. Hedgewar as to how many of them were untouchables. Dr. Hedgewar said, "Let's take a look." On reaching there, Babasaheb said, "I can't see any untouchable here." Babasaheb asked the Swayamsevaks, "Let the untouchables among you take a step forward." No one came forward as which Babasaheb was surprised. But, Dr. Hedgewar said, "We never consider anyone as untouchable. However, you can ask them to come forward with the name of your favourite caste." Then Babasaheb asked the volunteers, "If there is an untouchable, a Mang or a Chamar (a cobbler) in this class, then come one step forward." Many came forward at this announcement and their number was more than a hundred!

Pandit Nehru had banned the Sangh out of hatred, falsely accusing it of assassinating Mahatma Gandhi. Babasaheb, Sardar Patel and Syama Prasad Mookherjee made efforts to lift the ban. The ban was removed in July 1949, when Guruji met Babasaheb in Delhi in September, 1949 to thank him for his efforts.

On hearing the news of the leader of the Hindu Mahasabha, former Chief Minister of the United Provinces Dr. N.B. Khare's detention on the radio, Dr. Ambedkar, the then Law Ministerr went to Dr. Khare's residence. Dr. Khare has written in his autobiography, "Law Minister Bhimrao Ambedkar came to me and said, 'You have been deliberately put into this situation due to your strong opposition of Gandhiji and Gandhism. It may be possible that your friends and relatives will be scared to visit you because of the strict watch of CID at your place. But, you are always welcome to my place (1 Harding Avenue, now named Tilak Avenue) to visit me whenever you feel bored. No Maharashtrian friend except Babasaheb Ambedkar came to me to say a word of consolation during the days of house-arrest. My conversation with Babasaheb Ambedkar multiplied my respect for him'."

Even the leaders of the Sangh gave credit only to Sardar Patel for lifting the ban on the Sangh. The coordination and arrangement between the Home Department and the Law Department was essential for the lifting of the ban on the Sangh. Guruji Madhav Sadashivrao Golwalkar (1906-1973) understood this very well and thus often met Bhimrao Ambedkar during the period 1940-1949. It is also recorded on p. 409 of Dhananjay Keer's book that Guruji met Dr. Ambedkar at his residence in September 1949. This is also mentioned in the late Sohanlal Shastri's book, *Babasaheb Ambedkar ke Sampark mein Pachis Varsh.*

Prof. Thakkar applied for the post of a professor at Milind Mahavidyalaya (Milind College). Babasaheb asked him at the time of appointment, "What were you doing before?" Thakkar said, "I was a professor in a college at Nashik." When asked why he had left the place, Thakkar replied, "I lost my job because of participating in the Sangh's *satyagraha* (agitation)." Babasaheb patted Thakkar on his back and said, "Well! Then I have made the right choice!"

Babasaheb Ambedkar used to have frequent discussions with the Swayamsevaks. Once Moropant Pingale, Balasaheb Sathe and Professor Thakar met Dr. Ambedkar in Aurangabad. He made extensive inquiries about the Sangh (like how many branches were there, how many were there then, etc.) He then told Moropant, "I visited your Sangh Shiksha class. The strength you had at that time does not seem to have increased at a required pace over the years. The pace of progress is low. My society can't wait that long."

He understood that the Sangh's stance on casteism was in line with his views and many other Hindutva devotees, but he was saddened that the pro-Hindu leaders whom Babasaheb favoured did not have enough influence on the Sanatani society which believed in untouchability and casteism. Those who influenced Sanatani society were not approved by Babasaheb and his efforts to change the mindset of such leaders were unsuccessful.

Dattopant Thengadi and Babasaheb Ambedkar

Dattopant Thengadi, a leader connected with many sub-organizations of Sangh including 'Samajik Samrasta' recalls his memories with Babasaheb Ambedkar. "I asked him just a few days before conversion, 'It is a fact that there have been some atrocities in the past. There may be some pros and cons. But are you aware that we young people are trying to make a new society by atonement for them?'

"'You mean RSS?' He knew I was a Sangh Pracharak (preacher).

"He said, 'Do you think I have not given thought on this matter?'

"I said 'How can we say that about you? You must have thought about everything.'

"Then he asked 'When was the Sangh founded? How many years have passed? '

"I said 'The Sangh was founded in 1925. Today it marks 27-28 years.'

"'I know,' he said, 'but tell me one thing. How many people do you have?'

"I replied, 'I can't say.'

"'Don't give the answers like at the press conference, give a definite answer,' he said.

"'Really, I don't know,' I said again.

"Ambedkar said, 'Suppose your people number around 27-28 lakhs. How many years will it take to unite the whole society as it took them 27-28 years to gather so many people?'

"When I was about to say something, he just said, 'You don't say anything. I know that arithmetic and geometric development are not the same. But no matter how much a frog swells, it cannot become an ox. This will take many years. Is it possible to wait until then? Shall I sit idle? The issue before me is to give a definite direction to my society before my death. Because that society has been oppressed, deprived and exploited till now. There is a renaissance in it now. It is natural to have an annoyance, a rage.

That kind of society becomes the prey of communism. It is a cannon fodder for communism. I don't want Scheduled Caste societies to fall victim to communism. Therefore, from the point of view of the nation, it is necessary to give it some direction. You are making necessary efforts from the point of view of a unified nation, but keep in mind that between Scheduled Caste and communism, Ambedkar is the barrier and between caste Hindus and communism, Golwalkar (because he is a Brahmin) is the barrier.' He said further 'Am I right or not? So, if I could not give them the right direction before my death, a large chunk of the Scheduled Caste society would be ready to split in the direction of communism. You cannot bring them back into our national mainstream. Because, the question is not whether you are doing right or wrong or true or false; but, since that is done by upper caste people, my society will not listen to you. And that is why I have to make this arrangement before I die'."

Illusion about Socialists was Shattered

This decisive experience that gave impetus to this idea (good relations with socialists is an illusion) got him through during the first election in 1952 in accordance with the new constitution of Independent India. Babasaheb was a candidate of Scheduled Caste Federation from Mumbai. Babasaheb and all the people of the backward class believed that the Samajwadi Party was more progressive than the rest of the parties. So the Federation made an election alliance with the Samajwadi Party. Ashok Mehta was the Samajwadi Party candidate. Voters had the right to cast two votes on the basis of preference in that election. Both Ashok Mehta and Babasaheb Ambedkar lost in the election.

Babasaheb had caste statistics of all the assembly seats in his constituency. Analysing the statistics and the votes received, it came to his notice that as per the agreement, almost all the backward classes (of the Federation) had given their votes to Ashok Mehta, but the Samajwadi Party could not persuade its people to vote for Babasaheb. So the illusion of the Federation activists about the Samajwadi Party was shattered and they became convinced that it was impossible to bridge the gap between the untouchables and the upper castes. 'Their votes can't come here and our votes can't go to them' – that belief made casteism very strong in the minds of the people of the Federation, but Babasaheb saw the strong need to build an all-inclusive party instead of a caste-based party.

Dattopantji notes: "In the 1952 elections, the United Front of Bharatiya Jana Sangh, S.C. Federation and the Samajwadi Party was formed only for Madhya Pradesh. In that election, some incidents in Vidarbha became shocking. In one city, there were 40 activists sloganeering and demanding votes. But the number of votes cast at the same polling station was only 18. So it turned out that something was wrong. We people tried and got three ballot boxes from the government treasury. There was one Lok Sabha and two Legislative Assemblies ballot boxes. After much effort and with the help of experts, it became clear that ballot boxes could be tampered with. The Election Commissioner at that time was Shri P.K. Sen. He sent Regional Election Commissioner Mr. Mehra to Nagpur to check the veracity of our claim. Mr. Mehra wrote that our claim was true. Then came the letter from Mr. P.K. Sen. He wrote, "We accept that your claim is true, but you have to prove that special tampering has taken place in a certain place." People of the Federation and Samajwadi Party were with us over this issue. Eventually, Babasaheb also obtained complete information on the issue. He called me when he came to Nagpur. I had a personal relationship with him from then until the last moment of his life. It was like a relationship between a young guy and an elderly person. He considered me as a child of his own.

"Bhandara (Maharashtra) by-election was held after the Mumbai elections. The Mumbai duo of Ashok Mehta and Babasaheb returned to the field. The Bhandara constituency had a large number of untouchable voters, yet it was clear that it was impossible for Babasaheb to be elected only on the basis of their votes. Everyone was sure that the votes of the untouchables would go to Ashok Mehta, but even if we do not get a single vote from Ashok Mehta's party, we would have to give our second vote to Ashok Mehta because there was no other option. If that happens, the history of Mumbai will be repeated in Bhandara.

"A meeting of Federation activists took place. The activists decided that they would let our second vote go blank. Babasaheb arrived while the meeting was going on. He asked, 'What is going on?' Party workers explained the whole situation and said, 'We have decided to keep the second vote blank, because otherwise you will lose the election.' Babasaheb became very annoyed on hearing this. He said, 'I accept defeat in the election, but I will not allow your second vote to go blank. I have drafted the Constitution of India. I cannot tolerate such irresponsibility in the constitutional system.' But the question was how to cast your second vote. People suggested that another upper caste candidate should be fielded and another vote should be given to him. I was also present at that meeting, so naturally my name was discussed. Babasaheb said, 'You run for the election.' Being a Sangh Pracharak, there was no question of running in the election. I said, 'I don't have the money or the resources.'

"Babasaheb said, 'We will manage everything.' Finally I said, 'I have to ask my officers.' I told everything to revered Guruji. He said, 'This opportunity is good, but if you run for the election, you will not take advantage of this opportunity. Because all our workers will work for Babasaheb with all their heart; yet, people will say that because you are running for the election, the people of Sangh are working for Babasaheb. So neither you run for the election nor let any of us run for it. Instead, gather all our workers from Bhandara constituency and work for Babasaheb. The fact that the people of the Sangh are working for Babasaheb should come to the notice of Babasaheb and other untouchables. If that happened, then we would all be benefiting from the intended social convergence'."

Satisfaction at the Sangh's Efforts

During the by-election of Bhandara, all the Swayamsevaks of Bhandara district campaigned for Babasaheb. However, he had to face defeat in this election but when he analysed the polling figures and checked how many votes were received from which booth, it then dawned on him that he had received far more votes than the number of untouchables in the Bhandara constituency. He was very much satisfied that many upper caste people had voted for him.

Some leaders of the Federation came to meet him at the Shyam Hotel on the second day of the initiation ceremony at

Nagpur. Babasaheb told them, "You are more interested in politics and I am more interested in religion. I am not so sad about my loss in the Bhandara election, as I was expected to lose. But, one positive change is seen in this election–that the barriers between untouchables and upper caste society are demolished in this election. I have also got votes from upper caste Hindus, apart from votes of untouchables. Now it is time to change our thinking. We shall not just organise the untouchables and the backward classes; we shall organise programmes to reach out to the whole society."

It shows that Babasaheb realised that the barrier between untouchable and upper caste society had been knocked down and all this was the result of the work done by the Swayamsevaks in accordance with the guidance provided by Guruji following the policy of the Sangh of comprehensive goal of social harmony. This triggered the idea of a new political strategy in Babasaheb's mind.

Sangh's Views towards Ambedkar

Guruji, the second Sarsanghchalak (president) of the RSS harboured special respect for Dr. Babasaheb Ambedkar, who used to keep him updated about the work of the Scheduled Caste Federation and its leaders. There is an incident related to Dr. Ambedkar's prime follower from Vidarbha who was part of the Scheduled Caste Federation. The meeting to discuss arrangements of the public function of the third year Sangh Shiksha class was going on at the Sangh office in the presence of Guruji. A Sangh leader, Bapurao Vahadapande raised the issue as to who should be invited as the chief guest at this public function. Names of dignitaries of Nagpur were in discussion by other members, but Guruji proposed the name of Pandit Rewaram Kwade. Everyone at the meeting was surprised to hear this not-so-known name, but Guruji was well aware of this great personality. He was one among the only two activists and Dr. Ambedkar's followers who was interested in matters related to religion. The other one was Shri Vamanrao Godbole. The above incident showed how closely he was watching Dr. Babasaheb and his activities as well as the activists.

The thought expressed by Guruji in the special issue of *Gaurav* on the occasion of the 73rd birth anniversary of Dr. Babasaheb

Ambedkar, in 1962, shows how highly he regarded Babasaheb. The way the message was presented while paying the homage to this great personality is a testament to the harmonious relationship between Dr. Bhimrao Ambedkar and Rashtriya Swayamsevak Sangh. Guruji wrote in his message: "Swami Vivekananda did a great job of awakening the society and called for social renewal. Even Dr. Ambedkar, annoyed by the social and political outlook, repeated the same call in strong words. It instilled a sense of self-respect in that vast section of society – the class that is living a life of ignorance, misery and deprival. His success in this way was phenomenal. Dr. Babasaheb Ambedkar has done a great favor to the nation through his great work.

"His gratitude is such that society cannot pay it back. Gautama Buddha also sharply attacked the then society for the sake of social reforms and for the betterment of religion. But their purpose was not to create any kind of isolation. In the same way, Dr. Ambedkar also did immense work for the welfare of the society. He tried to reform the existing Hindu religion and purify the society but it was not his intention to separate the Scheduled Caste from the rest of the society, nor was it his intention to form a separate sect. Considering Dr. Ambedkar as the successor of Lord Buddha, I pay homage to his sacred memory, inspired by his faith in him from a distance."

After Babasaheb Ambedkar's conversion, most of his followers turned to politics; there were only two persons who were attracted to matters related to religion. One of them was Shri Vamanrao Godbole, secretary of the Buddhist Federation of India and the other was Pt. Revaram Kwade. Babasaheb had given him the title of Pandit because of his knowledge on the rituals of Buddhism.

Pt. Kwade was invited as a chief guest for the Sangh Shiksha Varg ceremony. Many of his friends advised him not to attend the Sangh's programme, but Mr. Kwade attended the programme. Before the programme, Mr. Kwade became emotional when Guruji offered him a cup of tea made by himself. He also praised the gesture in his speech.

Ambedkar-Sangh consensus on the word 'Harijan'

Babasaheb's opinion about the word 'Harijan' given by Mahatma Gandhi is well known. In this context, Guruji said, "It would not be appropriate to insist on the new word 'Harijan' to remove the feelings of people who have been deliberately isolated from the society. When I met Gandhiji, I expressed my apprehension and told him that 'the literal meaning of the word 'Harijan' was very good, but finding a new word for a particular class would make them feel a little different."

Some so-called progressives spread rumors full of misconceptions about relations between Rashtriya Swayamsevak Sangh and Babasaheb Ambedkar in order to create a schism between them. One best example of such rumors was that Babasaheb had chosen Nagpur for his *diksha* (initiation) to Buddhism because Nagpur is the headquarters of the Rashtriya Swayamsevak Sangh and to show his power to the RSS. However, the real reason was entirely different. This propaganda had a detrimental effect on the Dalits as well as the upper castes until the day of conversion. Such false propaganda had already come to Babasaheb's notice, so he started his speech on the initiation day by explaining that the choice of Nagpur for initiation was purely scriptural. He said that the spread of Buddhism has been associated with the Nag people (of that time) and that was the reason that Nagpur (a city of Nag people) had been chosen. He said, "Some people say that there is a big platoon of RSS, aka Rashtriya Swayamsevak Sangh is situated in Nagpur, so we have deliberately held this meeting on their chest in this city, but that is not true."

The mob of so-called secularists tried to spread rumours even on the day of his *diksha* ceremony on 14 October, 1956 at Nagpur. However, at the very outset of the discourse, Dr. Babasaheb Ambedkar denied all rumours and presented the proud history of Nagpur and Naga people, commenting, "I don't have time to explain every rumour but this is what I felt to be clarified." Hadn't it been clarified by Babasaheb himself, the false propaganda of Leftists would surely have been succeeded in its objective.

Leftists are the Enemy of the Country

Leftist activists have always been notorious for spreading false propaganda. During the time of Dr. Bhimrao Ambedkar and even today, they have been spreading lies about Ambedkar and that too by spreading lies under the name of Dr. Ambedkar. They have always been anti-Constitution, anti-Ambedkar and anti-nation since their rise in this country. Dr. Ambedkar has written a lot about their distorted mentality and here are some of his quotes:

- The communists have always exploited the labourers. I am a staunch enemy of the communists. (Bahishkrit Jilla Sammelan [District Convention of Excluded], Masur, District Satara, September, 1937). We must maintain the independence of our country. We can make our country prosperous only by maintaining independence.
- If we offer communism to the country, the independence of our country will be endangered (Speech in Nashik, *Janata* magazine: 8h December, 1951), Buddhism is the right way of life for everyone. Buddhism will survive only if it is explained how Buddhism is better than communism. Communism will take you to the jungle, to chaos. Communism does not hesitate to kill its opponents for its own establishment. Communists are chaotic; they love the path of violence. (Dr. Ambedkar, World Buddhist Conference, Kathmandu, Nepal, 20 November, 1956). This belief of Babasaheb Ambedkar about the leftists lasted till the last breath of his life. Unfortunately, today these Leftists are defaming India all over the world by taking the name of Bhimrao Ambedkar but acting against him.

Goal has been Expanded but...

Dr. Ambedkar's goal was not confined to the oppressed class or, in other words, the Dalit society; his goal was vast and to the benefit of all his fellow countrymen. He laid out his idea of future action in front of his key activists and presented his wish that the Scheduled Caste Federation was no longer useful in achieving the wider goal, even its name indicates a particular caste or group of castes. He said, "We need a large and extensive base to achieve our goal." He was confident of changing the direction of India's future with the help of the entire Indian society, but that desire remained only in his thoughts. Unfortunately, he passed away shortly after he came up with this idea.

Dr. Ambedkar knew that the basis of India's unity was cultural and social, and only that cultural and social consciousness could bring about a change. His statement is as relevant today as it was earlier–"Any time when human civilisation witnessed a political revolution, it witnessed social and cultural revolutions before that. And that determines the success and significance of the political revolution." Citing the example of India, he said, "Political revolution of Chandragupta Maurya was followed by the social and cultural revolutions of Buddha; similarly contribution of monks and saints of Maharashtra who accelerated cultural and social change, triggered the political revolution of Shivaji Maharaj." He also cited an example of Guru Nanak's cultural-social enlightenment and its influence in this context. His basic insistence was on cultural and social revolution.

Dr. Ambedkar described in his research paper 'Caste in India' presented at Columbia University in 1916 that "India has ubiquitous cultural unity. Although society is divided into innumerable castes, it is bound by one culture. A nation cannot survive only on cultural unity. Social cohesion is also important for the nation to survive."

Just as he connected culture with the nation, the basis of his social *satyagraha* on Dharma was the *Bhagavad Gita*. Dr. Babasaheb said during the *satyagraha* of Chavdar Lake in Mahad quoting the *Bhagavad Gita*:

"The *satya*-the truth, prevails where there is morality, equality and collectivity. *Satyagraha* (an agitation for truth) is a step towards these principles. This is my definition of *satyagraha*. *Satyagraha* is not my own idea, I have read about it in the *Gita*. Many people may be wondering why I resort to *Gita* for satyagraha. Many believe that *satyagraha* is not the subject of the *Gita*, but that is not true. In fact *satyagraha* is the basic principle of the *Gita*. Think carefully about why Lord Krishna gave his message in the form of the *Gita* and that will make you understand that what I am telling is true. Just recall, what advice did Lord Krishna give to Arjuna when he got down from the chariot and was sad to see his elders and gurus in front of him in the battle? Lord Krishna said, 'Do not be sad; be ready to fight for your rights with those who have taken away your land.' Then Arjuna asked, 'Tell me how the truth is what you are saying and how my demand is *satyagraha*?' The *Gita* is the answer of this one question of Arjuna. There is no other principle in the *Gita*, but only *satyagraha*. That is why I have made the *Gita* the basis of our demand for equal rights for the untouchables. Another reason to make the *Gita* as the basis of *satyagraha* is, and it is acceptable to both the parties, untouchables and upper castes, that if we had chosen any other scripture, that may have given the upper castes an excuse to reject our demands; but this *satyagraha* of the untouchables has gone through the test of the *Gita*, so they don't have any excuse now because rejecting our demands would be the rejection of the *Gita*. It now remains to see the results of the test of our *satyagraha*."

"Why do Indian billionaires believe in poor monks? The history of India shows that the source of power is religion. Religious leaders in India have a strong influence over the common man, and often even over the magistrates ...Here everything, even strikes and elections, can easily be given a religious twist. Socialists are under the illusion that if the source of power in European society is wealth, the same can happen in India."

—(*Annihilation of Castes*, written by Dr. Babasaheb Ambedkar)

India did not have to Endure Slavery

Nation building entails team work and the team for this work is the entire nation. All the people of the country should participate in the nation's work. This is how a bond is created among the people of the nation and the nation gets built. If just one class of people rules and the others have no participation, then the tendency of indifference is created. People, other than the ruling class, begin to think that they don't have to lose anything even if the rule doesn't last forever. That is the biggest obstacle in building a nation. Dr. Ambedkar believed that such a tendency was also responsible for the slavery of the nation. While giving a speech in the Convention of Untouchables in Satana village of Nashik district, on 12 February, 1938 he said, "Invaders like Alexander and Mohammad Tughlaq attacked and took over part of India. But, the *chaturvarna* system of our society taught the Hindus that no one except the Kshatriyas could wield weapons and protect the country; neither those handful of Brahmins nor Vaishyas or Shudras have that right to fight. That has been responsible for the downfall of India. If everyone with fire under their belly and strength in their wrists had freedom to take up arms, this scourge of slavery could have been avoided." Babasaheb fought to develop the national spirit and participation of all in the national work throughout his life. Following are some of his statements in this respect:

- "Efforts should be made for it if you want the upliftment of the nation and want that we should be respected among the major nations of the world. Moreover, there should be internal unity in the society of the nation" (*Mooknayak* magazine, issue 13, 31 July, 1920).
- "I don't believe in any kind of discrimination, even I don't accept 'I am Indian first, then Hindu or Muslim'. In fact, I am firstly Indian and lastly also Indian. Such an attitude is conducive to India's independence" (Mumbai Legislative Assembly at the time of partition of Karnataka, 4 April, 1938).
- "I have more love for the nation... and that is the true feeling of any nationalist. The nation is greater than the individual" (Vol. I, pp. 209-210; writings, speeches).
- "The work for the upliftment of untouchable society is the greatest work for the nation–a service to the country. To strive for their upliftment is to serve the Indian nation and the world" (*Janata* magazine, 15 June, 1932).
- "Living without self-esteem is not a sign of vigour. It may be difficult, but learn to live with self-respect by enduring it. The idol takes shape out of stone only when it suffers pain. The idol attains the place of divinity after enduring that pain. Pain must be endured for the betterment of society" (speech at the Ratnagiri Zilla Parishad meeting at Chiplun on 13 April, 1929).

Dr. Babasaheb used to say, "It is required to develop social equality and sense of brotherhood among the society if we want the upliftment of our nation and respect for our nation from the nations of the world." It was his dream to build a new India (after Independence). He presented the water policy and solution for the problem of water scarcity. He also provided a vision for energy policy and a way for power generation. He Further also suggested a way to solve the economic problems besides introducing India's strong foreign policy. He even chalked out India's industrial policy to enable India to become a world power. He drew up the Constitution of India which laid the foundation of social equality, harmony and national unity. He wished for all round development through the *mantra* of equality, affection and brotherhood. His outlook was always positive and he aimed at unity of the nation and society. He worked for the welfare of the people eking out a living at the bottom of the society. He placed his points firmly and said that social injustice and inequality would weaken the society and the country as a whole. He prioritised labour interests and called for women empowerment. He was concerned about protection of India's borders and warned the nation of traitors of the nation. His ideas for education of the masses are still an inspiration today. He gave four *mantras* of success for youth–education and self-esteem, purity of character, hard work and self-confidence. The prime mantra behind his contributions for the other fields was 'Nation first and last also nation'. He used to say, "We are Indians firstly and lastly."

His life and ideology has the potential to make the dream of a new India come true with the ideology directed towards building a harmonious society and nation building.

On 4 April, 1942, Babasaheb's 50th birthday was celebrated in Mumbai and major cities of Maharashtra. "Dr. Ambedkar is a revolutionary man of modern India. Hardly anyone else has done as much as he has done for the emancipation of the Dalits," wrote Mumbai's *Prabhat* daily.

But it was Veer Savarkar who published a true assessment of the work done by Dr. Ambedkar by saying, "Babasaheb Ambedkar's personality, his erudition, his organisational skills and his leadership qualities would have made him a major pillar of the country today. But he spent his life trying to eradicate untouchability. He instilled confidence in the untouchables. His work is enduring, patriotic and humanitarian. A great man like Dr. Ambedkar is born among the untouchables and will not rest without eradicating despair in the minds of the untouchables. I express my respect for Babasaheb's personality and work. I wish him a long and healthy life."

This Country Lagged because of Casteism

The main message of Dr. Bhimrao Ambedkar was to uplift the morality of Hindu society and urgently at that. It meant that there was an urgent need to build a new philosophical foundation for Hindu society and which would be based on democratic values, such as freedom, equality and fraternity. The basic concept, values as well as outlook of Hindu society had to be altered. He concluded that Hindus were a diseased race and would not be able to sustain freedom for long if it was achieved without gaining power. And such power had to be acquired for the country's defence provided by became a single-*varna* society. He was not the only one to raise his voice against the *varna* system; even leaders like Swami Shraddhanand, Lala Lajpat Rai, Raja Rammohun Roy, Bhai Parmanand, Jyotirao Phule, Acharya Prafullachandra Rai, Rameshchandra Dutt, Bipin Chandra Pal, Jadunath Sarkar, Lala Hardayal, Veer Savarkar to name only a few gave a similar message. Well-known historian Jadunath Sarkar opined that the spirit of nationalism had been destroyed due to the practice of casteism as it worked against the spirit of national unity. "The caste system is a curse for India," said Lala Hardayal, a well-known revolutionary leader. "Neither the Muslims nor England destroyed India; casteism within us has became our enemy. Priesthood and casteism have destroyed us." As long as we continue to practice casteism, it will be difficult to preserve India's Independence. India's great historians, sociologists, thinkers and social reformers also blamed casteism for the destruction of Hindus.

In this context, the statements made by Babasaheb Ambedkar in his *Mooknayak* and *Bahishkrit Bharat* magazines are still valuable for the unity of India. We can see the vision of the best Hindu reformer through his thoughts expressed in most of the editorials of *Bahishkrit Bharat*. He said in one of the editorials:

"The power of Hindu society has been eroded by casteism. We, all the people of the nation, are brothers. We are all Indians, regardless of caste. Work of the nation should not be disrupted. If motives of all religions are the same then why hatred for another? Compassion is the root of religion, serving the countrymen, helping common people, taking care of them is the true religion."

(*Mooknayak* magazine: Issue 10, 5 June, 1920)

"When the varna *system came into existence in the era of Puranas, rules were not so strict then. A person could change varna, could go from one varna to another through his own deeds. Sages, like Vishwamitra, Valmiki, Vashishtha, Tank, etc. are proof of this. In the course of time, selfish, hypocritical and heresy people erected a whole barbed wire fence between different* varnas *and further even between different castes and the result is the emergence of a whole lot of castes. As these castes came into existence, some patriarchs, in order to maintain their dominance, resorted to the* Puranas *and the* Smritis *to create these higher/lower distinctions by adding some fictitious and imaginary commands."*

(*Mooknayak* magazine, 14 August, 1920)

"In Mahad, we have come together with the aim to eliminate inequality from Hindu society and to unite it. We shall adopt programmes to end the tradition of varnashrama *of Hinduism. We have to adopt a programme to create a single strong* varna *by uniting all the five* varnas. *Untouchability will not end and there will never be equality in society unless there is a single* varna."

(*Bahishkrit Bharat, December, 1927*)

"Sociologists say that caste discrimination has weakened Hindu society. Social works are being considered as an out-caste activity because of the belief that one has to have 'birth in the same caste, death in the same caste, food in the same caste, marriage in the same caste.' The more a man stays away from other people, the more his caste is considered pure. Caste discrimination in social cohesion is like scissors. Caste discrimination does not allow the spirit of unity and made the lives of Hindus terrible. People of different castes have become indifferent to each other. In all their public dealings, it has been customary to think of advantage for one's own caste and detriment of other castes. This policy, no matter how unjust, is followed and as a result, an atmosphere of distrust has been created among the Hindu castes."

(*Bahishkrit Bharat,* editorial, 21 December, 1928)

"Hatred among castes cannot be vanished as long as there is a caste discrimination in existence. That has increased the fight between different castes instead of alliance between castes. Even the social reforms are at halt due to caste discrimination. People are not ready

to understand that the tradition of caste is wrong. And that is up to the extent that those who act against this false tradition are socially ostracized. The development of Hindu society has stalled because of the caste discrimination and that has weakened the society."

(*Bahishkrit Bharat*, editorial, 21 December, 1928)

"It is a general belief that untouchables cannot produce the right and dutiful people. But, upper caste people seem to forget that higher efforts are not possible without high ambition and great work cannot be done without higher efforts. When you set all the boundaries for untouchables in the name of social restraints, those who have been left behind by way of untouchability for thousands of years do not have mental powers to cross their own boundaries. And these boundaries have deprived them of the seed of ambition as well."

(*Bahishkrit Bharat*, editorial, 21 December, 1928)

"In my opinion untouchability and caste indicating names should be abolished, all the people should give up such caste based names and adopt simple names. There should not be mention of castes like Brahmin, Maratha, Chamar in names; being called Hindu should be enough. No one will treat others in a roguish way if this happens."

(Mumbai Province , Excluded Class Council, Barshi district: Solapur, 24 March, 1924)

"Is it not treason to be loyal to one's own caste even though one is a citizen of a nation?"

(*Annihilation of Castes* by Babasaheb Ambedkar)

"Our movement for the abolition of untouchability is a nation-building movement in true sense... The human body is meant to do something good so that the country and society can be salvated. '

(Presidential address, Berar Province Untouchable Council, Amravati, 13 November, 1927)

"We want the country to prosper and the country to have a higher position."

(Honours programme, Mumbai, 2 October, 1930)

"Compassion is another name for fraternity. Humanity and fraternity are other names for religion."

(Akashwani, Delhi discourse, 3 October, 1954)

While participating in the Mahad's *satyagraha*, he explained in detail the reason for the *satyagraha* and how people would gather for it, what the organisation of Hindus be like. If freedom was granted, then upon getting freedom the untouchables would not only make progress but use their ability, intelligence and skills for the prosperity of the country. Seen in this light, the movement for the abolition of untouchability was not just a movement for their upliftment but truly a people's movement. If untouchables wanted to save their interests, there should have been no need for a movement like *satyagraha* as the equality they have been fighting for even today can be achieved through conversion and the energy they are spending to eradicating untouchability can be used for their own educational and economic advancement.

Declaration of Hindu Unity

As long as Dr. Babasaheb considered that the excluded class was a part of Hindu society, he thought of the Hindu society as a whole. At the meeting of *satyagrahis* at Mahad, where he released his manifesto on 25-26 December, 1927, he declared:

"This assembly is of the view that the present Hindu society is a clear and pathetic example of how the nation collapses due to social injustice, religious hatred, political degradation and economic slavery. The main reason for such a dire plight of the Hindu society is that the broader society has not shown readiness to know what the birthright of human beings is and has not taken care to keep it intact and has not stopped the conspiracies of selfish people.

"Understanding one's innate rights, protecting them in adverse times and taking care not to disregard them in their interactions are all the basic needs and ultimate duty of every human being in the society. The following manifesto is being published for the information of all in the witness of, and with the blessings of the almighty God; who is the eye-witness of all Hindus.

1. "All human beings are of equal status by birth and will remain of equal status till death.
2. "The ultimate goal of the State system and social system should be to perpetuate the above-mentioned innate human rights.

3. "The whole community is the source of all kinds of rights as well as power. The exclusive rights of any individual, community or race, if granted by the broader society, are not acceptable on any basis, be it political or religious.
4. "Everyone has the right to freedom of opinion and expression; restrictions may be imposed on a person as long as other persons have the opportunity to exercise similar rights. This limit should be determined by the law made by the public itself.
5. "Only those things that are fatal to society should be prohibited by law. Everyone should have the freedom to do things that are not legally forbidden.
6. "Laws are not obligations imposed by a particular class. The entire society or their representatives should have the right to determine what the law is. This law, whether protective or regulatory, should be applied equally to all and the social structure should be built on the foundation of equality, not only that but caste should not interfere in all matters including respect of individual, individual rights and individual profession."

Issues Raised by Babasaheb are as Relevant Today Despite His Conversion

Does this declaration of birthright of all Hindus have importance only as a historical document? Babasaheb renounced Hindutva and Hindu society in his later life. It was a tendency among the so-called progressives at that time to paint Babasaheb as anti-Hindu society or anti-Hinduism. Also many may also have said that the significance of this declaration is no longer there, but the reality is different.

The existence of Hindu society is a fact. Even if Babasaheb were to remove a section of untouchables out of Hindu society, Hindu society would still exist under the name 'Hindu'. The problems of inequality are the same today as they were in 1927. The problem of congenital inequality in urban areas or in rural life may not have been as acute as it was in 1927, but it has not completely vanished. As long as there is a problem of social inequality, as long as there is untouchability and as long as a large section of society is deprived of civil rights, the significance of this declaration remains.

This manifesto continues to guide the Hindu society in the direction of 'social equality' until it is achieved. Dr. Babasaheb had asserted the birthright of all Hindus in this manifesto; it was not only for the birthright of untouchables; his struggle was for liberation from untouchability but the demand for rights was meant for the entire Hindu society.

"Self-esteem is the most important component in life. Any Person is zero without it. One has to overcome difficulties in order to live with self-esteem. And people can gain strength, confidence and identity only through hard work and perseverance. It is like drowning in the water to live without self-esteem and patriotism."

—(presidential speech, Session II, Ratnagiri district, Bahishkrit Council, Chiplun, 13 April, 1927)

Babasaheb considered the philosophy of Hinduism to be the best but also said that it was zero in practice

In one of the editorials of his magazine, *Bahishkrit Bharat* (22 April, 1927) under the title 'Principles of Hinduism', Dr. Babasaheb wrote: "The doctrine of Hinduism is many times more egalitarian than the doctrine of Christianity and Islam. Hinduism says fearlessly that humans are the child of God, they are the form of God. All here are the forms of God, no one is higher or lower here-that is the great principle of this religion. There is no greater basis for establishing an empire of equality. Despite this, the social equality that is found in Christian or Muslim nations is not seen in Hindu society. If anyone tries to establish social equality, it is opposed by Hindus. So it is clear how much Hindus know the true Hindu religion...We are not saying that religion is a confluence of morals; sometimes there are gaps, but when the practice of religion differs from the principles of religion, it becomes necessary to change the religious practices and bring them in line with the religious principles."

Dr. Babasaheb was undoubtedly one of the best Hindu reformers as is reflected by his thoughts expressed in most of the editorials of *Bahishkrit Bharat*. Once he said in an editorial: "The power of Hindu society has been eroded due to casteism." So he wanted a radical change in Hinduism through *satyagrahas* at Mahad Chadar lake and for temple entry. He set out to break the false traditions and that is why it was not an easy task. The tradition did not permit entry into temples by untouchables and no drawing of water from public ponds and wells for them. Babasaheb wanted to break all such traditions; in a sense, it was a rebellion against traditions that had been instilled in the society for ages in the name of religion. His revolt was to bring in a social revolution for social equality. Dr. Babasaheb had said, "Until now, like Mahatma Gandhi, we also considered untouchability a stigma of Hinduism, but now our outlook has changed and now we consider it as a stigma on us, on our body."

The Outrage against Double Standards

Babasaheb Ambedkar's opposition was not to the noble elements of Hinduism, but to those religious leaders and clergies who on the one hand advocated the best elements of Hinduism and on the other, supported the social system that created inequality and slavery in society. He took over the classical basis of the struggle to create awareness of human rights. He said in clear words in his book, *Annihilation of Castes*: "Progress is not possible without restructuring Hindu society on the basis of equality." His aim was to raise the status of untouchables against centuries of atrocities and injustice and to fight for their rights. In fact, from his ideas it becomes clear that his movement was not for any particular society or section of society; it was for the welfare of the nation. He conducted all his movements with this idea in mind. The basis of the Mahad *satyagraha* was also the same.

However, the Hindu society failed to comprehend this role of Babasaheb. His struggle was not to divide the society, but to unite it. Yet, he led some significant struggles and found success. On 17 March, 1937 the untouchables secured legal permission to fetch water from the lake. The monopoly of the Hindus dealt a severe blow to the fundamentals of Hinduism as well as its liberal spirit. And the sun of social equality could not shine.

He wanted the movement against untouchability to be a medium to recreate the entire Hindu society on the basis of these three points – freedom, equality and fraternity. His movement was for restoration of a truly Hindu religion by removing distortions in Hinduism. He launched a movement in 1929 to seek entry of untouchables at public festival of Ganeshotsav so that they too could celebrate it.

The untouchable Hindus did not have access to the Ambadevi temple in Amravati. A conference chaired by Bhimrao Ambedkar was held on 13 November, 1927 at Amravati to deal with the issue. He advocated social equality, saying, "Untouchables do not want entry only to worship the deity, but they want to prove that their entry does not defile the temple and does not diminish the sanctity of the idol." He launched the *satyagraha* with full strength and patience with the help of local activists for entry into the Kalaram temple at Nashik.

Addressing the workers at the beginning of this *satyagraha* on 2 March, 1930, he said, "The issue of prevention of untouchability is religious, social, political as well as economic. It is not that just an entry into the temple will resolve the issue. This *satyagraha* is to challenge the psyche of upper-caste Hindus." Such a social *satyagraha* has yielded pleasant results. The RSS is sincerely trying to make Bhimrao Ambedkar's dream come true. At the Kalaram temple of Nashik, where Dr. Ambedkar carried out his *satyagraha* to obtain entry into the temple, a *yajna* was held by the RSS efforts. The priest, Sudhir Maharaj (grandfather of him was a *pujari* at the time of Dr. Ambedkar's *satyagraha*) also called upon Dalit followers of the deity to participate in the *yajna*. He took them to the sanctum sanctorum of the temple, where no one other than the priest was allowed. They offered a *pooja* through the priest and the priest also apologised for the mistake committed by his ancestors.

Six-and-a-half decades have passed since the death of Dr. Babasaheb Ambedkar and it will be almost a hundred years since the establishment of the Sangh, there is still a lot of work to be done. Dr. Ambedkar's dream of a 'single-*varna* Hindu society' and Dr. Hedgewar's dream of a 'harmonious Hindu society' have not yet been fulfilled, but yes, the Hindu society has definitely changed, though a lot remains to be done still. The only true tribute to these two great personalities would be to speed up the work in that direction.

□

17

Dream: Liberty-Equality-Fraternity

Dr. Babasaheb Ambedkar was endowed with a multidimensional personality. There are many different aspects of each of these dimensions but his greatness and worthiness did not come to the fore in his lifetime. Only two of his characteristics–a great Dalit leader and the creator of the Constitution have found mention after his *mahanirvana* (journey to heaven). He was criticised for coming down heavily on Hinduism, on Hindu society and Hindu theology, but his critique was not motivated with any political interest. There are different forms of criticism–one of them hatred and motivated with vested interest; the other is like a mother's love. It is not considered hateful to rebuke kids for their misdeeds and mistakes. Babasaheb's criticism was criticism full of love. Had it been hateful, the country would have been shocked on his adoption of a foreign religion instead of Buddhism, but he never took a single step to the detriment of this nation. 'Nation first' has been at the centre of his every action and thought–he thought only of India.

Concerned about the development of the nation, he wrote in *Mooknayak* magazine (Issue 15, 28 August, 1920): "Have a look at the condition of our vast nation and then look at Japan. This small country was also devastated, but Japan developed rapidly and now made its position in leading developed countries of the world. The caste distinction that exists in our country today, a similar situation existed there in Japan also. Samurai were considered at the highest position in the caste system of Japan, but they gave away their rights of upper caste and created such an environment of fraternity, that they ended up making their ignorant and miserable brethren prosperous and happy. This created a new national spirit of self-sacrifice in them and finally contributed to the betterment of the motherland there." Babasaheb wrote extensively on topics like religion, society, politics, economics, etc. and all of which reflect his national outlook. (Who is Kremlin? Kremlin is a building in Russia).

A nation-building leader needs to have the following seven qualities: (1) clear vision about the nation, (2) dedication to nation building, (3) in-depth study and knowledge of society and nation building, (4) excellent character, (5) awesome ability to organise people, (6) a roadmap to nation building, (7) extraordinary ability to lead. All these qualities were abundantly present in Babasaheb.

India is an ancient nation with only one culture and all belong to the same religion; yet, it does not have social unity, or equality, or harmony. The social life has been polluted by the caste system and also the race system. Society has become dilapidated. We raise the slogan 'God lives in All', but we have temples, right to education, lakes and wells and walkways confined to the higher castes; human-to-human distinctions are made; people of one are made untouchables and left to live a life that of slaves. Babasaheb, while participating in the parliamentary debate in the Rajya Sabha in 1953, said: "What is untouchability? As far as my understanding is concerned, it is a mental illness. It is not a common disease or a tumour that can be removed by medicine or surgery; it is a mental illness. How can this distortion be removed, which has been prevailing in Hindu society for thousands of years? It is difficult to heal unless treated in a mental hospital."

All the established religions of India possess spiritual knowledge to create unity, harmony and equality among human beings, but as Babasaheb said, 'This best element of knowledge does not come in practice.' This spiritual knowledge did not end social slavery; people did not get rid of that mental illness that had penetrated into their psyche. Poverty was not slayed, nor everyone in society was shown respect and nor everyone had the freedom to enjoy equal rights. Political power, religious power, economic power were in the hands of a few. Babsaheb believed that this could only be ended with spiritual philosophy!

If this nation is to be empowered, then every person should be granted liberty, equality and fraternity. Social life should be managed on the principle of justice and this requires a Constitution that manages the society well. The law which governs social life is the religion and this terminology of this religion can be defined well. Therefore, the Constitution that governs the society is the modern scripture of the country.

This nation should run on the elements of democracy, but democracy should not merely be political. Political democracy is known as the democracy of the electorate. Babasaheb insisted that this such a democracy would not make the nation strong; the power of the nation lay in social democracy. Social democracy meant that there should not be any kind of artificial bondage for the individual. All forms of racial and caste-based discriminations must be ended so that people could interact with each other on grounds of equality. Babasaheb also insisted on the third type of democracy and that was economic democracy. The influence of wealth and lack of wealth were fatal. Influence of wealth creates monopolies, which lead to amassing of wealth mostly through exploitation. Lack of wealth destroys a person's humanity, rendering him helpless. It was in the interest of the healthy society to get rid of both these situations, and that could be done through equal distribution of wealth. This has to be done by the ruling government. The State should formulate policies that do not create the influence of wealth or lack of wealth. How it can be achieved is shown in the guiding principles of the Constitution.

Babasaheb gave a speech at a convention for untouchables on 12 February, 1938 in a Satana village of Nashik district. He said, "Invaders like Alexander and Mohammad Tughalq could attack and occupy our country, but, the *chaturvarna* (system) taught the Hindus that none except the Kshatriyas could fight and protect the country. A handful of Brahmins could not take up arms. This teaching is responsible for the decline and downfall of India. This catastrophe of slavery could have been avoided if everyone capable of fighting had the freedom to take up arms." He advocated participation of all in national work in order to develop a national spirit.

Dr. Babasaheb Ambedkar's contribution as a visionary can be gauged from the following departments that were constituted:

• Employment Exchange	• Employees State Insurance
• Working Hours Limit	• Maternity Leaves
• Compulsory recognition to Trade Union	• Dearness Allowance
• Paid leaves	• Health Insurance
• Legal Strike Act	• Provident Fund
• Labour Welfare Fund	• Technical Training Scheme
• Central Irrigation Commission	• Provision of Finance Commission
• Right to Vote	• Indian Statistical Law
• Central Technical Power Board	• Hirakund Dam
• Damodar Valley Project	• Orissa River Project
• Bhakra Nangal Dam	• Son River Valley Project
• Reserve Bank of India	• Indian Constitution

His invaluable contribution to the development of the nation has been forgotten after his death. The Congress, a handful of Dalit leaders and the 'red salute' are bent on balkanising India.

Another commendable achievement was his step to seek refuge at the feet of Lord Buddha by converting himself to Buddhism. Like Buddhist monks, Babasaheb spread peace, compassion, love, affection and sympathy. The world today needs a Buddha and not a *yuddha* (war). This means social cohesion along with brotherhood and the feeling that 'every Indian is my brother'. A revolution comes through non-violent ways and by propagating peace and good faith around the world.

Babasaheb cited the example of Tathagata Buddha to guide every Indian's life by saying, "There is a message by Mahatma Buddha to his Bhikkhu Sangh (followers) before his *mahanirvana* (going to heaven) and is mentioned in the *Mahanirvana Sutta*.

Once, after recovering from illness, the Lord was taking rest under a tree. His disciple Anand came to him and said, 'I have seen Lord in states of sickness and in happiness. Lord's current illness made me disturbed and there is no peace in my mind. I cannot focus on Dhamma, but I am gratified and at peace that Lord will not accept *parinirvana* without giving his message to his Sangh."

"God replied: 'Anand! What does the Sangh want from me? I have taught Dhamma with an open mind; nothing is hidden'."

"What else does the Tathagata say to Bhikkhu Sangh? 'Anand, be your own radiance like the Sun. Do not depend on others for light, like the Earth. Believe in yourself. Don't rely on another. Be truthful. Always take refuge in the truth and do not surrender to anyone." After giving this example, Babasaheb said, "I too take refuge in these words of Lord Buddha. Be your own guide. Use your own discretion. Do not listen to the advice of others. Be truthful. Take refuge in the truth. Do not surrender to anyone."

If we follow this message of Lord Buddha, the future of India will be bright and victory would touch our feet.

□

Dr. Babasaheb Ambedkar– Summary of Life

Bhimaro Ramji Ambedkar was born on 14 April, 1891 in the military cantonment of Mhow in the Central Provinces (currently Madhya Pradesh). He was the fourteenth and last child of Ramji Maloji Sakpal and Bhimabai Murbadkar. His family belonged to the Hindu Mahar caste, who were treated as untouchables and subjected to intense socio-economic discrimination. His ancestors were serving for the British East India Company, while his grandfather and father served the British Army. His father rose to the rank of Subedar. British government was insistent on educating children of their employees and they established special schools for them. Subedar Ramji Sakpal thus received a degree in Marathi and English, and also encouraged his children to get educated. That ensured good education for Dr. Bhimrao Ambedkar, who would have otherwise been denied this by virtue of his caste.

Having immense faith in Kabir Panth, Ramji Sakpal encouraged his children to study the Hindu classic scriptures, especially the *Mahabharata* and the *Ramayana*. He used his position in the army to ensure the education of his children in the government school, as they faced resistance because of their caste. Although able to attend school, Ambedkar and other untouchables were segregated and given no attention or assistance from the teachers. Ramji Sakpal retired in 1894 and the family moved to Satara two years later. Dr. Ambedkar's mother passed away shortly after their shifting to Satara. Their life became miserable; however, their paternal aunt began to take care of the children. It was unfortunate that only five out of 14 kids of Ramji Sakpal survived–sons Balaram, Anandrao and Bhimrao and two daughters-Manjula and Tulasa. Bhim was the only sibling who passed his school examination and went on to high school graduation and obtained a college degree. His Devrukhe Brahmin teacher, Krishnaji Keshav Ambedkar, who loved him because of his inclination towards learning, changed his surname from Ambavedkar to his own Ambedkar in school records.

Ramji Sakpal remarried in 1898 and the family moved to Mumbai (then Bombay), where Ambedkar became the first untouchable student of the Government High School near Elphinstone Road. Although excelling in his studies, Ambedkar was constantly disturbed at his racial segregation and discrimination. He passed his matriculation examination and entered the University of Mumbai in 1907. He was the first among the untouchables to enter the college in India. This success led to celebration within his community and he was awarded a book, *Biography of the Lord Buddha* by his teacher, Krishnaji Arjun Keluskar aka Dada Keluskar, a Maratha scholar. Bhim Ambedkar's marriage was arranged as per Hindu custom, a year before he entered the university, to Ramabai, a nine-year old girl from Dapoli. He passed out from the Elphinstone College in 1908 and obtained a scholarship of Rs. 25 a month from the Gaekwad ruler of Baroda, Sayaji Rao III to go in for higher studies in the USA. By 1912, he obtained his degree in economics and political science, and was now ready to take up employment with the Baroda state government. His wife gave birth to his first son, Yashwant in the same year. Ambedkar had just moved to Baroda with his young family, and he had to rush back to Mumbai to see his ailing father, who died on 2 February, 1913.

Bhim noticed that he and his family were treated differently at the workplace. Even at school, he was given a separate corner to sit; no desk was given except for a rough mat. He was not allowed to drink water from the common water fountain and common cups used by other students. He had to use his hands to drink water poured by the school peon. Bhim was surprised at such an indifferent treatment given to him at the school. What was wrong with him? He faced indifferent treatment on many occasions. Once, he and his elder brother were travelling to Goregaon to spend summer holidays with their father, who was working there as a cashier. They got off the train and were waiting for their father to receive them at the station. Somehow, Ramji Sakpal couldn't arrive; the station master, a kind gentleman, asked them who they were and where they were heading. The boys were very well dressed, clean, and polite. Bhim, without thinking twice, told him they were Mahars (a group classed as untouchables). The station master was stunned–his face changed, his behaviour became indifferent and he went away.

Bhim finally decided to hire a bullock-cart to reach their father (there were no motor taxis at that time) but somehow the coachman had heard that the boys were untouchables and he also ignored them. Finally, they offered to pay double the usual fare and even offered to drive the cart themselves, while the coachman travelled on foot beside it. The coachman was not ready to touch these 'untouchable' boys, as he thought that he would become impure by their mere touch. However, the extra money persuaded him that he could have his cart 'purified' later! Bhim was constantly trying to understand as to what was wrong with them, throughout the journey, but he couldn't fathom the reason. Both he and his brother were neat and clean and nicely dressed–how was it possible that whatever they touched would become impure?

Bhim never forgot this incident along with many similar incidents. He realised, as he grew up, that untouchability in Hindu society was stupid, cruel and senseless. He couldn't even go to the barber to get a haircut because they were 'untouchables'. His sister had to do this at their home. He got the only answer whenever he asked his sister, 'Why are we untouchables?' 'That is the way it has always been.' Bhim could never be satisfied with the answer. He knew that this was the way the society had been behaving since ages that it had become a tradition. It was also painful to learn that this unjust tradition had to stay forever. Couldn't it be changed?

Being a student from the untouchable community and of a lower caste, Bhim faced numerous insults at the school. Those were really tough days for the young Bhim, particularly as his mother was already dead and father was working far away from the village of his school to give him solace. His teachers, Ambedkar and Pendse, were the only ones in the entire school who were kind and affectionate to him, though, both of them belonged to the higher caste. They encouraged him and praised his good work at the school. His teacher sometimes even shared his lunch with him–something that would have horrified most higher-caste Hindus.

Bhim missed his mother and was very upset when his father decided to remarry. He wanted to run away from home and go to Bombay. One night he woke up without making any sound and managed to steal his aunt's purse; unfortunately he found only one small coin in her purse. Bhim was ashamed of his act. He put the coin back and vowed to himself to study very hard and become independent.

Soon he won the highest praise and admiration from all of his teachers. They urged Ramji Sakpal to give the best education to his son Bhimrao. Ramji Sakpal then moved with his family to Bombay. Their living conditions were different in this big and crowded city as the entire family had to live in a small room located in the poorest of the poor neighbourhoods of Bombay. However, Bhim was able to get admission at the Elphinstone High School, one the best schools in the country. His room was obviously crowded all the time and the streets outside were noisy and filthy. Bhim wanted to study hard but there was no environment for studying. He then found a unique way to carry on his studies at home. He would go to bed as soon as he returned home from the school and his father would wake him up at 2 at midnight. Everything would be quiet in those late hours and he was able to complete his homework and study in peace. Compared to the village, life was different but the label of 'untouchable' didn't leave him. He was an untouchable in this modern city as he was in his small village and was also treated indifferently even at this most famous school.

Bhim was an above the average student. He became fond of gardening and, whenever he could, he bought saplings and with great devotion nurtured them to full growth. While studying in Satara, many of his classmates left for good jobs in Bombay. He too wanted to go to Bombay and get a job to become independent. He realised that if he ever were to be successful, he would have to concentrate more on his studies. He became interested in reading. He read not just the prescribed books in school, but any book in general. His father was too pleased when he digressed from school books and never said 'no' when Bhim wanted a book.

One day, when the teacher called him to the blackboard to do a sum, all the other boys jumped up and made a big fuss. Their lunch boxes were stacked behind the blackboard–they complained the Bhim's touch would make their food impure! He was also barred from choosing Sanskrit as a second language to study; he was told that it was a language of Hindu holy scriptures and it was forbidden to untouchables. He forcibly chose Persian. But, he later studied Sanskrit by himself and was able to even speak fluently in the language.

In due course, Bhim passed his matriculation examination. He was the first from his untouchable community to reach this stage. So, a gathering was arranged to congratulate him by the people who wanted to improve the society.

Bhim was 17-years old at that time. An early marriage was very common in those days, so he was also married to Rambai the same year. He, however, continued to study hard and passed the intermediate examination with distinction. However, further study was costly and Ramji Sakpal was unable to pay the school fees. Bhim was recommended to the Maharaja Sayajirao Gaekwad of Baroda through some kind persons who were interested in his further progress. The Maharaja, looking at his credentials and his enthusiasm to study, granted a monthly scholarship to him. Bhimrao cleared his B.A. in 1912 with this help. (The suffix 'Rao' was added to his name, which is a sign of respect in Marathi language in Maharashtra). He joined the civil services soon after his college graduation but had to rush back to Bombay to take care of his ailing father in just two weeks from joining. Ramji Sakpal couldn't survive and died soon. He was truly a great father, who did everything for his sons within his capacity. He laid the foundation for Bhimrao's future achievements.

The Maharaja of Baroda was providing scholarships to outstanding scholar students for further studies abroad. Selected students had to sign an agreement to serve Baroda State for 10 years on finishing their studies. Of course, Bhimrao was selected and he went to the USA in 1913 where he studied at the world-famous Columbia University, New York. The freedom and equality he experienced in America cast a very strong impression on him. It was so refreshing for him to be able to lead here a normal life, free from the caste prejudice of India. He could do anything he wanted to, but he devoted his time to studies. He studied 18 hours a day; his favourite means of entertainment was to visit bookshops!

He did his M.A. within a short period of two years with Economics and Sociology as major. He also completed his Ph.D. thesis the following year. He left Columbia University and joined the London School of Economics in England. However, he had to leave London before finishing his studies due to the expiration of his scholarship granted by the State of Baroda. Bhimrao had to wait three years before he could return to London to complete his course.

The famous British Museum in London has a huge library, which opens at 8 o'clock every morning; Ambedkar never missed the time; he would surely be there by 8 a.m. every day and leave at 5 p.m. He came in touch with an Indian student named Asnodkar in London. He hailed from a rich family and was not interested in studies. Ambedkar told him, "Your folks may have made plenty of money, but what are you going to achieve as a human being? Goddess Saraswati (goddess of learning) will not come to you on your will; seek her blessings and get educated when she is in front of you." Ambedkar became a barrister in 1922 and moved back to India next year.

He had to serve Baroda State as he had agreed while availing the scholarship for higher studies. So, he took up a job in the Baroda Civil Services. Bhimrao was holding a top degree in doctorate and was also trained for the top job. He again faced the same problem of Hindu caste system–untouchability on returning to Baroda State. It was now more painful because he had been abroad for the past four years and seen the world outside of Hindu society as well, leaving behind his label of 'untouchable'.

The working atmosphere at the office was very miserable for him. No one would hand over files and papers hand to hand to him–the peon used to throw them on to his desk. Nor would they give him water to drink. No respect was given to him merely because of his caste. He had to go from hotel to hotel, looking for a room to stay, but none of them would take him in. At last he had found a filthy small place to live in a Parsi guesthouse, only because he had finally decided not to disclose his original caste. Living conditions over there were not comfortable; it was a small bedroom with a tiny bathroom attached without any facility for hot water. He was all alone there, with no one to talk with. There were no electrical lights or even oil lamps, so the place was completely dark at night. Bhimaro was hoping to find some other place to live through his civil service job, but before he could, one morning he faced a crowd of angry people with sticks outside his room, just as he was about to leave for his job. They accused him of defiling the hotel and told him to leave the place by evening–or else! What could he do? He could not stay with either of the two acquaintances he made in Baroda for the same reason–his low caste. Bhimaro felt totally distressed and rejected.

He had no choice but to return to Bombay after only 11 days at his new job. He tried to start a small business there, advising people on investments but that too failed once the customers learned of his caste. In 1918, he joined Sydenham College in Bombay as a lecturer. His students recognised him as a brilliant teacher and scholar. Within this period he also managed to found a Marathi newspaper, *Mooknayak* (Leader of the Dumb) to advocate the cause of the untouchables. He also began to organise and attend conferences, knowing that he had to proclaim and publicise the humiliations he had to suffer as a Dalit–'his own life had taught him the necessity of the struggle for liberation.'

In 1920, with the help of some friends, he was able to return to London to complete his studies in Economics at LSE. He also enrolled as a Barrister at Gray's Inn. In 1923, Bhimrao returned to India with a doctorate in Economics from the LSE; he was perhaps the first Indian to have earned a doctorate from this world-famous institution. He also qualified as a Barrister-at-Law. He knew that nothing had changed back home. His qualification meant nothing as far as the practice of untouchability was concerned–it was still an obstacle to his career. However, he had received the best education that anyone in the world could get and was well equipped to be a leader of the Dalit community. He could argue with and persuade the best minds of his time on equal terms. He was an expert in law and could give convincing evidence to British commissions as an eloquent and gifted speaker. Bhimrao dedicated the rest of his life to this task. He became known by his increasing number of followers–those untouchables he urged to awake–as he knew the great value and importance of education. He founded a society called Bahishkrit Hitakarini Sabha (Society for Interests of Excluded). This set up hostels, schools and free libraries. To improve the lives of Dalits, education had to reach everyone. Opportunities had to be provided at grass-root level because knowledge is power.

Leading the Peaceful Agitation: In 1927, Bhimrao presided over a public meeting at Mahad Kolaba district, where he said: "It is the time we uproot the idea of 'higher & lower' out of our minds; we shall attain our own self-respect." He himself had experienced humiliation and injustice due to the dark-age tradition of untouchability in Hindu society; so he knew that no one would grant justice to them and which had to be attained by themselves. The Bombay Legislature had already passed a Bill allowing everyone to use water from public tanks and wells. (We had seen earlier how Bhim was denied water at school, at his office and other places because of the superstition of being 'impure' as he was an untouchable.)

Leading to the Legislature Bill, Mahad Municipality had already made the local water tanks open to all people four years back, but so far not a single untouchable had dared to drink or draw water from that tank due to the fear of tradition and fear of 'higher'-caste people. Bhimrao led the procession after a public meeting on a peaceful demonstration at the Chowder public water facility. He knelt down, took a handful of water and drank it. That was a historical act which provided courage to thousands of other untouchables who too followed him. Thus history was created at the Chowder public water facility. Now untouchables were free to use the public water facilities for which they were forbidden for hundreds of years.

Resistance to such an act was obvious. So they faced a violent attack from the upper-caste Hindus, but Bhimrao insisted to his fellowmen that violence would not help; he gave his word to keep the demonstration peaceful and all his fellowmen did not even resist the violent attack on them. Bhimrao had been publishing a magazine for his Bahishkrit Hitkarini Sabha and he had titled it as *Bahishkirt Bharat* ('Excluded India'). He once urged his people to hold the *satyagraha* (non-violent agitation) to secure the right to enter the Kalaram temple at Nasik as it was forbidden to untouchables just as thousands of other Hindu temples. They were told that they would be able to take part in the annual festival after about a month of peaceful non-violent agitation at Kalaram temple. But, that was not accepted by all the upper-caste devotees and stones were pelted at them when they tried to participate in the celebration at the temple. They were driven away and disallowed to take part. So, they resumed their peaceful non-violent agitation with courage. As a result, the temple could not opened to the public for about a year, as the peaceful agitators had blocked the entrance.

The Round Table Conference and Gandhi: Meanwhile, the Indian freedom movement had gained momentum under the leadership of Mahatma Gandhi. The Round Table Conference was held in London by the British Government In 1930 to decide the future of India. Dr. Bhimrao Ambedkar represented the untouchable community of India. He said in his presentation, "The Depressed Classes of India also join the demand for replacing the British Government by the government of the people and by the people...Our 'wrongs' have remained as open sores and have not been 'righted' although 150 years of British rule have rolled away. Of what good is such a government to anybody?"

The British had done nothing to alleviate the status of the depressed classes. He said that India must have a minimum of dominion status. He canvassed for a separate electorate for the depressed classes.

Soon a second conference was held, which Mahatma Gandhi attended on behalf of the Congress Party. Babasaheb met Gandhi in Bombay before they went to London. Gandhi told him that he had read what Dr. Ambedkar had said at the first conference and considered Ambedkar to be a real Indian patriot. At the Second Conference, Bhimrao asked for a separate electorate for the Depressed Classes–"Hinduism," he said, "has given us only insults, misery, and humiliation." A separate electorate would mean that the untouchables would vote for their own candidates and be allotted their votes, separate from the Hindu majority. Bhimrao was made a hero; now known as Babasaheb by thousands of his followers on his return to Bombay, even though he always told people not to idolise him. The news broke that the British Government granted the separate electorate for the depressed class of India and this really created turmoil in Hindu society as well as political leaders of the Congress, especially Mahatma Gandhi. He clearly felt that this was a division of Hindu society into untouchables (whom he called Harijans) and upper class and it pained him grievously. And to oppose the same, he declared a 'fast unto death'.

The Fast of Mahatma: Mahatma Gandhi was jailed at the Yerawada Jail when the granting of a separate electorate for the depressed class of India was announced by the British Government. Mahatma Gandhi felt that separate electorates would only separate the Harijans from the Hindus. The very thought that the Hindus would be divided pained him much. He started a fast against separate electorates, saying that he will fast unto death, if necessary. That created anxiety in the country, especially among the leaders of the Congress. They approached Dr. Ambedkar to take back his demands and to save Gandhiji. He said, "Gandhiji did not fast to oppose when Muslims, Christians and Sikhs were given separate electorates. What is the other solution, if you are not willing to give separate electorates to untouchables? I understand that it is essential to save Gandhiji's life. But I am not prepared to give up the interests of the backward classes just to save him." He further said, "I will give up the claim for separate electorates if you agree to reserve a larger number of seats for the untouchables than what British Government has given."

Later he visited Gandhiji at the Yerawada Jail. Gandhi persuaded Babasaheb, giving him the assurance that Hinduism would change, leaving its bad practices of untouchability. Finally Babasaheb agreed to sign the historical Poona Pact with Gandhiji in 1932. Instead of separate electorates, more representation was to be given to the depressed classes. However, later it became obvious that this did not amount to anything concrete.

The progress in Babasaheb's life was by way of his library collection of over 50,000 books and a house named Rajgriha at Dadar in north Bombay. He lost his beloved wife Ramabai in 1935. The same year he was appointed Principal of the Government Law College, Bombay. The Dalit public meeting was also held at Yeola in the same year. Babasaheb said at the meeting, "We have not been able to secure the barest of human rights... I am born a Hindu. I couldn't help it, but I solemnly assure you that I will not die a Hindu." This was the first time that Babasaheb emphasised on the importance of conversion from Hinduism for his people–for they were only known as untouchables within the fold of Hinduism. Babasaheb was appointed Labour Minister by the Viceroy during the Second World War, yet he always remained with his roots. He never lost his ethics nor became corrupt or crooked. He said he was born poor and he would remain absolutely unchanged in his attitude towards his friends and the rest of the world. The All-India Scheduled Caste Federation was formed in 1942 to mould all untouchables into a united political party.

Architect of the Constitution: After the war, Babasaheb was elected to the Constituent Assembly to decide the way that India–the country of millions–should rule. How should elections take place? What are the rights of the people? How are laws to be made? Such important matters had to be decided and laws were to be made. The Constitution answers all such questions and lays down rules. When India became independent in August 1947, Babasaheb Ambedkar became the first Law Minister of Independent India. The Constituent Assembly made him the chairman of the committee formed to draft the Constitution for the world's largest democracy. All his study of law, economics, and politics made him the best qualified person for this task. A study of law, knowledge of the history of India and of Indian society–all were essential aspects to chalk out the Constitution; and he carried the whole responsibility alone. He alone could complete this huge task.

The British Parliament passed the act of India's Independence on 15 July, 1947 and India became a free country on 15 August, 1947. The Constituent Assembly of independent India appointed a drafting committee with Dr. Ambedkar as its Chairman to draft the Constitution of India. Dr. Ambedkar was also invited to join the cabinet as the Minister of Law. He worked on both fronts and toiled over the drafting of the Constitution while taking care of his ministry. He presented the first draft Constitution before the people of India in February, 1948, but, he soon fell ill and was admitted to a nursing home in Bombay. Here he met Dr. Sharda Kabir and married her in April 1948. He presented the final draft of the Constitution on 4 November, 1948 to the Constituent Assembly, and that was adopted in the name of the people of India on 26 November, 1949. He said on that occasion; "I appeal to all Indians to be a nation free from 'idea of castes', which have brought separation in social life and created heartburn and hatred among the people of this country."

Conversion to Buddhism: He visited a Buddhist conference in Sri Lanka in 1950. He spoke on his return to Bombay at the Buddhist temple, "People should embrace Buddhism in order to end their hardships. I am going to devote the rest of my life to the revival and spread of Buddhism in India."

Why did he choose Buddhism?: Ambedkar told his friend Dattopant Thengadi: "At the eve of my life, I can see the rush of ideas for our people from all corners of the world, from every country and from every culture. Our people may be confused in this flood of ideas. I can see strong attempts to separate people who are struggling hard, from the mainstream of this country and to attract them towards other cultures and countries. The tendency is growing at a very fast pace. Some of my colleagues and friends who were disgusted with untouchability, poverty and inequality are ready to flow with this flood. What about others? They should not be separated from the mainstream of this nation's life' and I must show them the path. At the same time, we need change in our economic and political life, and that is why I have decided to follow Buddhism. There is a way of life which has come down as a steady stream in India for thousands of years, and Buddhism has not opposed it. The backward-class people must rebel against the injustice done to them; they must wipe it out. But, untouchability is a problem of the Hindu society. Bharat must remain intact while solving this problem. Buddhism is the best solution for that."

He never believed in the theory of Aryans and Dravidians and that Aryans came to this land from outside and defeated the Dasyus (Dravidians) of this land. He also proved that there is no basis of this in the *Vedas*, where the word 'Arya' appears only 33 or 34 times. The word has been used in the *Vedas* as an adjective, meaning 'the noble' or 'the elder'. *Mahabharata*, in the same way, says that 'Dasyus' can be found in all *varnas* (castes) and *ashramas* (stages of life). He announced in May, 1956 on the occasion of Buddha's anniversary, that he will embrace Buddhism on 14 October, 1956. And finally on that day, at the big function in Nagpur, in the presence of thousands of spectators, he, his wife and his three lakh followers officially became Buddhists. When he was asked at this occasion, 'why?', then Dr. Ambedkar replied, "Why don't you ask this question to yourself and....your forefathers?"

He led a huge gathering in the ceremony on 14h October, 1956 at Nagpur to embrace Buddhism, and over half a million people converted their faith, following him. He knew that Buddhism was a true part of Indian history and to revive it was to continue India's best legacy. For the next five years, Babasaheb carried on a relentless fight against social evils and superstitions.

A Legacy Marking Indian Socio-political History: Ambedkar's legacy, as a socio-political reformer, has been long-lasting in modern India. In post-Independence India, his socio-political thought gained respect across the political spectrum and influenced various spheres of life, like socio-economic, education and government policies for affirmative action through socio-economic and legal incentives.

Dr. Ambedkar administered untouchable political parties and social organisations, and served in the Legislative Council of British India. He intensified his criticism of orthodox Hindu society as well as of slavery and exclusivism in Islam. Despite this, his reputation as a scholar led to his appointment as independent India's first Law Minister, and chairman of the committee responsible to draft the Constitution. Dr. Ambedkar's work would guarantee political, economic and social freedom for untouchables and other ethnic, social and religious communities of India. His polemical condemnation of Hinduism and attacks on Islam made him unpopular and controversial, although his conversion to Buddhism revived interest in Buddhist philosophy in India.

In 1926, he became a nominated member of the Bombay Legislative Council. By 1927 Dr. Ambedkar decided to launch active movements against untouchability. He began with public movements and marches to open up and share drinking from water resources to which until then the untouchable communities had no access; also he put up a struggle for entry into Hindu temples as it was not allowed by upper-caste communities.

Historical Poona Pact: Ambedkar had become one of the most prominent untouchable political figures of that time. He had grown increasingly critical of mainstream Indian political parties for their perceived lack of emphasis om the eradication of the caste system. Ambedkar criticised the Indian National Congress and its leader Mahatma Gandhi, whom he accused of reducing the untouchable community into a picture of pity. Ambedkar was also dissatisfied with the failures of British rule, and advocated a political identity for untouchables, separate from both the Congress and the British. At a Depressed Classes Conference on 8 August, 1930 Ambedkar outlined his political vision: "Safety of the Depressed Classes pivoted on their being independent of the government and the Congress, both. We must shape our course ourselves and only by ourselves. Political power cannot be a panacea for the ailment of the Depressed Classes. Their salvation lies in their social elevation; they must cleanse their evil habits; they must improve their improper ways of living. They must be educated. There is a great necessity to ruffle their pathetic contentment and to instill that divine discontent into them, which is the stream of an ascendency."

Born in a class considered low and outcast, Dr. Ambedkar fought untiringly for the downtrodden. The boy who suffered bitter humiliation became the first Minister of Law in independent India and chalked out the country's Constitution. A determined fighter, a deep scholar, humane to the tips of his fingers he was!

We Need Dharma but Casteism should Go: "Untouchability is an offspring of casteism; untouchability will not be removed until casteism is wiped out." This was Dr. Ambedkar's firm belief. He argued that political power was very necessary to wipe out casteism. He believed that Dharma too was essential for the people, but he revolted against those who, in the name of Dharma, treated some of their fellowmen like animals. Many people criticised him; some newspapers even tried to scare him. Dr. Ambedkar knew from his own experience that even a bright man could not come up in life because of casteism. Believers of such useless tradition prioritise caste and quality of person for them, rendering the person powerless.

Ambedkar fought casteism. He was disgusted to find how difficult it was to secure justice and to find how many men were narrow minded. He even said that it would be better to give up the Hindu Dharma itself.

Muslim and Christian priests and missionaries learnt about this declaration and tried hard to attract Ambedkar. They assured him that the untouchables who were willing to change their religion would be given equal status in their society.

He died as an unhappy man at his failure to change the society.